THE DAILY STUDY BIBLE

(OLD TESTAMENT)

General Editor: John C. L. Gibson

DEUTERONOMY

DEUTERONOMY

DAVID F. PAYNE

THE WESTMINSTER PRESS
PHILADELPHIA

Published by
The Saint Andrew Press
Edinburgh, Scotland
and
The Westminster Press®
Philadelphia, Pennsylvania

PRINTED IN THE UNITED STATES OF AMERICA
2   4   6   8   9   7   5   3

Library of Congress Cataloging-in-Publication Data

Payne, David F. (David Frank), 1931–
Deuteronomy.

(The Daily study Bible series)
Bibliography: p.
1. Bible. O.T. Deuteronomy—Commentaries. I. Title.
II. Series: Daily study Bible series (Westminster Press)
BS1275.3.P39 1985   222′.15077   85-13653
ISBN 0-664-21832-6
ISBN 0-664-24580-3 (pbk.)

CONTENTS

vi *CONTENTS*

ISRAEL IN THE TIME OF DEUTERONOMY

Full map below. For detail, see opposite page.

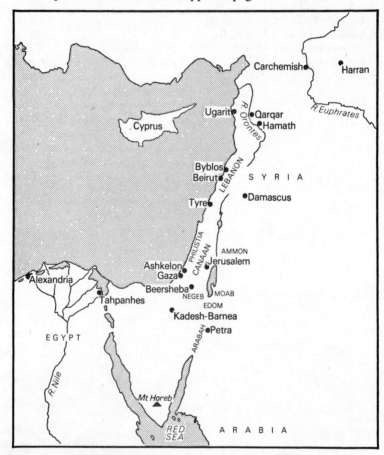

The diagram above is adapted from *Old Testament Illustrations,* C M Jones, Cambridge University Press and redrawn by William Ross, Edinburgh.

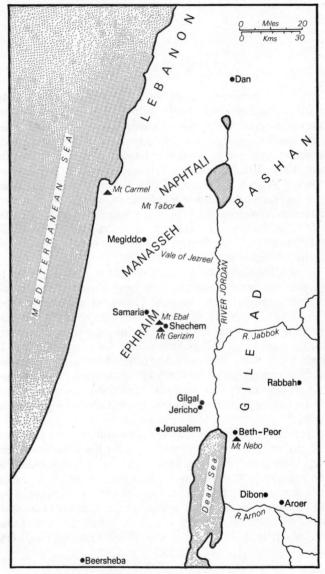

The diagram above is adapted from *Old Testament Illustrations*, C M Jones, Cambridge University Press and redrawn by William Ross, Edinburgh.

GENERAL PREFACE

This series of commentaries on the Old Testament, to which Mr. Payne's volume on *Deuteronomy* belongs, has been planned as a companion series to the much-acclaimed New Testament series of the late Professor William Barclay. As with that series, each volume is arranged in successive headed portions suitable for daily study. The Biblical text followed is that of the Revised Standard Version or Common Bible. Eleven contributors share the work, each being responsible for from one to three volumes. The series is issued in the hope that it will do for the Old Testament what Professor Barclay's series succeeded so splendidly in doing for the New Testament—make it come alive for the Christian believer in the twentieth century.

Its two-fold aim is the same as his. Firstly, it is intended to introduce the reader to some of the more important results and fascinating insights of modern Old Testament scholarship. Most of the contributors are already established experts in the field with many publications to their credit. Some are younger scholars who have yet to make their names but who in my judgment as General Editor are now ready to be tested. I can assure those who use these commentaries that they are in the hands of competent teachers who know what is of real consequence in their subject and are able to present it in a form that will appeal to the general public.

The primary purpose of the series, however, is *not* an academic one. Professor Barclay summed it up for his New Testament series in the words of Richard of Chichester's prayer—to enable men and women "to know Jesus Christ more clearly, to love Him more dearly, and to follow Him more nearly." In the case of the Old Testament we have to be a little more circumspect than that. The Old Testament was completed long before the time of Our Lord, and it was (as it still is) the sole Bible of the Jews, God's first people, before it became part of the Christian Bible. We must take this fact seriously.

Yet in its strangely compelling way, sometimes dimly and sometimes directly, sometimes charmingly and sometimes embarrassingly, it holds up before us the things of Christ. It should not be forgotten that Jesus Himself was raised on this Book, that He based His whole ministry on what it says, and that He approached His death with its words on His lips. Christian men and women have in this ancient collection of Jewish writings a uniquely illuminating avenue not only into the will and purposes of God the Father, but into the mind and heart of Him who is named God's Son, who was Himself born a Jew but went on through the Cross and Resurrection to become the Saviour of the world. Read reverently and imaginatively the Old Testament can become a living and relevant force in their everyday lives.

It is the prayer of myself and my colleagues that this series may be used by its readers and blessed by God to that end.

New College   JOHN C. L. GIBSON
Edinburgh   General Editor

AUTHOR'S PREFACE

The author is deeply grateful to the general editor for the invitation to contribute to the Daily Study Bible series. The incomparable achievement of the late William Barclay in the New Testament volumes has been a beacon and a challenge—but incomparable it was. Nevertheless it is only right that this notable series should encompass the Old Testament as well. The temptations of Christ, the Gospels tell us, were confronted and rebutted with the words and message of the Old Testament—and, to be more precise, with texts drawn from Deuteronomy.

Deuteronomy, then, is not a book the Christian should neglect; and yet it seems in many of its detailed laws and prescriptions to be alien and remote, a hangover from another world. This small commentary endeavours to penetrate to the timeless principles underlying the ancient precepts, and to explore some of their relevance to the modern Christian. However, these principles *are* to be found, and perhaps this point should be emphasized.

To most modern biblical scholars, Deuteronomy was a product of the seventh century B.C. or somewhat later; to many generations of churchmen and laymen, it was the work of Moses in the thirteenth century B.C. (probably). The argument remains alive, but it can only detract from the message of Deuteronomy if we make this issue our only concern and interest; arguments about dates are ultimately irrelevant to timeless truths. The author hopes that readers of both schools of thought can find profit in the pages that follow.

Finally I would like to give my warm thanks to the general editor and the Press for their patience, to Mrs Vivien Craigan for undertaking so much secretarial labour under pressure of time, and to my wife and family for all their encouragement and self-sacrifice.

Queen's University   D. F. PAYNE
of Belfast

INTRODUCTION

Deuteronomy is one of the most important books in the Old Testament. It is a pivotal book, bridging the gap between the Law and the Old Testament account of the history of Israel. It is the *final* book of the five that make up the "Law of Moses" (known also as the *Pentateuch*, and in Jewish circles as the *Torah*), so that we can view it as the climax of the Law. But it could equally be read as the *first* book of a group which scholars nowadays call the "Deuteronomistic History": *ie* Deuteronomy itself, Joshua, Judges, 1 and 2 Samuel, and 1 and 2 Kings. These books do bear a certain family relationship to each other, so that we can reasonably consider Deuteronomy as the basic book in this group.

THE NAME

The name *Deuteronomy* is unfortunately not the most attractive or easy of the names of biblical books. It is really a pair of Greek words run together: *deuteros* meant "second", and *nomos* meant "law", and the combined word *deuteronomion* ("second law" or "repetition of the law") occurs in Deuteronomy 17:18 in the ancient Greek Bible (known as the *Septuagint*). This is really an inaccurate translation, because the verse is speaking about a *copy* of the law, not a repetition of it, as the RSV makes clear. Still, the title for the book is not really far wrong, because the greater part of Deuteronomy is in fact a restatement of the laws contained in Exodus, Leviticus and Numbers. The laws in these three books are linked with the law-giving by Moses at Mount Sinai, very soon after the Israelite people had left Egypt and crossed the Red Sea. The laws in Deuteronomy are still linked with Moses, but a generation later, at a time when the Israelites were on the verge of the Promised Land and about to occupy it. The last chapter of Deuteronomy records the death of Moses.

DATE AND AUTHORSHIP

The alternative title for Deuteronomy in the RSV—as in the Authorized Version before it—is "The Fifth Book of Moses". This is not an ancient title, but it does express the very ancient conviction that Moses was the book's author. The reason for this belief is clear enough. Quite apart from the tradition that Moses wrote all five books—Genesis to Deuteronomy—the reader will soon notice that Moses is stated to be the *speaker* of nearly all of Deuteronomy (see 1:1, 5:1, 27:1, 27:11, 29:2, 31:1, 31:30, 33:1): indeed, most of the book is written between inverted commas. Chapter 31 goes further, and speaks of Moses as the *writer* of "this law" (31:9, 24); a phrase which may refer to the book as a whole, although this is uncertain. Clearly Deuteronomy claims to represent the words of Moses.

Moses lived in the thirteenth century B.C., but most scholars are of the opinion that Deuteronomy was written some centuries later. The actual date is disputed. Many have argued that the book found in the Jerusalem temple in the reign of Josiah (late seventh century) was Deuteronomy, or part of it; cf. 2 Kings 22:8. If so, then arguably the book was written and deposited in the temple a relatively short time before its discovery. But all this is only speculation, and is denied both by scholars defending a much earlier date and by scholars who argue for a later date than Josiah's reign. There has also been much argument about whether the book is a unity; perhaps some parts of it are later than others. (Even those who argue that Moses was the author of the rest of the book would admit that he did not write the account of his own death in chapter 34.)

Readers may study detailed commentaries and reach their own conclusions on such matters. All that need be asserted here is that the message of the book, although in many ways timeless, must have been particularly relevant when the Israelite or Jewish people had suffered political disasters, but had the opportunity of a fresh start. The end of the Babylonian Exile (fifth century B.C.) was one such time; the returning exiles found themselves in a very similar position to the Israelites at the end of Moses' life

—about to enter the Promised Land into an unknown future. As a completed book, Deuteronomy probably had its major impact then, in the fifth century. However, much in it is far older than that, and a substantial link with the laws of Moses need not be denied.

Even if as a book Deuteronomy was relatively late, nobody is accusing its authors of perpetrating some pious fraud. In any society, law is something which develops constantly, to meet new situations and changing circumstances, but its basis remains the same. The Jews hold to this day that all their laws and practices are simply the outworking of the laws of Moses, over 3000 years ago. So if Deuteronomy was chiefly an elaboration of older laws, the nucleus of which came from Moses himself, it was perfectly reasonable to attach the name of Moses to it. Whatever its date, it is true to say that the book is more concerned with the *authority* of Moses than the *authorship* of Moses. In the United Kingdom, we do not ask who actually drafted a new law; it is sufficient that it stands in the name of the Queen and therefore has full force and authority. The real authorship of Deuteronomy is equally unimportant.

THE NATURE OF DEUTERONOMY

So far we have spoken of Deuteronomy as a law book, but this is only partly true. Deuteronomy is in fact three things at once: it is a book of laws, it is a book of sermons, and it is a historical book. As a historical book, it follows on from the book of Numbers and carries the story forward to the death of Moses and the appointment of Joshua as his successor. So the framework of Deuteronomy consists of historical narrative; but in fact the book is nearly all speech, not events. Many individual laws are given, but we also find a number of sermons or addresses—long exhortations given by Moses to Israel. The laws are included in one of these speeches. So we observe that the laws are inside the speeches, and the speeches are inside the historical framework. The following table will make this clearer:

1:1–5	Introductory narrative
1:6–4:40	Moses' first address to Israel
4:41–43	Brief narrative
4:44–28:68	Moses' second address (including the Laws, 12:1–25:19)
29:1–30:20	Moses' third address
31:1–29	Narrative
31:30–32:43	Song of Moses
32:44–52	Narrative
33:1–29	Blessing of Moses
34:1–12	Narrative

What exactly is Deuteronomy then? It may be read as part of an on-going story; the long story of ancient Israel from its beginnings as a nation down to the Babylonian Exile. Its purpose in this setting is to explain why that story was such a wretched one, in spite of a bright and promising start. The answer it gives is that God had to punish Israel for its failure to keep its promises (in the Sinai covenant) and to keep his laws. At the same time it provides a reminder of many of those laws, so that the next generation is exhorted to follow them and, as a consequence, to reverse the direction of Israel's history, gaining God's blessing instead of his punishment. So the book is an explanation, a reminder, and a sustained exhortation.

THE NATURE OF THE LAW

The core of Deuteronomy is its law code (12:1–25:19), and without question the laws were of central importance. In our world today, although we all approve of "law and order" and realize the necessity of law in any large society, we tend in practice to make light of it. It is in any case secular, so that we do not consider any of its provisions to be God-given, and we are well aware that no law is final and immutable. Probably, too, our thinking is affected by our acquaintance with the New Testament and its insistence that Christians are not "under law". Perhaps, then, it would be worthwhile to explore briefly the nature, the purpose and the value of the Old Testament Law of Moses.

The first thing to notice is that the Law incorporated things that we would keep separate. A great many laws were civil, dealing with matters like theft and murder. Others were religious, such as those prescribing for the annual festivals and holy days. In Deuteronomy especially, many are social, concerned with the welfare of the poor. Some are moral, such as the precept not to "covet" (Deut. 5:21). Some are admonitions rather than laws; pleas to act justly and behave generously. Such a mixture seems to have been unique in the ancient world. All of these varied laws are promulgated in the name of *Yahweh*, the God of Israel—they are the expression of his will. The Law is not only his will but his "instruction", the basic sense of the Hebrew word *Torah*, which is generally translated "Law". So the Law is both what God wanted from his people Israel at a specific period in history, and also a general design and guide for living. As a result, much of it could not apply literally and directly to us in our very different circumstances; but the general principles are timeless. Jesus himself gave his authority to "the two great commandments of the law": loving God and loving one's neighbour.

The New Testament critique of the law was no criticism of it, but of some attitudes towards it. There were two things in particular which the New Testament writers did criticize. The first was an inflexible and over-literal use of it. Laws must always be adapted to meet changing needs; if one obeys just the *letter* of the law, then the *spirit* of the law can be neglected and even disobeyed. The second complaint was even more serious: too many Jews of New Testament times made the Law the route to God, instead of the outworking of an already existing right relationship with him.

Deuteronomy, then, will not lead us to God—only faith in Christ can do that. But once we know and love God, we gain great profit from the principles enshrined in the laws of a book like Deuteronomy. They show us, in very practical terms, how we may obey God's will in many areas of daily life, provided that we adapt the precepts given to the very different social and political circumstances of the twentieth century.

WORDS WORTH PONDERING

Deuteronomy 1:1

¹These are the words...

The title of the Book of Deuteronomy is not an attractive one. "Deuteronomy" is a long and cumbersome word, meaningless to the man in the street, and certainly does not suggest that the book is likely to be interesting. Our forefathers translated the title of the previous book into English—"Numbers"—and it is a pity they chose to leave the title of this Fifth Book of Moses in its Greek form, untranslated. It means "Second Law" in Greek.

The traditional Hebrew name for the book is at least in plain language—"Words". This title was chosen simply because it is the first word of consequence in the first sentence of the book. We might well think it a strange Jewish custom to pick out the first word of a document to serve as its title, but in this case it is in fact a remarkably appropriate title. A glance through the pages of Deuteronomy in an RSV Bible shows that there is scarcely a paragraph which does not begin with inverted commas.

So the Hebrew name seems much better than the English one; and yet, for many people, "Words" could be just as forbidding a title. In today's world we are bombarded with words, and are not disposed to quarrel with the saying that "silence is golden". Are we really likely to find much interest or profit in a book that is nearly all *words*? "What sort of words?" we might inquire suspiciously; and the answer, "laws and sermons", is not likely to reassure us! But a moment's thought would remind us that the powers of thought and speech are fundamental to all human civilization and communication, a God-given blessing which lifts us above the animal kingdom. There are of course millions of words uttered which are stupid and silly, shoddy and pointless, useless and downright evil; but as Proverbs 25:11 points out, "A word fitly spoken is like apples of gold". Deuteronomy's claim to contain words worth pondering was endorsed by Jesus himself, for he considered it a book worth quoting repeatedly. Deuteronomy's words merit close attention.

Besides which, we must not lose a sense of proportion. Deuteronomy may be a book of words, but it stands in a whole series of books which recount events—the history of Israel during many generations and centuries. From Genesis through to 2 Kings, we find the consecutive record of major events in Israel's national life; here among that list we find Deuteronomy, a pivotal book which offers principles and reflections relevant to the on-going life of the nation. We find ourselves in a very different historical situation today; but if we find any profit in reading the historical books of the Old Testament, we should certainly be willing to study Deuteronomy to see what lessons it drew from history and brought to history.

A MESSAGE FOR CHANGING CIRCUMSTANCES

Deuteronomy 1:1–4

¹These are the words that Moses spoke to all Israel beyond the Jordan in the wilderness, in the Arabah over against Suph, between Paran and Tophel, Laban, Hazeroth, and Dizahab. ²It is eleven days' journey from Horeb by the way of Mount Seir to Kadesh-barnea. ³And in the fortieth year, on the first day of the eleventh month, Moses spoke to the people of Israel according to all that the Lord had given him in commandment to them, ⁴after he had defeated Sihon the king of the Amorites, who lived in Heshbon, and Og the king of Bashan, who lived in Ashtaroth and in Edre-i.

(i)

Deuteronomy begins by promising us *words*, as we have noted; but we are not told that they are timeless truths, nor even that God was the speaker. *Moses* is the speaker, we are told; and remarkably specific information about the occasion is added. We are told the audience, the location, the date and the situation.

Of course all this information must seem very remote to the modern reader. A small percentage of readers of this commentary may perhaps be citizens of Israel, and a handful of readers may even live in the general region described, namely, in the Negev wilderness to the south of Palestine; but even to them, Moses, and the events briefly referred to here, are impossibly remote. To the great majority of readers, all of this information seems very obscure and totally irrelevant. What is the point of it all?

Indeed the ancient Israelite readers might have asked much the same question. Although they lived very much nearer to the locations and to the events, nearness is only relative. Even at the geographical level, it is worth remembering that before the advent of modern transport, one hundred miles of barren terrain would have been an awesome and forbidding barrier. There can have been few Israelites who, like Elijah (1 Kings 19:3–9), ever made the journey south to *Horeb*—and he needed supernatural provisions! To generations of Israelites, Moses and the Exodus were as much ancient history as they are to us. The chief difference between them and us is that they looked back to Moses with feelings of pride and kinship—and obligation. They did not perceive the same cultural gap that we do.

What then is the relevance of all this detailed information? Several points can be made. (1) Deuteronomy is concerned with *facts*. God has not revealed himself by signs of some sort in the sky, but in very down-to-earth and practical ways. We are reading about real events and real places and real people. (2) Deuteronomy is concerned with *history*. Unlike some of the great oriental religions, the religion of the Bible teaches that the march of events in human history is unique and important. We are not helplessly caught in "the ever-circling years", but we find ourselves in a particular place at a particular time; and God has his purposes and goals for human history. History is going somewhere, and so are we. (3) God is concerned about *situations*. The Bible as a whole consists of God's revelations, given at many different times to many different people. (That explains why there are so many varied types of literature in the Bible.) He gave the guidance and direction necessary at the time to the people in a particular situation. As times changed, therefore, God's written guidance would need to be reconsidered, reapplied to meet changing circumstances. However, the Bible still needs careful consideration and careful application: it is not a fixed code of unchangeable laws, for instance, and it is certainly no book of magic spells.

(ii)

The situation portrayed is just outside Palestine, at a very significant time in the history of the Israelite people. Behind them lay the Exodus from Egypt and the years of homelessness in the wilderness; behind them lay the formative experience of the giving of the Law at *Horeb* (better known by the name Sinai). Before them lay the conquest of the "Promised Land", with its attendant dangers and difficulties; they had recent experience of hostility and battles on the borders of the land (v. 4). It was then a most appropriate moment for retrospect and reflection, for challenge, warning and guidance; and that is very largely what the book of Deuteronomy is going to offer.

The audience hearing Moses' words is described as "all Israel". This phrase emphasizes two things—the intended unity of Israel and also the relevance of the message to each individual Israelite, throughout the generations. The readers, of course, were not facing the same challenges, for they were already settled inside Palestine; but they were invited to put themselves in the position of their ancestors, and to consider their own subsequent history in the light of all that Deuteronomy had to say.

Finally, the speaker deserves attention. *Moses* was the great national leader who had led the Israelites out of Egypt and brought them to the borders of their homeland. He had made them a nation and given them a constitution. But above all, perhaps, we should stress his rôle as a prophet. No leader or politician is infallible; but the biblical record states emphatically that to certain men God chose to speak directly, giving them a message to pass on to others. The man is fallible, but his source of authority was not—and is not. The reader, ancient or modern, can have this assurance at the outset that the book of Deuteronomy commands attention not because of its human wisdom or shrewd insights, but because it offers divine revelation. The words will need interpretation and application, but their thrust and ultimate message bear the stamp of God's own truth and authority.

EXPERIENCES OF GOD'S CARE

Deuteronomy 1:5–25

⁵Beyond the Jordan, in the Land of Moab, Moses undertook to explain this law, saying, ⁶"The Lord our God said to us in Horeb, 'You have stayed long enough at this mountain; ⁷turn and take your journey, and go to the hill country of the Amorites, and to all their neighbours in the Arabah, in the hill country and in the lowland, and in the Negeb, and by the seacoast, the land of the Canaanites, and Lebanon, as far as the great river, the river Eu-phrates. ⁸Behold, I have set the land before you; go in and take possession of the land which the Lord swore to your fathers, to Abraham, to Isaac, and to Jacob, to give to them and to their descendants after them.'

⁹"At that time I said to you, 'I am not able alone to bear you; ¹⁰the Lord your God has multiplied you, and behold, you are this day as the stars of heaven for multitude. ¹¹May the Lord, the God of your fathers, make you a thousand times as many as you are, and bless you, as he has promised you! ¹²How can I bear alone the weight and burden of you and your strife? ¹³Choose wise, understanding, and experienced men, according to your tribes, and I will appoint them as your heads.' ¹⁴And you answered me, 'The thing that you have spoken is good for us to do.' ¹⁵So I took the heads of your tribes, wise and experienced men, and set them as heads over you, commanders of thousands, commanders of hundreds, commanders of fifties, commanders of tens, and officers, throughout your tribes. ¹⁶And I charged your judges at that time, 'Hear the cases between your brethren, and judge righteously between a man and his brother or the alien that is with him. ¹⁷You shall not be partial in judgment; you shall hear the small and the great alike; you shall not be afraid of the face of man, for the judgment is God's; and the case that is too hard for you, you shall bring to me, and I will hear it.' ¹⁸And I commanded you at that time all the things that you should do.

19"And we set out from Horeb, and went through all that great and terrible wilderness which you saw, on the way to the hill country of the Amorites, as the Lord our God commanded us; and we came to Kadesh-barnea. 20And I said to you, 'You have come to the hill country of the Amorites, which the Lord our God gives us. 21Behold, the Lord your God has set the land before you; go up, take possession, as the Lord, the God of your fathers, has told you; do not fear or be dismayed.' 22Then all of you came near me, and said, 'Let us send men before us, that they may explore the land for us, and bring us word again of the way by which we must go up and the cities into which we shall come.' 23The thing seemed good to me, and I took twelve men of you, one man for each tribe; 24and they turned and went up into the hill country, and came to the Valley of Eshcol and spied it out. 25And they took in their hands some of the fruit of the land and brought it down to us, and brought us word again, and said, 'It is a good land which the Lord our God gives us.'"

The bulk of the book of Deuteronomy will provide us with a detailed account of the *law* (v. 5); but first a long historical prologue, containing its own lessons, is incorporated. This continues to the end of chapter 3. This long section is therefore full of allusions to events and situations recorded in the books of Exodus and Numbers, the books which recount the story of Israel's wilderness wanderings over many years between Egypt and Canaan, their home-to-be (described by its various parts in vv. 7ff.). As Exodus tells the story, the definitive law had been given at Sinai (or Horeb) and the definitive covenant between God and Israel had also been inaugurated at the sacred mountain. Why then, we may ask, is Deuteronomy necessary, with its "second law" and covenant? The internal logic of Deuteronomy provides one answer to this question: Israel's forthcoming entry into the Promised Land would create a dramatic break with the past, as a wandering people became a settled nation, with an entirely different way of life. So Israel's great leader, Moses, takes great pains to make sure that Israel will be faithful to her God-given law and covenant, and will remember her formative past.

Another answer is provided by a consideration of the function of the book of Deuteronomy. It was not written to serve as a record of events long ago in Transjordan; on the contrary, it was a programme, a call to action. Just as the people of Israel in Moses' time needed to reconsider their position before embarking on their unseen future in Palestine, so too would later readers see in Deuteronomy a challenge and a programme of action. Above all, readers are invited to renew their covenant with their God; or in other words, to examine their hearts and lives, and then to reassert their loyalty to God's calling and service—a loyalty not so much in words as in practical day-to-day living. In a Christian context, the communion service should have a similar effect on our thinking and our conduct.

In this section, three reminders of past events are given.

(a) *The Promised Land* (v. 8). Israel faced a great many battles and hardships before the land would be won and settled, but the important thing to remember was that God had promised them ultimate victory. (Christians find similar reassurances in Heb. 11.) Later readers could cling to that exact promise when that same land would be threatened by all sorts of invaders, such as Philistines, Assyrians and Babylonians. In some sense, at least, God's people would never be homeless.

(b) *A thorough organization* (vv. 9–18). No single individual, however gifted, could personally look after a whole nation's needs; but God had already given his approval to a careful system of leadership and control. Every generation has its "wise, understanding, and experienced men"; not even a Moses is indispensable. So even in this historical section there is a note of promise. (The emphasis here is on the judicial sphere, as is appropriate in a book chiefly concerned with laws.)

(c) *A rich prospect* (vv. 19–25). There was a very great contrast between "all that great and terrible wilderness"—Israel's home since they had left Egypt—and the "good land" ahead of them in Palestine. Representatives of all the tribes had gone ahead to establish this fact, so that every tribe could be sure of a good home. Later readers probably needed this reminder of God's generosity in giving them such a home. It is all too easy to take life's blessings for granted, and even to grumble at them.

WRONG ATTITUDES

Deuteronomy 1:26–45

26"Yet you would not go up, but rebelled against the command of the Lord your God; 27and you murmured in your tents, and said, 'Because the Lord hated us he has brought us forth out of the land of Egypt, to give us into the hand of the Amorites, to destroy us. 28Whither are we going up? Our brethren have made our hearts melt, saying, "The people are greater and taller than we; the cities are great and fortified up to heaven; and moreover we have seen the sons of the Anakim there."' 29Then I said to you, 'Do not be in dread or afraid of them. 30The Lord your God who goes before you will himself fight for you, just as he did for you in Egypt before your eyes, 31and in the wilderness, where you have seen how the Lord your God bore you, as a man bears his son, in all the way that you went until you came to this place.' 32Yet in spite of this word you did not believe the Lord your God, 33who went before you in the way to seek you out a place to pitch your tents, in fire by night, to show you by what way you should go, and in the cloud by day.

34"And the Lord heard your words, and was angered, and he swore, 35'Not one of these men of this evil generation shall see the good land which I swore to give to your fathers, 36except Caleb the son of Jephunneh; he shall see it, and to him and to his children I will give the land upon which he has trodden, because he has wholly followed the Lord!' 37The Lord was angry with me also on your account, and said, 'You also shall not go in there; 38Joshua the son of Nun, who stands before you, he shall enter; encourage him, for he shall cause Israel to inherit it. 39Moreover your little ones, who you said would become a prey, and your children, who this day have no knowledge of good or evil, shall go in there, and to them I will give it, and they shall possess it. 40But as for you, turn, and journey into the wilderness in the direction of the Red Sea.'

41"Then you answered me, 'We have sinned against the Lord; we will go up and fight, just as the Lord our God commanded us.' And every man of you girded on his weapons of war, and thought it easy to go up into the hill country. 42And the Lord said to me, 'Say to them, Do not go up or fight, for I am not in the midst of you; lest you be defeated before your enemies.' 43So I spoke to you, and you would not hearken; but you rebelled against the command of the Lord, and were on, away from our brethren the sons of Esau who live in Seir, away from the Arabah road from Elath and Ezion-geber.

"And we turned and went in the direction of the wilderness of Moab. ⁹And the Lord said to me, 'Do not harass Moab or contend with them in battle, for I will not give you any of their land for a possession, because I have given Ar to the sons of Lot for a possession.' ¹⁰(The Emim formerly lived there, a people great and many, and tall as the Anakim; ¹¹like the Anakim they are also known as Rephaim, but the Moabites call them Emim. ¹²The Horites also lived in Seir formerly, but the sons of Esau dispossessed them, and destroyed them from before them, and settled in their stead; as Israel did to the land of their possession, which the Lord gave to them.) ¹³'Now rise up, and go over the brook Zered.' So we went over the brook Zered. ¹⁴And the time from our leaving Kadesh-barnea until we crossed the brook Zered was thirty-eight years, until the entire generation, that is, the men of war, had perished from the camp, as the Lord had sworn to them. ¹⁵For indeed the hand of the Lord was against them, to destroy them from the camp, until they had perished."

This section traces the movement of the Israelite people from *Kadesh-barnea* (1:46) to the *brook Zered* (2:14), and covers a period of thirty-eight years (2:14). The map on page xii shows that this slow journey brought them into close contact with two other ethnic groups—the Edomites, called "the sons of Esau" in this passage (vv. 1–8), and the Moabites (8–12). Both names occur frequently in the Old Testament, since both of these small states remained close neighbours of Israel for centuries. Relationships varied over these centuries; on the whole, little love was lost between Israel and these other groups. The book of Genesis reveals that the Israelites had a contemptuous view of the origins of the Moabites (as also the Ammonites), as Genesis 19:30–38 explains; but at the same time it is frankly acknowledged that the Edomites (cf. Gen. 36:1), Moabites and Ammonites were closely related to Israel. Other peoples mentioned in this section of Deuteronomy were perceived as foreigners—the Amorites (1:44) and the Horites (2:12), for instance. From an objective historical standpoint it would seem that the Israelites, Edomites, Moabites and Ammonites were part of one and the same movement of related tribes who settled in the south-eastern sector of

Syria–Palestine, to some extent displacing earlier populations (and to some extent filling sparsely-inhabited terrain), and who gradually evolved into small kingdoms. The Old Testament writings show awareness of this history, and it is interesting to note that Deuteronomy here explicitly acknowledges the rights of both Edom and Moab to the land they occupied. The people of Israel had no right at all to encroach upon "the territory of [their] brethren" (2:4), and more than that, they must seek to avoid giving any offence to them, or any cause for hostilities. It is important to observe that the Old Testament's attitude to peoples other than Israel is a varied one, and that it draws some careful distinctions.

These other peoples did not worship Israel's God, nor offer him any allegiance—they had their own tribal gods. However, Israel's God is said here to have been responsible for giving them territory (2:9). To the author of Deuteronomy, there was no other God, so Yahweh alone could have given the Moabites and others their lands. The Moabites, we may say, had a "Given Land"; the big difference was that Israel received a "Promised Land", since God chose to reveal his purposes to them beforehand. The other peoples were out of touch with the true God, but that in no way diminished their rights before God. In the same passage we see God giving lands to those who did not serve him, while denying land to a generation of Israelites who had seriously disobeyed him. This is an interesting contrast, and warns us against any naïve idea that God will automatically grant Christian individuals (or nations) every success in life, or that he will casually ignore the needs and rights of non-Christians. None of his relationships with men and women is casual; they are all governed by his principles of working and by his purposes, although both may be hidden from us at the time.

ISRAEL'S FIRST VICTORY

Deuteronomy 2:16–37

¹⁶"So when all the men of war had perished and were dead from

among the people, [17]the Lord said to me, [18]'This day you are to pass over the boundary of Moab at Ar; [19]and when you approach the frontier of the sons of Ammon, do not harass them or contend with them, for I will not give you any of the land of the sons of Ammon as a possession, because I have given it to the sons of Lot for a possession.' [20](That also is known as a land of Rephaim; Rephaim formerly lived there, but the Ammonites call them Zamzummim, [21]a people great and many, and tall as the Anakim; but the Lord destroyed them before them; and they dispossessed them, and settled in their stead; [22]as he did for the sons of Esau, who live in Seir, when he destroyed the Horites before them, and they dispossessed them, and settled in their stead even to this day. [23]As for the Avvim, who lived in villages as far as Gaza, the Caphtorim, who came from Caphtor, destroyed them and settled in their stead.) [24]'Rise up, take your journey, and go over the valley of the Arnon; behold, I have given into your hand Sihon the Amorite, king of Heshbon, and his land; begin to take possession, and contend with him in battle. [25]This day I will begin to put the dread and fear of you upon the peoples that are under the whole heaven, who shall hear the report of you and shall tremble and be in anguish because of you.'

[26]"So I sent messengers from the wilderness of Kedemoth to Sihon the king of Heshbon, with words of peace, saying, [27]'Let me pass through your land; I will go only by the road, I will turn aside neither to the right nor to the left. [28]You shall sell me food for money, that I may eat, and give me water for money, that I may drink; only let me pass through on foot, [29]as the sons of Esau who live in Seir and the Moabites who live in Ar did for me, until I go over the Jordan into the land which the Lord our God gives to us.' [30]But Sihon the king of Heshbon would not let us pass by him; for the Lord your God hardened his spirit and made his heart obstinate, that he might give him into your hand, as at this day. [31]And the Lord said to me, 'Behold, I have begun to give Sihon and his land over to you; begin to take possession, that you may occupy his land.' [32]Then Sihon came out against us, he and all his people, to battle at Jahaz. [33]And the Lord our God gave him over to us; and we defeated him and his sons and all his people. [34]And we captured all his cities at that time and utterly destroyed every city, men, women, and children; we left none remaining; [35]only the cattle we took as spoil for ourselves, with the booty of the cities which we captured. [36]From Aroer, which is on the edge of the valley of the Arnon, and from the city that is in the valley, as far as Gilead, there was

not a city too high for us; the Lord our God gave all into our hands. [37]Only to the land of the sons of Ammon you did not draw near, that is, to all the banks of the river Jabbok and the cities of the hill country, and wherever the Lord our God forbade us."

The story of Israel's northward march continues, now reaching Ammonite territory and the region towards the north end of the Dead Sea. Eventually the Israelites were to cross the River Jordan just north of the Dead Sea, near the ancient city of Jericho; but the story of this crossing into Palestine proper is held back until the early chapters of the book of Joshua. The north-eastern corner of the Dead Sea is the geographical context for the remainder of Deuteronomy.

This whole region was of considerable political interest to Israel; it was frontier territory during the period of the monarchy, when at times Israel dominated and governed Ammon, Moab and Edom, while at other times her own tribal territories in Transjordan, to the north of Ammon, were threatened if not actually overrun by various enemies. The scene is set in this chapter, and in chapter 3, for such later conflicts. As with Moab and Edom, it is stressed that Israel has no right to the lands of the Ammonites; but a quite different situation is described with regard to the city of *Heshbon*, ruled by its king *Sihon*. Heshbon was later one of the Moabites' chief towns, but at this point in time it was a small *Amorite* kingdom. The Amorites were one of the more important ethnic groups inhabiting Palestine and soon to be dispossessed by Israel, so this passage sees it as appropriate that there was immediate conflict between Amorites and Israelites—with victory for Israel as a sign of things to come. (Verse 25 is really concerned with all the peoples under the skies of Palestine, as we might express it, not with the whole world.)

While the Israelites were forewarned of Sihon's hostility, and promised victory over him, Sihon too had his rights, and he could have avoided trouble and defeat if he had been reasonable (vv. 26–29). But just like Pharaoh in Exodus chapters 6–12, Sihon was implacably obstinate (v. 30) and brought trouble on himself. Verse 30 does not mean to imply that Sihon had no will of his own; rather, it emphasizes that Sihon's obstinacy served God's purposes all along.

Here, for the first time in Deuteronomy, we find a detailed story about the Israelites' engagement in warfare; and also we are shown, for the first time, the Israelites butchering "men, women, and children" (v. 34). The statement in this verse that Israel "utterly destroyed" the Amorites of Heshbon implies in Hebrew that they did so not in the blood-lust of the moment, but as a deliberate religious action, a sort of gift to Yahweh. Such conduct, which today strikes us as barbaric, was by no means unique to Israel in the ancient Near East. God had yet to reveal to Israel the areas in which they must repudiate the ways of other nations; and another lesson yet to be learned was the value of the individual in God's sight. At that time it seemed only natural that a whole community should either suffer or prosper together.

The important point for the writer of Deuteronomy was that nothing and nobody could or would thwart God's plans for his people. This message was as reassuring for Israelites of a later age as its New Testament counterpart has been for generations of Christians: what shall separate us from the love of Christ?

THE MASTERY OF TRANSJORDAN

Deuteronomy 3:1–17

> [1]"Then we turned and went up the way to Bashan; and Og the king of Bashan came out against us, he and all his people, to battle at Edre-i. [2]But the Lord said to me, 'Do not fear him; for I have given him and all his people and his land into your hand; and you shall do to him as you did to Sihon the king of the Amorites, who dwelt at Heshbon.' [3]So the Lord our God gave into our hand Og also, the king of Bashan, and all his people; and we smote him until no survivor was left to him. [4]And we took all his cities at that time—there was not a city which we did not take from them—sixty cities, the whole region of Argob, the kingdom of Og in Bashan. [5]All these were cities fortified with high walls, gates, and bars, besides very many unwalled villages. [6]And we utterly destroyed them, as we did to Sihon the king of Heshbon, destroying every city, men, women, and children. [7]But all the cattle and the spoil

of the cities we took as our booty. ⁸So we took the land at that time out of the hand of the two kings of the Amorites who were beyond the Jordan, from the valley of the Arnon to Mount Hermon ⁹(the Sidonians call Hermon Sirion, while the Amorites call it Senir), ¹⁰all the cities of the tableland and all Gilead and all Bashan, as far as Salecah and Edre-i, cities of the kingdom of Og in Bashan. ¹¹(For only Og the king of Bashan was left of the remnant of the Rephaim; behold, his bedstead was a bedstead of iron; is it not in Rabbah of the Ammonites? Nine cubits was its length, and four cubits its breadth, according to the common cubit.)

¹²"When we took possession of this land at that time, I gave to the Reubenites and the Gadites the territory beginning at Aroer, which is on the edge of the valley of the Arnon, and half the hill country of Gilead with its cities; ¹³the rest of Gilead, and all Bashan, the kingdom of Og, that is, all the region of Argob, I gave to the half-tribe of Manasseh. (The whole of that Bashan is called the land of Rephaim. ¹⁴Jair the Manassite took all the region of Argob, that is, Bashan, as far as the border of the Geshurites and the Maacathites, and called the villages after his own name, Havvoth-jair, as it is to this day.) ¹⁵To Machir I gave Gilead, ¹⁶and to the Reubenites and the Gadites I gave the territory from Gilead as far as the valley of the Arnon, with the middle of the valley as a boundary, as far over as the river Jabbok, the boundary of the Ammonites; ¹⁷the Arabah also, with the Jordan as the boundary, from Chinnereth as far as the sea of the Arabah, the Salt Sea, under the slopes of Pisgah on the east."

Moving on from Heshbon, the Israelites next clashed with the small kingdom of *Bashan*; this time apparently, there was no attempt to avoid conflict or to negotiate, so we may assume that the fighting at Heshbon had alarmed its northern neighbour, and the ruler of Bashan, King *Og*, determined to take the offensive against Israel. Bashan was another Amorite kingdom, and no doubt considered Israel to be hostile to all Amorites. At any rate, here too the Israelites were victorious, and the enemy not only crushed but exterminated (vv. 3, 6).

This second victory was evidently a particularly memorable one, for two reasons. The major reason was that it placed the whole of Transjordan in Israelite hands; the names *Gilead* and *Bashan* (v. 10) comprise the whole region north of Ammon up to

Mount Hermon (v. 8), which was, and is still, a major geographical barrier. The other reason was the memory of the abnormal height of the defeated king, Og, recorded visually in a startling museum piece, later to be seen in the Ammonite capital city *Rabbah* (v. 11), modern Amman. This relic, some four metres in length, was by general consent not a "bedstead of iron", but rather a basalt sarcophagus—a "coffin, made of stone" (GNB). There is plainly no religious teaching about a detail like this; it testifies to the absorbed interest the biblical writer had in the past history of his people; an interest which was rewarded by many religious insights. Nowadays many of us visit museums or ancient monuments with a certain interest, but very often it is a very detached interest; perhaps a war memorial will elicit our gratitude, if only momentarily, for the sacrifices made by an earlier generation. Israel's gratitude was towards God, for victories which she saw as entirely God-given and, at times, miraculous.

The speaker, we remind ourselves, is Moses; Moses is described in verses 12–17 as having organized the newly conquered Amorite territory as tribal holdings. Once Israel came to settle in the whole "Promised Land", most of the tribal districts lay to the west of the River Jordan, but Reuben and Gad were wholly in Transjordan, while Manasseh spanned the river, with half of its tribal holding in Transjordan (vv. 12ff.). In this paragraph, Israel's land in Transjordan is carefully charted. Moses died before the Israelites marched into Palestine proper, but it is made clear here that the victory over the Amorites and the organization into tribal regions had Moses' authority behind them: the Transjordanian settlement is symbolic of the whole conquest. To Israel it was important that Moses' authority lay behind their conquest, because he was not only their first national leader, but also a prophet; in other words, a man in direct touch with God. Thus they could be sure that the organization of Israel, as it developed, had God's blessing upon it.

Organization and structures are very important to any community; to the Christian Church as much as to ancient Israel. It is interesting to discover, however, that the New Testament does not offer us a clear blueprint for Church organization; on the contrary, even the important title of "apostle" is ill-defined and problematic. No second Moses stands behind the specific organization of *any* of our Christian denominations. The New Testament instead points to the on-going activity of the Holy Spirit as the divine sanction for our practices and procedures. Flexibility and willingness to adapt to new circumstances are the characteristics of the Church which truly acknowledges God's authority.

PLANNING FOR THE FUTURE

Deuteronomy 3:18–29

[18]"And I commanded you at that time, saying, 'The Lord your God has given you this land to possess; all your men of valour shall pass over armed before your brethren the people of Israel. [19]But your wives, your little ones, and your cattle (I know that you have many cattle) shall remain in the cities which I have given you, [20]until the Lord gives rest to your brethren, as to you, and they also occupy the land which the Lord your God gives them beyond the Jordan; then you shall return every man to his possession which I have given you.' [21]And I commanded Joshua at that time, 'Your eyes have seen all that the Lord your God has done to these two kings; so will the Lord do to all the kingdoms into which you are going over. [22]You shall not fear them; for it is the Lord your God who fights for you.'

[23]"And I besought the Lord at that time, saying, [24]'O Lord God, thou hast only begun to show thy servant thy greatness and thy mighty hand; for what god is there in heaven or on earth who can do such works and mighty acts as thine? [25]Let me go over, I pray, and see the good land beyond the Jordan, that goodly hill country, and Lebanon.' [26]But the Lord was angry with me on your account, and would not hearken to me; and the Lord said to me, 'Let it suffice you; speak no more to me of this matter. [27]Go up to the top of Pisgah, and lift up your eyes westward and northward and southward and eastward, and behold it with your eyes; for you shall not go over this Jordan. [28]But charge Joshua, and encourage and strengthen him; for he shall go over at the head of this people, and he shall put them in possession of the land which you shall see.' [29]So we remained in the valley opposite Beth-peor."

This section brings to an end the historical prologue; indeed, it is a forward-looking passage, envisaging the full conquest of Palestine and the leadership of Joshua (after the death of Moses), and it sets the stage for Moses' death; he was to be buried "in the valley opposite Beth-peor" (v. 29, cf. 34:6). As a narrative, Deuteronomy 3 links directly with chapter 34, with 34:1 an immediate sequel to 3:29; but the book has been shaped to incorporate all the laws which make up the bulk of Deuteronomy, beginning in chapter 4.

Verses 18–20 concern the able-bodied men of Reuben and Gad, who had just acquired their tribal holdings to the east of the Jordan, and who might well have abandoned the major struggle for possession of Palestine; they had many herds (v. 19) which required constant tending, and the temptation must have been strong to settle down and enjoy their possessions. The reminder that Israel was a unity, and that all the tribes must fight the nation's battles, was a lesson of much wider application. Israel was a confederacy of tribes, and there was a permanent danger of disunity and disintegration; there are some parallels with the issues that brought about the American Civil War. Strength, as always, lies in unity; sectional interest must never be allowed to override national needs and responsibilities.

The instructions to *Joshua* (vv. 21ff.) are summed up in the phrase "You shall not fear". This was a natural and sensible enough message for the eve of a major campaign, and it was no trite and pointless remark, because it was based on experience, the experience of very recent victory. Victory was not a hope but a promise. The message was for every generation of Israel, moreover, for she was, and would remain, a small nation often threatened by bigger ones. Not that she would always gain victories—far from it. But a key term, not to be overlooked, is to be found in verse 20: God planned to give his people *rest* . In the context, this single word conveniently sums up victory, ensuing peace, and settlement in the Promised Land, which would speedily be known no longer as "the land of Canaan", but as "the land of Israel". Whatever the political vicissitudes of the years and centuries ahead, it would still be *their* land, even when they were the heavily taxed subjects of a foreign emperor. Even after the up-rooting of many people in the Babylonian Exile of the sixth century, the way back would one day present itself: the land of Israel would always be "home". As Hebrews 4 recognizes, this national "rest" would be partial and incomplete; but that is not the issue in Deuteronomy 3.

Finally, the chapter prepares the reader for the death of Moses. It is very likely that the Israelites always felt that Moses had died at an inopportune time and in an inappropriate place; similarly every British schoolboy is aware that Nelson was killed just before his greatest victory was accomplished. It is the sort of detail that a nation remembers and passes down from generation to generation. At any rate, this is not the only Old Testament passage which discusses Moses' death, and emphasizes that God determined it. Numbers 20:12 describes Moses' premature death as a punishment upon *him*; this passage prefers to say that it was a punishment upon Israel (v. 26). Even so, the nation would not be left leaderless (v. 28). Whatever their failings, God's people are never deprived of his guidance, nor are his promises cancelled.

THE LETTER OF THE LAW

Deuteronomy 4:1–8

[1]"And now, O Israel, give heed to the statutes and the ordinances which I teach you, and do them; that you may live, and go in and take possession of the land which the Lord, the God of your fathers, gives you. [2]You shall not add to the word which I command you, nor take from it; that you may keep the commandments of the Lord your God which I command you. [3]Your eyes have seen what the Lord did at Baal-peor; for the Lord your God destroyed from among you all the men who followed the Baal of Peor; [4]but you who held fast to the Lord your God are all alive this day. [5]Behold, I have taught you statutes and ordinances, as the Lord my God commanded me, that you should do them in the land which you are entering to take possession of it. [6]Keep them and do them; for that will be your wisdom and your understanding in the sight of the peoples, who, when they hear all these statutes,

will say, 'Surely this great nation is a wise and understanding people.'
7For what great nation is there that has a god so near to it as the Lord
our God is to us, whenever we call upon him? 8And what great nation
is there, that has statutes and ordinances so righteous as all this law
which I set before you this day?"

Chapter 4 serves as an introduction to all the laws of the chapters
that follow; it marks the start of a major section of Deuteronomy
(chapters 4–28). Chapter 3 has completed the historical retrospect, although there are some flashbacks in chapter 4 as well.
The call to "give heed" (v. 1) to God's laws is set against the grave
disregard of them which some Israelites had displayed at a place
called *Baal-peor* (v. 3): the story is told in Numbers 25. (Possibly
Baal-peor and Beth-peor, 3:29, were one and the same place.)
Baal-peor was a town dedicated to pagan worship; there was a
shrine there to the Canaanite god *Baal* (v. 3). The Israelites were
poised to enter the land of Canaan, where Canaanite culture and
religious customs would make a strong appeal to the less sophisticated Israelites; so the importance of fidelity to Yahweh could not
be emphasized too strongly. There was no doubt a clear message
here for the Jewish exiles as well, who returned from Babylonia to
their own land in the sixth century B.C.; they too were urged, as
they made a new beginning in their homeland, to be faithful to the
divine laws, recognizing that disobedience would bring fresh
disaster.

On the face of it, verse 2 invites a rigid legalism, for it seems to
put great emphasis on the letter of the law, and to allow no room
for modifications of it. There is no doubt that verses such as this
have been used to sanction a dead and restrictive legalism in some
areas and strands of Judaism, and for that matter Christianity too,
in spite of numerous New Testament passages warning against
such an attitude (especially Rom. 7:6; 2 Cor. 3:6). However,
several points must be made.

(a) *The instruction is given to the populace, not to legisla-
tors.* There was nothing to stop or hinder normal processes of the
development of law; but ordinary Israelites are urged not to
break laws.

(b) *We are dealing with secular laws as well as religious*; plainly no society would permit the ordinary citizen to play fast and loose with such laws as "You shall not kill" (5:17). The law code of Deuteronomy attached just as much importance to the First Commandment (5:7); to *add to* or *take from* this law would inevitably produce polytheism (or atheism).

(c) *The laws of Deuteronomy were a mark of "wisdom"*; a code visibly superior to those of surrounding nations (v. 6). If so, then these laws could not be arbitrary, meaningless rules and regulations. If they became irrelevant in the course of time, they would lose their meaning and become devoid of all wisdom. If our self-imposed religious rules ever strike the rest of mankind as meaningless and foolish, we ought to pause and ask ourselves whether *God* may not wish to add to, or diminish, their precise formulation.

(d) *The laws of Deuteronomy were a mark of "righteousness"* (v. 8). This verse too refutes any idea that the laws were arbitrary and apparently meaningless. The ethical standards of the law of Moses, handed down for generations, still proved attractive to many non-Jews in the Roman Empire in the first century, many of whom became Christians.

The primary intention of verse 2 is certainly not to fossilize religious customs for all time; it is rather to urge that God's laws should be taken with the utmost seriousness, and that we are not at liberty to adjust them to suit our own selfish, thoughtless or misguided, whims and schemes.

THE DANGERS OF IDOLATRY

Deuteronomy 4:9–24

⁹"Only take heed, and keep your soul diligently, lest you forget the things which your eyes have seen, and lest they depart from your heart all the days of your life; make them known to your children and your children's children—¹⁰how on the day that you stood before the Lord your God at Horeb, the Lord said to me, 'Gather the people to me, that I may let them hear my words, so that they may learn to fear me all

the days that they live upon the earth, and that they may teach their children so.' [11]And you came near and stood at the foot of the mountain, while the mountain burned with fire to the heart of heaven, wrapped in darkness, cloud, and gloom. [12]Then the Lord spoke to you out of the midst of the fire; you heard the sound of words, but saw no form; there was only a voice. [13]And he declared to you his covenant, which he commanded you to perform, that is, the ten commandments; and he wrote them upon two tables of stone. [14]And the Lord commanded me at that time to teach you statutes and ordinances, that you might do them in the land which you are going over to possess.

[15]"Therefore take good heed to yourselves. Since you saw no form on the day that the Lord spoke to you at Horeb out of the midst of the fire, [16]beware lest you act corruptly by making a graven image for yourselves, in the form of any figure, the likeness of male or female, [17]the likeness of any beast that is on the earth, the likeness of any winged bird that flies in the air, [18]the likeness of anything that creeps on the ground, the likeness of any fish that is in the water under the earth. [19]And beware lest you lift up your eyes to heaven, and when you see the sun and the moon and the stars, all the host of heaven, you be drawn away and worship them and serve them, things which the Lord your God has allotted to all the peoples under the whole heaven. [20]But the Lord has taken you, and brought you forth out of the iron furnace, out of Egypt, to be a people of his own possesson, as at this day. [21]Furthermore the Lord was angry with me on your account, and he swore that I should not cross the Jordan, and that I should not enter the good land which the Lord your God gives you for an inheritance. [22]For I must die in this land, I must not go over the Jordan; but you shall go over and take possession of that good land. [23]Take heed to yourselves, lest you forget the covenant of the Lord your God, which he made with you, and make a graven image in the form of anything which the Lord your God has forbidden you. [24]For the Lord your God is a devouring fire, a jealous God."

This passage recalls the formative experiences of Israel as a nation: the rescue of the Israelites from slavery in *Egypt* (v. 20) and the subsequent law-giving ceremony at the mountain called *Horeb* or Sinai (vv. 10–14)—the whole book of Exodus is devoted to these twin events. The brief summary given here emphasizes the harshness of the conditions they had endured in Egypt, and the fact that Israel, rescued from such a *furnace*, had exchanged it for a binding relationship with a God who was "a devouring fire" (v. 24). Such a powerful God was as much to be feared (v. 10) as any political foe—Egypt or Assyria or Babylon. Unlike Egypt, this God was to be loved as well as feared (cf. 6:5); but the first lesson Israel must learn was the reality of his existence, and all that it implied.

The main thrust of this section is a stern warning against various forms of idolatry (vv. 15–24), including idols made to represent Yahweh himself. The religious objects and exercises discussed in verses 16–19, all too familiar in the ancient world and not least among the Amorites and Canaanites, are totally alien in today's Western world; but the basic distinction made here between such practices and the worship of Yahweh is still relevant and important. The distinction is between what is seen and what is unseen. We in our age are well aware of the tremendous invisible power of electricity, for instance, and ancient peoples were no less aware of the mysterious power of the fertility of the soil, for example; but in every age, man is all too prone to trust what he can *see*, to give his attention to what is in front of him, and to neglect more intangible realities. We plan for tomorrow rather than next week; we prefer to treat surface symptoms and ignore the hidden infections. We prefer, it may be, to worship money, comfort, convenience, or status, rather than the challenging God who continues ever and again to bring his *words* (v. 12) to our attention. It is much easier to worship an idol, bow to a crucifix, send a cheque to the local church, than it is to listen to the voice of the invisible God. The Israelites were by no means the only ones who were inclined to choose a *form* rather than a *voice* (v. 12).

A key word in this passage is *covenant* (vv. 13, 23). Other peoples as yet knew no better than star-worship and suchlike (v. 19), but Israel had already entered into a solemn agreement to worship Yahweh and no other god. They now belonged to him exclusively (v. 20), just as a married man *belongs* to his wife, and vice versa. Any such solemn agreement has its stipulations, and the basic conditions of Israel's agreement were *the ten commandments* (v. 13), which will be listed in chapter 5. The Jews never forget that they are people of the covenant; Christians often need reminding that they are bound by the terms of "the new covenant" and the law of Christ (Heb. 9:15; Jas. 1:22–25).

THE AFTERMATH OF IDOLATRY

Deuteronomy 4:25–31

25"When you beget children and children's children, and have grown old in the land, if you act corruptly by making a graven image in the form of anything, and by doing what is evil in the sight of the Lord your God, so as to provoke him to anger, 26I call heaven and earth to witness against you this day, that you will soon utterly perish from the land which you are going over the Jordan to possess; you will not live long upon it, but will be utterly destroyed. 27And the Lord will scatter you among the peoples, and you will be left few in number among the nations where the Lord will drive you. 28And there you will serve gods of wood and stone, the work of men's hands, that neither see, nor hear, nor eat, nor smell. 29But from there you will seek the Lord your God, and you will find him, if you search after him with all your heart and with all your soul. 30When you are in tribulation, and all these things come upon you in the latter days, you will return to the Lord your God and obey his voice, 31for the Lord your God is a merciful God; he will not fail you or destroy you or forget the covenant with your fathers which he swore to them."

Two different periods of Israel's history are here brought together, telescoped in a single verse (26) which brings into one and the same perspective, Israel's occupation of Palestine (thirteenth century B.C.) and her experience of exile from it nearly seven hundred years later. The theme of the danger of idolatry, introduced in the previous paragraph, is continued and developed. Persistent idolatry will put the conquest of Palestine into reverse; that is the clear warning of verse 27, but the chief thrust of the passage is not so much a warning as an appeal. Before considering this appeal, however, we may fairly ask the question whether it is true that it was idolatry which caused the Babylonian Exile. Of course, major historical events have a whole network of causes behind them, and no doubt historians can suggest a whole series of causes. It is certainly true that idolatry plagued Israel between the Conquest and the Exile; and that after the humbling experience of the Exile, pagan worship was increasingly rejected by the Jewish people as a whole. We, who ourselves claim to worship the God of Israel, would be foolish indeed to deny his hand in history. It is also reasonable to argue that Israel's idolatry both weakened the moral fibre of the nation, and dissipated its inner strength and unity, making it easier prey for powerful nations like Assyria and Babylon.

Those Israelites of the sixth century who found themselves in exile, had no opportunity of worshipping their God in the established ways of temple rites and sacrifices, because they were located hundreds of miles away from their homeland. If temple rituals were what they wanted, then idolatry was now their only option (v. 28)! They had this choice; but this section of Deuteronomy makes a solemn and heartfelt appeal to the exiles to make a different choice: *ie* to "seek the Lord" (v. 29). The phrase was almost a technical one, meaning to make pilgrimage to a shrine; since that was physically impossible, verse 29 is appealing for a spiritual pilgrimage, a journey of the *heart* and *soul*: that is, the emotions and the will. "True worshippers", said Jesus, "worship the Father in spirit and truth", not (necessarily) in Jerusalem or in Samaria (John 4:23). We might have expected a promise that those who responded to this appeal would return to their homeland; instead, they are invited to "return to the Lord" (v. 30), although verse 31 adds that God will not *forget* his earlier promises to Abraham and the other patriarchs of Genesis—promises which first and foremost included the Promised Land. It is far more important to be in close touch with God than to live in any particular place on earth, however sacred to God or dear to us.

GOD AND HIS LAWS

Deuteronomy 4:32–49

[32]"For ask now of the days that are past, which were before you, since the day that God created man upon the earth, and ask from one end of heaven to the other, whether such a great thing as this has ever

happened or was ever heard of. [33]Did any people ever hear the voice of a god speaking out of the midst of the fire, as you have heard, and still live? [34]Or has any god ever attempted to go and take a nation for himself from the midst of another nation, by trials, by signs, by wonders, and by war, by a mighty hand and an outstretched arm, and by great terrors, according to all that the Lord your God did for you in Egypt before your eyes? [35]To you it was shown, that you might know that the Lord is God; there is no other besides him. [36]Out of heaven he let you hear his voice, that he might discipline you; and on earth he let you see his great fire, and you heard his words out of the midst of the fire. [37]And because he loved your fathers and chose their descendants after them, and brought you out of Egypt with his own presence, by his great power, [38]driving out before you nations greater and mightier than yourselves, to bring you in, to give you their land for an inheritance, as at this day; [39]know therefore this day, and lay it to your heart, that the Lord is God in heaven above and on the earth beneath; there is no other. [40]Therefore you shall keep his statutes and his commandments, which I command you this day, that it may go well with you, and with your children after you, and that you may prolong your days in the land which the Lord your God gives you for ever."

[41]Then Moses set apart three cities in the east beyond the Jordan, [42]that the manslayer might flee there, who kills his neighbour unintentionally, without being at enmity with him in time past, and that by fleeing to one of these cities he might save his life: [43]Bezer in the wilderness on the tableland for the Reubenites, and Ramoth in Gilead for the Gadites, and Golan in Bashan for the Manassites.

[44]This is the law which Moses set before the children of Israel; [45]these are the testimonies, the statutes, and the ordinances, which Moses spoke to the children of Israel when they came out of Egypt, [46]beyond the Jordan in the valley opposite Beth-peor, in the land of Sihon the king of the Amorites, who lived at Heshbon, whom Moses and the children of Israel defeated when they came out of Egypt. [47]And they took possession of his land and the land of Og the king of Bashan, the two kings of the Amorites, who lived to the east beyond the Jordan; [48]from Aroer, which is on the edge of the valley of the Arnon, as far as Mount Sirion (that is, Hermon), [49]together with all the Arabah on the east side of the Jordan as far as the Sea of the Arabah, under the slopes of Pisgah.

The appeal to the exiles is again made on the basis of earlier history; verses 32–38 stress in a vivid way how good God had been to Israel since the dawn of time, and challenge the listener or reader to find any comparable experience on the part of other nations and their gods. The ultimate truth was, indeed, that there was *no other* God; this clear expression of monotheism is the climax of the paragraph, in verse 39. If the returning exiles would learn this lesson thoroughly, then their successors would be able to rest secure in their homeland (v. 40). The appeal was thus a very practical one.

Fidelity to Yahweh meant not only the repudiation of idolatry but also full obedience to the whole law, in all its "statutes" and "commandments" (v. 40). Deuteronomy is undeniably *law* in our sense of the term; prohibitions and positive demands, with penalties for infringement attached. But what was the law understood to be? Verse 36 describes it as the *voice* of God, speaking in order to educate his people; *instruct* would be a better translation than "discipline." It seems that the basic sense of the Hebrew word *torah* (usually translated "law") is "teaching" or "instruction". The God-given laws of the Old Testament, no less than the Sermon on the Mount in the New Testament, have been well entitled "Design for Life". This is a helpful way of understanding the purpose of the law and the purpose of Deuteronomy in particular. Perhaps we should add one further word to this title: Deuteronomy offered a design for *corporate* life, a scheme for a whole nation. Some of the punishments are, by modern standards, extremely severe (as we shall see), but it seemed vital to protect the well-being of society as a whole.

We could not apply the Deuteronomic Law code as it stands to any modern society; it was a code designed precisely for Israel, and precisely for the Israel that existed well over two thousand years ago. As it stands, it would not even be appropriate for the present-day State of Israel. Is it then a code of law which has been repealed, so to speak? To envisage it in this way would be to choose a half-truth; it is better to think of it as a book of instruction, from which we may learn as much as ancient Israel, provided that we are ready to adapt its teaching to our own times and situations.

Verses 44–49 provide the immediate context for the law-giving, and summarize the contents of chapters 2 and 3. The geographical context was Transjordan, the area allotted to the Reubenites, the Gadites and the half tribe of Manasseh (cf. 3:12–17); the editor of Deuteronomy found this a convenient juncture to mention *three* special *cities* of Transjordan which played an important rôle in the administration of law (vv. 41–43); this rôle is discussed more fully in chapter 19.

THE TEN COMMANDMENTS

Deuteronomy 5:1–21

¹And Moses summoned all Israel, and said to them, "Hear, O Israel, the statutes and the ordinances which I speak in your hearing this day, and you shall learn them and be careful to do them. ²The Lord our God made a covenant with us in Horeb. ³Not with our fathers did the Lord make this covenant, but with us, who are all of us here alive this day. ⁴The Lord spoke with you face to face at the mountain, out of the midst of the fire, ⁵while I stood between the Lord and you at that time, to declare to you the word of the Lord; for you were afraid because of the fire, and you did not go up into the mountain. He said:

⁶"'I am the Lord your God, who brought you out of the land of Egypt, out of the house of bondage.

⁷"'You shall have no other gods before me.

⁸"'You shall not make for yourself a graven image, or any likeness of anything that is in heaven above, or that is on the earth beneath, or that is in the water under the earth; ⁹you shall not bow down to them or serve them; for I the Lord your God am a jealous God, visiting the iniquity of the fathers upon the children to the third and fourth generation of those who hate me, ¹⁰but showing steadfast love to thousands of those who love me and keep my commandments.

¹¹"'You shall not take the name of the Lord your God in vain: for the Lord will not hold him guiltless who takes his name in vain.

¹²"'Observe the sabbath day, to keep it holy, as the Lord your God commanded you. ¹³Six days you shall labour, and do all your work; ¹⁴but the seventh day is a sabbath to the Lord your God; in it you shall not do any work, you, or your son, or your daughter, or your man-servant, or your maidservant, or your ox, or your ass, or any of your

cattle, or the sojourner who is within your gates, that your manservant and your maidservant may rest as well as you. 15You shall remember that you were a servant in the land of Egypt, and the Lord your God brought you out thence with a mighty hand and an outstretched arm; therefore the Lord your God commanded you to keep the sabbath day.

16"'Honour your father and your mother, as the Lord your God commanded you; that your days may be prolonged, and that it may go well with you, in the land which the Lord your God gives you.

17"'You shall not kill.

18"'Neither shall you commit adultery.

19"'Neither shall you steal.

20"'Neither shall you bear false witness against your neighbour.

21"'Neither shall you covet your neighbour's wife; and you shall not desire your neighbour's house, his field, or his manservant, or his maidservant, his ox, or his ass, or anything that is your neighbour's.'"

(i)

All Israel is *summoned* to hear God's laws publicly declared—or rather, publicly repeated, for a new generation. The law code of Deuteronomy, although it has its own distinctive features, is not radically different from the laws contained earlier in the Bible: the Ten Commandments, to begin with, are the same as those listed in Exodus 20, despite some modifications in the expression of them. Moreover, it is plain that the biblical writer considered it to be exactly the same law code, but now proclaimed to a new generation—the Israelites about to enter the Promised Land. It is strongly emphasized in verse 3 that these laws were no relic from a previous era (like Og's "bedstead"!), but had direct and immediate relevance to the listeners. (Verse 3 would be better translated "It was not so much with our fathers that the Lord made this covenant as with us . . .") God's word is always for today. The first readers of Deuteronomy will have been challenged in the same way; they too were reminded of the immediacy of God's call to obedience.

We are so familiar with the Ten Commandments that we tend to take their structure and perhaps their contents for granted. They are certainly remarkable in a legal document; such documents are usually extremely impersonal, but here we find God speaking in the first person, and talking directly to his people, and what is more, addressing them as individuals. (The "you" in the Commandments is singular, as the "thou" of older English versions made clear). We find explanations, warnings, and even a promise (as the New Testament pointed out, cf. Eph. 6:2) interspersed with the commands themselves. The structure of the Ten Commandments (or let us use the briefer title, "the Decalogue") has raised a good deal of discussion among scholars; many believe that the Decalogue must have been a spoken exhortation from the beginning, rather than a law code, transmitted to the people by various human spokesmen. In that respect, it no doubt differs from the many individual laws and ordinances that follow it, both in Exodus and Deuteronomy. Both Exodus and Deuteronomy treat the Decalogue as fundamental to the whole law code; and both Jews and Christians have always considered it a foundation document.

These governing principles for the people of God have already been said to equal ten in number (4:13). There is some disagreement as to which is which (for example, Jews take v. 6 as the first, while the Christian traditions begin with v. 7), but there is no controversy over the fact that they number ten. The point in giving them a definite number is that they belong together—all the other laws can be considered simply the outworking of them. Taken together, they lay down the basic duties of man; or to consider the other side of the coin, they make clear basic human rights and also (indeed, first and foremost) basic *divine* rights. Only those who have entered into a covenant with God, can be expected to obey the earlier commandments in the list, although we should not underestimate the universal values enshrined in the Decalogue; but all those who are in such a relationship with God are expected to heed and respect these ten principles. Christians, as the New Testament assures us, are not subject to the wide range of regulations of the Jewish law; but the rights of God and man are neglected by Christians at their peril. Nor can we pick and choose among the ten; some Christians behave as if they can ignore their fellow men so long as they give God his due. James 2:10ff. has the answer to that attitude!

On the other hand, these principles need thoughtful consideration and careful application, for they are not entirely self-explanatory. For example, "work" (v. 13) is not defined, and the Jewish definition of it is very distinctive; how is such a principle meant to be honoured in a Christian context? Similar issues arise for all the commandments.

GOD'S DUE

Deuteronomy 5:6–11 (*cont'd*)

6" 'I am the Lord your God, who brought you out of the land of Egypt, out of the house of bondage.

7" 'You shall have no other gods before me.

8" 'You shall not make for yourself a graven image, or any likeness of anything that is in heaven above, or that is on the earth beneath, or that is in the water under the earth; 9you shall not bow down to them or serve them; for I the Lord your God am a jealous God, visiting the iniquity of the fathers upon the children to the third and fourth generation of those who hate me, 10but showing steadfast love to thousands of those who love me and keep my commandments.

11" 'You shall not take the name of the Lord your God in vain: for the Lord will not hold him guiltless who takes his name in vain.' "

(ii)

Verse 6 begins by indicating the basis for the demands that follow; God had claimed Israel's allegiance by rescuing them from Egypt. We are not called to honour God just because he exists, but because of his unfailing goodness to us, and because of the salvation he has provided in Christ. The first commandment (v. 7) follows logically: in a world where many gods were worshipped, Israel was called to the exclusive worship of the one and only God who had rescued his people. It is easy enough for us to have substitute gods today—money, pleasure, self—but perhaps, in the atheistic West of today, the equivalent command would be simply a call to worship. In the ancient world, the temptation was to follow the herd and worship at the shrines of false gods; in our world, the temptation is to follow the herd and neglect all forms of worship. God has the *right* to be worshipped, and men—not least those who profess to be Christians—have a *duty* to worship him.

God also has the right to be worshipped *properly*; that is the thrust of the second commandment (v. 8), which prohibited the Israelites from using pagan methods to worship the true God. (The verse also rules out idolatry of any kind.) There were two dangers in idolatry. The *first* was that the image would be confused with the deity it represented. (It is true that ancient pagan theologians did not make this confusion; but one imagines that many ordinary worshippers found the distinction an over-subtle one.) The *second* danger was the belief that God could be manipulated just as easily as an inanimate object, like an idol, could be moved about. The wish to manipulate God, and the foolish idea that it can be done, are by no means absent from the Churches today. The best word to describe the attempt to bend God to our wills is "magic"; true religion consists in the willingness to let God bend us to his will!

Another way of interpreting the second commandment is to see it as a warning against making God fit into the cultural norms of the day. To use the tag "God is love" to justify total sexual licence might be a particularly blatant illustration of such an attitude; but in fact there is always the insidious danger of limiting God to our ways of thinking, conditioned as we are by our cultural environment.

God's third right (v. 11) has often been misunderstood; this commandment had nothing to do with swearing and "bad language". Nor is it likely that it was a prohibition of false promises to other people, made in the name of Yahweh; if it was, it would belong with the other *human* rights, later in the Decalogue. More probably it refers to the use of God's name in incantations and magical rituals. In a sense, this was a misuse of power, since to utter aloud the name of any deity was thought at the time to have a powerful, frightening effect. It amounted to wrongful use of divine things to achieve one's own ends—often at the expense of other people. This commandment, then, attacks not the careless and casual use of God's name, but rather the deliberate use of it for evil purposes. True reverence would certainly avoid irreverent language; but more, it humbly acknowledges God's power and bows to it, never seeking to impose it upon others.

KEEPING THE SABBATH

Deuteronomy 5:12-15 (cont'd)

> [12]"'Observe the sabbath day, to keep it holy, as the Lord your God commanded you. [13]Six days you shall labour, and do all your work; [14]but the seventh day is a sabbath to the Lord your God; in it you shall not do any work, you, or your son, or your daughter, or your manservant, or your maidservant, or your ox, or your ass, or any of your cattle, or the sojourner who is within your gates, that your manservant and your maidservant may rest as well as you. [15]You shall remember that you were a servant in the land of Egypt, and the Lord your God brought you out thence with a mighty hand and an outstretched arm; therefore the Lord your God commanded you to keep the sabbath day.'"

(iii)

Sacred days were common enough in the ancient world, but it seems very probable that a weekly *sabbath* was unique to Israel. The human value of such an institution is widely recognized in practical terms, in that most of the world now divides time into weeks—and anticipates the weekend with a lot of pleasure! No doubt certain sacred practices marked the day, for it is described as "holy" (v. 12); and it is no accident that in due course, special synagogue services were held on the sabbath day among the Jews, and the early Christian Church followed the same pattern (although it came to prefer Sunday to Saturday as the holy day of the week).

Among other nations, sacred days were marked by taboos—arbitrary superstitious prohibitions in case the gods should be offended. The fourth commandment, however, prohibits one single thing—*work*—and does so on perfectly logical grounds. In Exodus 20:8-11, the Israelites are told to do no work on the sabbath because of the divine pattern set at creation; but here in

Deuteronomy, the motive is humanitarian. The liberated Israelites who had escaped from Egypt had known only too well the slavery of hard, ceaseless, unremitting toil; they must now make a weekly rest from work not just a benefit for themselves but, more particularly, a gift to their employees. Work is not defined, and rightly so; in an agricultural economy (and the Israelites in Palestine were largely an agricultural people) it is impossible to avoid *all* work on a Saturday, for cows have to be milked and livestock fed. The *principle*, however, was clear enough. If the farmer himself chose to work, he would almost certainly force his employees to work, since so many tasks on a farm require several pairs of hands.

One day each week, then, for worship and for rest, is a heritage for which to be profoundly thankful. But unfortunately by Christian times, the Jewish sabbath had attracted a multitude of rules and regulations; and this may be one reason why the Christian Church decided on a different holy day. Most of the commandments are negatives, but this one is positive—"Observe the sabbath day"—and there is something basically wrong when it is turned into a day of prohibitions. It is worth pondering that this commandment is not clearly endorsed in the New Testament; indeed Paul even seems to put a question mark against it in Galatians 4:9–11. It is important to take a balanced view of it. It is quite wrong to treat Sunday as if the other days of the week did not belong equally to God; it is quite wrong to make a fetish or an idol of the day; it is quite wrong to get *our* enjoyment of the day out of imposing irksome restrictions upon *others* (including, it may be, our own children). It is above all a day to enjoy, and to share with God.

SOCIAL OBLIGATIONS

Deuteronomy 5:16–21 (*cont'd*)

[16]"'Honour your father and your mother, as the Lord your God commanded you; that your days may be prolonged, and that it may go well with you, in the land which the Lord your God gives you.
[17]"'You shall not kill.

¹⁸ "'Neither shall you commit adultery.

¹⁹ "'Neither shall you steal.

²⁰ "'Neither shall you bear false witness against your neighbour.

²¹ "'Neither shall you covet your neighbour's wife; and you shall not desire your neighbour's house, his field, or his manservant, or his maidservant, his ox, or his ass, or anything that is your neighbour's.'"

(iv)

The remaining commandments "have to do with obligations to parents and with the life, person, property and reputation of one's fellows" (J. A. Thompson, see Further Reading). The first of them was of great practical importance in an age when the family unit provided not only the social fabric of the nation but also its whole welfare progamme. It is to be noted, however, that the instruction is not to *obey* parents, necessarily—the New Testament endorses obedience of children to parents (Eph. 6:1), but the Decalogue is primarily addressed to grown adults. The command is to *honour* them, which denotes an attitude of mind and an outlook; their dignity and well-being must be carefully considered and protected.

The prohibition against killing, adultery and theft, speak for themselves; but it should be noted that killing is literally "murder". This commandment is not discussing either killing in conditions of warfare, or capital punishment; both of which are in fact recognized as legitimate elsewhere in Deuteronomy. Here we see basic and unalterable laws for any society—and of course most societies have comparable laws on their statute books. These are not merely laws, however, but divine education, a design for life; so such simple and obvious instructions merit deeper thought. Jesus, no less, showed us the way to interpret them, when he linked murder with anger, and adultery with lustfulness (Matt. 5:21–30). The evil deeds, which we all spurn, begin with those inward thoughts and attitudes which we can so easily cover up and hide from others. Jesus had no need to explore the motivation that lies behind theft, because the last commandment, which bans all covetousness and greed, already does this for the reader. The ninth commandment concerns court cases, where false testimony, under the penal laws of the day, might often result in the execution of one's *neighbour*. If indeed an Israelite did covet his neighbour's wife, house, and so on, then, by bringing a malicious charge against the neighbour, he might well secure what he desired. At the very least, his neighbour's reputation was likely to suffer.

Widespread disobedience to these laws and principles would undermine the whole social fabric of Israel—or indeed, any nation or community. The list is remarkable in that it ends with a purely internal human failing—covetousness—a failing which plainly no courts, in Israel or anywhere else, could punish or correct. Some scholars, puzzled by this fact, have argued that a more practical and tangible action must be meant—in other words, theft of some sort—but verse 19 has already prohibited that. It seems that we are to see the tenth commandment as a principle of wide relevance rather than a law; its New Testament counterpart states that "the love of money is the root of all evils" (1 Tim. 6:10). A great many crimes and misdeeds are motivated by desires of various sorts; very few crimes are ultimately divorced from the emotions of pride or greed. The motto for the Christian is surely that of Paul: "I have learned, in whatever state I am, to be content" (Phil. 4:11).

TRUE OBEDIENCE

Deuteronomy 5:22–33

22"These words the Lord spoke to all your assembly at the mountain out of the midst of the fire, the cloud, and the thick darkness, with a loud voice; and he added no more. And he wrote them upon two tables of stone, and gave them to me. 23And when you heard the voice out of the midst of the darkness, while the mountain was burning with fire, you came near to me, all the heads of your tribes, and your elders; 24and you said, 'Behold, the Lord our God has shown us his glory and greatness, and we have heard his voice out of the midst of the fire; we have this day seen God speak with man and man still live. 25Now therefore why should we die? For this great fire will consume us; if we hear the voice of the Lord our God any more, we shall die. 26For who is there of all flesh, that has heard the voice of the living God speaking out of the midst of fire, as we have, and has still lived? ²⁷Go near, and hear all that the Lord our God will say; and speak to us all that the Lord our God will speak to you; and we will hear and do it.'

²⁸"And the Lord heard your words, when you spoke to me; and the Lord said to me, 'I have heard the words of this people, which they have spoken to you; they have rightly said all that they have spoken. ²⁹Oh that they had such a mind as this always, to fear me and to keep all my commandments, that it might go well with them and with their children for ever! ³⁰Go and say to them, "Return to your tents." ³¹But you, stand here by me, and I will tell you all the commandment and the statutes and the ordinances which you shall teach them, that they may do them in the land which I give them to possess.' ³²You shall be careful to do therefore as the Lord your God has commanded you; you shall not turn aside to the right hand or to the left. ³³You shall walk in all the way which the Lord your God has commanded you, that you may live, and that it may go well with you, and that you may live long in the land which you shall possess."

Both in Exodus and Deuteronomy, the Ten Commandments are treated as the fundamental laws or principles governing Israel's community life and its relationship with God; the many other rules and regulations are seen as the outworkings of the Decalogue. This section of Deuteronomy draws a distinction between the two. The Decalogue was declared to all Israel by the voice of God himself, and then written down, again by God himself, on two stone tablets (v. 22); the remainder of the law (yet to be outlined) is revealed to Moses, whose task it will be to teach it. It will serve as the foundation of life and conduct once the Israelites are in Palestine (v. 31). The Decalogue is the fixed basis, indelibly recorded in stone, years earlier; the rest of the law is more contingent, for it relates specifically to life in Palestine (and not, for instance, to life in the wilderness or life in exile). It may well be that, as a document, Deuteronomy was brought to the attention of the exiles returning from Babylon; if so, they will have known the Decalogue by heart, but the remainder of the law code will have been relatively new to them (at least as Deuteronomy expresses and explains it). Its relevance to their lives back in the Promised Land will have been made very clear in this passage, especially verse 33, which offers a conditional promise that they can avoid exile in the future.

To all generations of Israelites before Deuteronomy became known and accessible, the Decalogue held a special place. The two tablets were preserved in their holiest shrine, with their most sacred object, the ark of the covenant (10:5; 1 Kings 8:6); but their contents, the Ten Commandments in their shortest form, will surely have been known by heart. The tradition of the terrifying experience of God's presence at Sinai will also have been extremely well known. The every-day laws of the nation, by contrast, will have been administered in the law courts as and when they were relevant, and the Israelites will not have memorized them. So this passage emphasizes, above all, that God was just as much the author of the detailed laws as he was of the great principles enshrined in the Ten Commandments. The authority of Moses is also behind them, although that is ultimately less important.

The Israelite, then, was not free to act just as he pleased as long as he kept the Ten Commandments in his own fashion; verse 32 indicates that he must not *deviate* in any direction. By New Testament times there was a major disagreement between the Sadducees and the Pharisees about obeying the Law of Moses (not merely the Decalogue, of course). The Sadducees did feel a freedom to act as they pleased where the Law of Moses offered no rulings; but the Pharisees were truer to the spirit of this chapter when they insisted that God's rules for life went far beyond "the letter of the law". That is not to say that we should agree with, or follow, all their interpretations or their rules; but it is certainly true that to pay lip-service (however genuine) to broad principles only, can lead far too easily to all sorts of failures to perceive the will of God for all the varied circumstances of life. It is a laudable aim to seek to obey "the Word of God" in all respects; but as soon as we limit his Word to the literal words of Holy Scripture, we are, in fact, in serious danger of disobedience. True obedience consists in carrying out God's will for the precise circumstances in which we find ourselves.

PERMANENT REMINDERS

Deuteronomy 6:1–9

[1]"Now this is the commandment, the statutes and the ordinances which the Lord your God commanded me to teach you, that you may do them in the land to which you are going over, to possess it; [2]that you may fear the Lord your God, you and your son and your son's son, by keeping all his statutes and his commandments, which I command you, all the days of your life; and that your days may be prolonged. [3]Hear therefore, O Israel, and be careful to do them; that it may go well with you, and that you may multiply greatly, as the Lord, the God of your fathers, has promised you, in a land flowing with milk and honey.

[4]"Hear, O Israel: The Lord our God is one Lord; [5]and you shall love the Lord your God with all your heart, and with all your soul, and with all your might. [6]And these words which I command you this day shall be upon your heart; [7]and you shall teach them diligently to your children, and shall talk of them when you sit in your house, and when you walk by the way, and when you lie down, and when you rise. [8]And you shall bind them as a sign upon your hand, and they shall be as frontlets between your eyes. [9]And you shall write them on the door-posts of your house and on your gates."

(i)

The appeal to treat the full range of God's laws with the utmost seriousness and careful attention is reinforced in these two paragraphs, which contain some of the most well-known verses in Deuteronomy. Nobody could accuse devout Jews, down to our own era, of neglecting verses 4–9, which they seek to apply in the most thorough, and indeed literal, way. Small scrolls, containing verses 4–9 and some other brief Old Testament passages, are placed in small containers (known as "phylacteries", cf. Matt. 23:5) which are bound to the arm and forehead during prayer; and another similar container (called a "mezuzah") is set into the doorposts of Jewish houses. The duty of educating children in the Jewish faith (cf. v. 7) has also been taken very seriously indeed. Verse 5 is equally well-known in Christian circles, since our Lord described it as "the great and first commandment" (Matt. 22:37–38).

While it is not certain that the instructions of verses 8ff. were originally meant to be taken literally, as Jewish people take them, the instructions do seem too detailed and elaborate to be purely metaphorical. In any case, the real point of the instruction was not physical but symbolic: God's laws are meant to affect both the person and his home, day in, day out. The setting for these famous verses is important; this passage is part of the long preface to the detailed law code which begins in chapter 12, and it seeks to bring home to the reader the importance of reading, learning, obeying and applying not only the Ten Commandments of chapter 5, but all the lesser rulings of later chapters. The books of Kings maintain that it was ignorance of, neglect of, and disobedience to, God's laws, which led to the fall of Jerusalem in 587 B.C., and to the Babylonian Exile. The lesson for the returning exiles, later that century, was plain: from the start, as they re-entered their land, they must "learn, mark and inwardly digest" all God's laws. Then they would prosper and multiply (v. 3) and have no need to fear any further national disasters. It was vital, then, to keep those laws always in one's mind's eye (vv. 8–9), and to teach them in detail to every new generation (v. 7).

But why—apart from sheer self-interest—should the law code be obeyed? The motivation is supplied in verses 4 and 5. In the *first* place, there could be no other god for Israel. However, (as the RSV footnote shows) the exact sense of verse 4 is in some doubt, although the general tenor of it is clear enough. No other deity could have any laws for Israelites to follow. In the *second* place, the Israelites had a duty to *love* their God; the covenant bound them to him not only in obligation, but also in a close, warm relationship. The Christians' duty to God cannot be any less. The Bible by the bedside—or better still, in the livingroom—might well serve the purpose of providing the constant reminder of God's wishes, which we all need.

THE GREAT CHALLENGE

Deuteronomy 6:5 (*cont'd*)

[5]"And you shall love the Lord your God with all your heart, and with all your soul, and with all your might."

(ii)

This key verse deserves more thorough attention. The command to *love* is all too easy to take for granted, simply because the verse is so well-known. It was not the usual emotion towards a deity in the ancient Near East; fear was much more common. Indeed, the whole concept of loving God was drawn from the language of human relationships (and may even have been rather daring language when first applied to the Almighty). Israel's relationship with God was compared by Hosea to the relationship between man and wife; he and other Old Testament writers described idolatry in terms of illicit sexual relations—harlotry, in fact (*eg* Hos. 2). The bond of love between a man and a woman has two effects which are relevant to this section of Deuteronomy: (1) it is exclusive; (2) it is constant. That is to say, a man in love has but one object of his affections; and he wants to spend all his time with his loved one. Deuteronomy 6:5 then makes this claim upon Israel: as a people, Israel should acknowledge only one God, and spend all her time seeking to please him.

No half-hearted sentiment is good enough. Nothing could be more emphatic than the second half of the verse: "with all your heart, and with all your soul, and with all your might". In the New Testament repetition of this verse, the word "mind" is added to the list (Mark 12:30). Probably this is because the Greek words did not quite equate in meaning with the Hebrew words in Deuteronomy. In its literal sense, of course, the same thing is meant by the "heart", for instance, in any language; but figuratively speaking, "heart" denotes the emotions in English, while the Hebrew equivalent denotes the intellect (as in the phrase "foolish of heart"). Perhaps we should paraphrase "heart", "soul" and "might" in Deuteronomy 6:5 as *intellect, emotions* and *will-power*. Our love for God (as for our wives, children or parents) must *first* be practicable and intelligent; love that does not show itself in forethought and sensible actions is worth very little. *Second*, it must—of course—stir our emotions. Mere "going through the motions" of religious observances and rituals requires no emotion whatsover. The God who loved us and gave his

Son for us asks for a genuinely loving response. *Third*, true love for God will exercise our will-power. It is easy to make promises in the heat of an emotion—for example, during the experience of conversion, or when listening to a powerful sermon. To fulfil them afterwards, when circumstances are not so conducive, requires a certain determination. It is then that the reality of our love is tested.

Put together, these three challenging phrases add up to this: You shall love your God with all your being, with every aspect of your personality, without exception or reservation. An impossible target? It is certainly an ideal, but much depends upon the wishes hidden deep within us: do we really *want* to love God, or merely keep on the right side of him?

MAINTAINING DEVOTION TO GOD

Deuteronomy 6:10–25

[10]"And when the Lord your God brings you into the land which he swore to your fathers, to Abraham, to Isaac, and to Jacob, to give you, with great and goodly cities, which you did not build, [11]and houses full of all good things, which you did not fill, and cisterns hewn out, which you did not hew, and vineyards and olive trees, which you did not plant, and when you eat and are full, [12]then take heed lest you forget the Lord, who brought you out of the land of Egypt, out of the house of bondage. [13]You shall fear the Lord your God; you shall serve him, and swear by his name. [14]You shall not go after other gods, of the gods of the peoples who are round about you; [15]for the Lord your God in the midst of you is a jealous God; lest the anger of the Lord your God be kindled against you, and he destroy you from off the face of the earth.

[16]"You shall not put the Lord your God to the test, as you tested him at Massah. [17]You shall diligently keep the commandments of the Lord your God, and his testimonies, and his statutes, which he has commanded you. [18]And you shall do what is right and good in the sight of the Lord, that it may go well with you, and that you may go in and take possession of the good land which the Lord swore to give to your

fathers [19]by thrusting out all your enemies from before you, as the Lord has promised.

[20]"When your son asks you in time to come, 'What is the meaning of the testimonies and the statutes and the ordinances which the Lord our God has commanded you?' [21]then you shall say to your son, 'We were Pharaoh's slaves in Egypt; and the Lord brought us out of Egypt with a mighty hand; [22]and the Lord showed signs and wonders, great and grievous, against Egypt and against Pharaoh and all his household, before our eyes; [23]and he brought us out from there, that he might bring us in and give us the land which he swore to give to our fathers. [24]And the Lord commanded us to do all these statutes, to fear the Lord our God, for our good always, that he might preserve us alive, as at this day. [25]And it will be righteousness for us, if we are careful to do all this commandment before the Lord our God, as he has commanded us.'"

The call to utter devotion to God in verse 5 seems comprehensive enough, but one very common, almost universal, human failing is to slip backwards from high standards and from good intentions; imperceptibly, over the course of time, those standards and intentions become eroded. So although the Israelites, whether in the time of Moses or at the end of the Exile, may have responded to the appeal of verse 5 with enthusiasm and sincerity, the danger was that, in the course of time, they would *forget* (v. 12). It is particularly easy to forget to be grateful; prosperity in Palestine, even though the Israelites had done nothing to earn it, was likely to wipe out the memory of adversity in Egypt (vv. 10–12). To "forget the Lord" meant, in practical terms, turning to pagan *gods* (v. 14). It is a general truth that affluence tends to dull one's spiritual life and perceptions. A stern warning is given (v. 15): if God's gifts are not appreciated, they may be wrenched away again. This was no empty threat to Israel; small nations were always in peril of invasion by powerful neighbours.

The next exhortation is not to "put the Lord . . . to the test" (v. 16), recalling an incident at a place called *Massah* (see Exod. 17:1–7). One can *test* God in two ways: (1) one can put him on trial in times of anxiety or crisis, to see if he really will help; or (2) one can try his patience, testing him to see how much disobedience he will tolerate. Both are really signs of lack of faith and loss of love; both betray the fact that a certain distance has crept into the relationship between man and God. The remedy proposed by verses 17 and 18 is to immerse oneself in activities directed towards God: then he is never forgotten and the relationship remains unbroken. Some years ago, I asked a devout Jew what value he found in performing the trivial actions demanded by Jewish law—why, for instance, he refrained from switching on an electric light on a sabbath day. The answer was, "My instincts are to switch on the light when it grows dusk, naturally, but then I think of God and withdraw my hand; so this law, even if it seems trivial to you, constantly brings God to my mind." Plainly the Jewish people have taken to heart the guidance of Deuteronomy. It is probably rather easier for Christians, who see themselves as "not under law but under grace", to forget God in the ordinary affairs of daily life.

Verses 20–25 offer a very practical way of remembering to love God, and of preventing the passage of time from damaging a people's relationship with him. The failure to educate children in the faith will speedily erode the faith of a nation; it was particularly vital to remind the coming generations of the reasons for gratitude, love and obedience to God, for otherwise they would take for granted the gifts of national prosperity in Palestine. To obey God, for us as for them, is "for our good always" (v. 24). Verse 25 indicates the possibility, indeed the desirability, of *righteousness*: we should see this as an invitation, not to sinless perfection, but to a right, daily relationship with God.

"FIGHT THE GOOD FIGHT"

Deuteronomy 7:1–5

1"When the Lord your God brings you into the land which you are entering to take possession of it, and clears away many nations before you, the Hittites, the Girgashites, the Amorites, the Canaanites, the Perizzites, the Hivites, and the Jebusites, seven nations greater and mightier than yourselves, 2and when the Lord your God gives them over to you, and you defeat them; then you must utterly destroy them;

you shall make no covenant with them, and show no mercy to them. ³You shall not make marriages with them, giving your daughters to their sons or taking their daughters for your sons. ⁴For they would turn away your sons from following me, to serve other gods; then the anger of the Lord would be kindled against you, and he would destroy you quickly. ⁵But thus shall you deal with them: you shall break down their altars, and dash in pieces their pillars, and hew down their Asherim, and burn their graven images with fire."

This section presents a chilling picture of death and destruction; in letter and in spirit, it seems far removed from the New Testament. There is however one big difference between the Old Testament and the New: the Old Testament is concerned with the affairs of a nation, whereas the New Testament is not. The Old Testament is completely realistic about national and international affairs; and nearly two thousand years into the Christian era, we do not yet see a world free of warfare, nor is it likely that we shall in the near future. To say this is not to condone, or give approval to, warfare; it is rather to recognize that (due no doubt to man's innate sinfulness) wars seem as inevitable in international affairs as strikes are in industrial relations. Is it wrong for a nation to defend itself against an aggressor? Was the war against Hitler wrong? Are Christians who hold to Liberation Theology and preach armed conflict against totalitarian injustice completely wrong? Such questions are easier to pose than to answer with any assurance. Deuteronomy, at any rate, teaches "thou shalt not kill", but it does not teach pacifism. Many passages in both Testaments do teach that war is a horror, to be finally eliminated—in God's good time (*eg* Isa. 11:6–9; Rev. 21:22–22:5). On the other hand, evil is something that has to be fought, with whatever weapons which may be appropriate; often the problem is to identify and to isolate evil.

As we read verses 1–5, it is absolutely clear that the writer believed, without the slightest reservation or doubt, that the land of Palestine belonged to Israel as their God-given, long-promised heritage. But we must not take the words too literally; even though there was some fighting, it seems to have been on a limited scale, and a great many Canaanites and others survived and were gradually absorbed into the Israelite polity. We must remember that, as a book, Deuteronomy was brought to the attention of the Israelites centuries after the time of Moses, at a time when the Conquest was long since complete, and the *seven nations* listed in verse 1 had disappeared from the map. Deuteronomy was a book to meditate upon, not the battle orders for the Israelite army under Joshua. If indeed the first readers were the returning exiles, they entered the Promised Land as a weak, politically impotent group, who would not have dared to upset the stability of the region. So these verses were not practical politics, and their message was not a military one. In one sense it represents an "if only!": *if only* the Israelites on entering the land had swept the Canaanites out of it; *if only* they had avoided mixed marriages; *if only* they had avoided idolatry and smashed every pagan temple and symbol—then the Exile would never have happened in the first place! The message to Jews already in Palestine, or re-entering it, in later years was plain enough; the Hittites, Girgashites, and all the rest, may have disappeared, but pagan religious trappings were still all too readily available, and mixed marriages were easy enough (a major matter of concern to Ezra and Nehemiah, in the early post-exilic period). Take the strongest possible measures, says Deuteronomy, to avoid contamination of your faith.

It is a lesson we may well still need. In our modern world, where there are so many insidious dangers to the Christian faith, and where tolerance is often preached as a supreme virtue, we are often inclined to take no measures at all to protect our faith. But we must never forget that our weapons are to be spiritual ones (cf. Eph. 6:10–18).

THE LOGIC OF GOD'S CHOICE

Deuteronomy 7:6–16

6"For you are a people holy to the Lord your God; the Lord your God has chosen you to be a people for his own possession, out of all the peoples that are on the face of the earth. 7It was not because you were more in number than any other people that the Lord set his love upon you and chose you, for you were the fewest of all peoples; [8]but it is because the Lord loves you, and is keeping the oath which he swore to your fathers, that the Lord has brought you out with a mighty hand, and redeemed you from the house of bondage, from the hand of Pharaoh king of Egypt. [9]Know therefore that the Lord your God is God, the faithful God who keeps covenant and steadfast love with those who love him and keep his commandments, to a thousand generations, [10]and requites to their face those who hate him, by destroying them; he will not be slack with him who hates him, he will requite him to his face. [11]You shall therefore be careful to do the commandment, and the statutes, and the ordinances, which I command you this day.

[12]"And because you hearken to these ordinances, and keep and do them, the Lord your God will keep with you the covenant and the steadfast love which he swore to your fathers to keep; [13]he will love you, bless you, and multiply you; he will also bless the fruit of your body and the fruit of your ground, your grain and your wine and your oil, the increase of your cattle and the young of your flock, in the land which he swore to your fathers to give you. [14]You shall be blessed above all peoples; there shall not be male or female barren among you, or among your cattle. [15]And the Lord will take away from you all sickness; and none of the evil diseases of Egypt, which you knew, will he inflict upon you, but he will lay them upon all who hate you. [16]And you shall destroy all the peoples that the Lord your God will give over to you, your eye shall not pity them; neither shall you serve their gods, for that would be a snare to you."

This passage invited Israel (in any generation) to do some self-examination; to consider what they were, what they should be, and what their future could be. They were a *holy* and *chosen people* (v. 6); they ought to be carefully obedient to their God (v. 11); and their future could be one of idyllic prosperity (vv. 13–15). There is a clear logic in the sequence of ideas. God had chosen Israel; he must therefore have a purpose for its people, which could only be for their good. They must respond by falling in with his plans; otherwise they would be thwarting God. Disobedience to him must therefore be punished; but if the nation worked with him, in harmony and obedience, then God was bound to bless them with every prosperity.

We nowadays tend to stumble over two aspects of this teaching. In the *first* place, the so-called "doctrine of election" is unpopular, since it suggests that God is guilty of favouritism. *Second*, the mechanical idea that goodness is inevitably rewarded and evil always punished in this life, is simply not true to human experience, and is indeed challenged in the Old Testament itself by the book of Job as a whole. Let us first explore what is meant by "election".

(i)

The doctrine of election is, in the first place, an expression of faith and religious experience. The individual (or nation, in Israel's case) who has experienced an encounter with God which has revolutionized his whole being and life and sense of purpose, is left with a feeling of awe and wonder at God's grace. He has been signally blessed and favoured; and at some stage he is bound to ask "Why *me*?", when he observes other people who have never had such an enriching and transforming experience. This question is unanswerable, indeed puzzling, as verse 7 hints; but the facts of the experience are not to be denied, and the Bible uses the word "choose" to describe God's self-revelation to those who have received it. It is a metaphor from human relationships; when a man "chooses" a woman to be his wife (or vice versa!), the choice may even be inexplicable to others, but we recognize it as an outworking of his love for her, and we do not think it at all *unfair* to others. We could add that the marriage might create a home in which countless other people could be entertained, helped, guided and blessed; and if so, that man's "choice" will be to the good of the neighbourhood. Similarly, God's choice of Israel, although a unique and wonderful experience in itself, unshared at the time by other nations, was not God's final act among men; and many other passages indicate God's intentions to bless the world through Israel. At this stage, however, Israel was only finding its feet among the nations, and God's fuller and wider plans lay in the future: the horizons of Deuteronomy's vision are more or less limited to Israel.

AUTOMATIC REWARDS?

Deuteronomy 7:6–16 (*cont'd*)

(ii)

Verses 6 and 7 use language which fits in very well with the analogy of the marriage relationship: God "set his love" upon Israel, and chose her "for his own possession"—"to have and to hold"—for all time (note the "thousand generations" in v. 9). In this context, "holy" means primarily *separate*, just as a wife willingly cuts herself off from a full relationship with any other man but her husband. In Israel's case, to be *holy* meant, first and foremost, to separate herself from idolatry (v. 16); but from the positive viewpoint, it meant to be obedient to all God's wishes, namely his laws. God was utterly *faithful* (v. 9), and no less was demanded of Israel. Verse 10 uses startling language to describe those Israelites who were, or would be in the future, disobedient to God's will; they are said to "hate him". Here, as often, the Bible puts things in stark black-and-white terms; if one does not *love*, one *hates*—the matter is as simple as that.

This, then, is the context in which we find the promise of incredible prosperity, on condition that Israel keeps covenant (vv. 12–15). Is it true to life? Of course it is not—but then Israel plainly did not keep her side of the bargain, so the situation never arose. Once again, we need to recall that, as a book, Deuteronomy was read centuries after the time of Moses, when readers knew perfectly well that Israel had experienced disaster and adversity, far from unparalleled prosperity. The real lesson of the paragraph is to persuade unconvinced or thoughtless Israelites long afterwards that the *reason* for all Israel's ills was her failure to keep covenant with God; and to persuade them to learn the moral from this lesson.

But what of the problem noted earlier—the doctrine of mechanical rewards and punishments in this life? Probably this is unfairly stated to begin with. The word "mechanical" is our word, not Deuteronomy's; Deuteronomy would prefer to say that God's rewards or punishments are certain, which is not quite the same thing. Also, while it is true that Deuteronomy's perspective is *this* life, it in no way sets out to deny the reality of life after death. Given that perspective (which is elaborated chiefly in the New Testament), the doctrine appears somewhat different. It states that *ultimately* God is bound to punish evil and to reward good; and this doctrine seems essential to a belief in the justice of God. How God will deal with evil, and how far justice may be tempered with mercy and forgiveness, are matters which lie in his hands. He is the God of both justice and compassion.

If we believe in an omnipotent and loving God, we can scarcely be cynical about the glowing picture offered in verses 13–15. Living in a world where disease and starvation afflict millions, we surely must believe that the world God wants to create is one where such evils do not exist. A pious hope? Deuteronomy 7 insists that the responsibility is partly ours.

GLITTERING ATTRACTIONS

Deuteronomy 7:17–26

¹⁷"If you say in your heart, 'These nations are greater than I; how can I dispossess them?' ¹⁸you shall not be afraid of them, but you shall remember what the Lord your God did to Pharaoh and to all Egypt, ¹⁹the great trials which your eyes saw, the signs, the wonders, the mighty hand, and the outstretched arm, by which the Lord your God brought you out; so will the Lord your God do to all the peoples of whom you are afraid. ²⁰Moreover the Lord your God will send hornets among them, until those who are left and hide themselves from you are destroyed. ²¹You shall not be in dread of them; for the Lord your God is in the midst of you, a great and terrible God. ²²The Lord your God will clear away these nations before you little by little; you may not make an end of them at once, lest the wild beasts grow too numerous for you. ²³But the Lord your God will give them over to you, and throw them into great confusion, until they are destroyed. ²⁴And he will give their kings into your hand, and you shall make their name perish from under heaven; not a man shall be able to stand against you, until you have destroyed them. ²⁵The graven images of their gods you shall burn with fire; you shall not covet the silver or the gold that is on them, or

take it for yourselves, lest you be ensnared by it; for it is an abomination to the Lord your God. 26And you shall not bring an abominable thing into your house, and become accursed like it; you shall utterly detest and abhor it; for it is an accursed thing."

The Israelites, poised to march into Canaan, faced hostile forces of unknown and frightening dimensions; the exiles returning from Babylon in the sixth century faced unknown obstacles and difficulties. It is but human nature to suppose that problems and difficulties are greater than they really are, and in this case the hostile forces were real enough and powerful enough. The *first* exhortation (v. 18) is "you shall not be afraid"; but that is easier said than done. The *second* is more important, therefore: "remember what the Lord your God did". God's goodness in the past is the proof that he will take care of the future—or rather, that he will take care of his people in the future. Israel's foundation experience was their rescue from Egypt, which to them was wholly miraculous. Exodus 1–15 records these events for us, and tells of a number of specific miracles, not least the removal of the sea from the Israelites' path (Exod. 14:21ff.). It may be that some of the stories can be explained in non-supernatural terms: for instance, Exodus 14:21 refers to the effects of a strong east wind. Be that as it may, the undeniable fact is that the Israelite nation was convinced, and with good reason, that, but for God's direct intervention, they would never have escaped from slavery in Egypt. Deuteronomy 7 builds on this earlier experience and this strong conviction: God would do no less in the future than he had done in the past. It was as much God's will for the Israelites to have a homeland as it had been his will to take them out of Egypt and make them a viable national entity. Thus the passage is a call to trust God; and it also develops the logic of God's covenant with Israel.

Verse 22 is a warning that the obstacles and dangers will not disappear overnight. We should probably take the language as symbolic rather than rigidly literal: obstacles can even have positive value for the time being. The "hornets" of verse 20 should certainly be understood figuratively—if indeed the obscure

Hebrew word even means *hornets*. The Good News Bible begins verse 20, "He will even cause panic among them", and that is the gist of the promise here. The picture in these verses is sometimes described as "holy war". God's personal involvement in Israel's battles is a natural development of the belief that he cared for their national welfare. The important lesson is the recognition of the greatness of God and the love of God; the New Testament counterpart to this section is found in Romans 8:32: "He who did not spare his own Son but gave him up for us all, will he not also give us all things with him?"

Once again, the danger of being tempted into idolatry is emphasized in verses 25ff.; there is also a warning against the lure of *silver* and *gold* in themselves. The culture of Canaan, much more sophisticated than that of the Israelites with their desert background, proved a heady attraction to the Israelites in all too many respects. It is still true that, if we admire a person's accomplishments, we tend to accept his values too. The glitter and glamour of Hollywood, for instance, have deceived many into giving credence and tacit approval to its moral standards.

DESERT EXPERIENCES

Deuteronomy 8:1–10

¹"All the commandment which I command you this day you shall be careful to do, that you may live and multiply, and go in and possess the land which the Lord swore to give to your fathers. ²And you shall remember all the way which the Lord your God has led you these forty years in the wilderness, that he might humble you, testing you to know what was in your heart, whether you would keep his commandments, or not. ³And he humbled you and let you hunger and fed you with manna, which you did not know, nor did your fathers know; that he might make you know that man does not live by bread alone, but that man lives by everything that proceeds out of the mouth of the Lord. ⁴Your clothing did not wear out upon you, and your foot did not swell, these forty years. ⁵Know then in your heart that, as a man disciplines his son, the Lord your God disciplines you. ⁶So you shall keep the commandments of the Lord your God, by walking in his ways and by

fearing him. [7]For the Lord your God is bringing you into a good land, a land of brooks of water, of fountains and springs, flowing forth in valleys and hills, [8]a land of wheat and barley, of vines and fig trees and pomegranates, a land of olive trees and honey, [9]a land in which you will eat bread without scarcity, in which you will lack nothing, a land whose stones are iron, and out of whose hills you can dig copper. [10]And you shall eat and be full, and you shall bless the Lord your God for the good land he has given you."

Here begins another sermon on the importance of keeping God's law (see Introduction, pp. 3, 4). Chapter 7 looked back to Israel's experience in Egypt as its basis for argument and exhortation; chapter 8 recalls the more recent experience of the desert through which the people had lived and journeyed for *forty years* (v. 2). Palestine, as a country, lies very close to barren and arid land, and the Israelite people were very conscious of the *wilderness*, never forgetting that their ancestors had once lived there. They remembered different things about it; one of the psalmists recalled a long list of wilderness situations when Israel had rebelled against God (see Pss. 106), while some of the prophets preferred to remember that, in general, the Israelites had been very dependent on God to supply their daily needs there, and, as a result, had been closer to him than at any later time. Deuteronomy 8 has its own way of interpreting the wilderness years.

(a) *The passage draws attention to God's unfailing care.* Thanks to their God's miraculous provison (vv. 3ff.) they had been able to cope with the wilderness conditions and to survive them. He had given what was essential for survival, but not much else; the Promised Land, with all its potential for agriculture and industry, now offered a glowing contrast to the wilderness, and it too came from the good hand of God.

(b) *The passage describes the desert as a humbling and testing experience.* God used the relative hardships of the desert to make the Israelites recognize their total dependence on his care and provision; they could not, in the desert, take any pride in their own achievements. In this way the experience tested their willingness to accept God's gifts gratefully and to respond by loving obedience (v. 2).

(c) *The passage describes the desert as a discipline.* God is depicted in verse 5 as a parent punishing, correcting and guiding his son. No doubt the verse has in mind some of the rebellions listed in Psalm 106: revolts against God which he had to punish. So, by the time the Israelites reached the Promised Land, they would be well schooled in obedience to their God.

Hardship is everyone's experience from time to time—perhaps for long periods of our lives. There are two ways of responding to it: at one extreme, there are those who rebel against it and against God; at the other extreme, there are those who humbly learn from the experience, and can acknowledge God's goodness throughout.

This paragraph contains a key verse: verse 3 was quoted by Jesus himself as a weapon against temptation (Matt. 4:4). Those who live their lives on the philosophy that man does "live by bread alone" have no inner defences against adversity. More than that, life that is lived purely for material ends has no direction or value. The ideal is to live by "everything [we cannot pick and choose] that proceeds" from God's lips: that is, the guidance he reveals in the spoken and written word.

THE DANGERS OF PROSPERITY

Deuteronomy 8:11–20

[11]"Take heed lest you forget the Lord your God, by not keeping his commandments and his ordinances and his statutes, which I command you this day: [12]lest, when you have eaten and are full, and have built goodly houses and live in them, [13]and when your herds and flocks multiply, and your silver and gold is multiplied, and all that you have is multiplied, [14]then your heart be lifted up, and you forget the Lord your God, who brought you out of the land of Egypt, out of the house of bondage, [15]who led you through the great and terrible wilderness, with its fiery serpents and scorpions and thirsty ground where there was no water, who brought you water out of the flinty rock, [16]who fed you in the wilderness with manna which your fathers did not know, that he

might humble you and test you, to do you good in the end. [17]Beware lest you say in your heart, 'My power and the might of my hand have gotten me this wealth.' [18]You shall remember the Lord your God, for it is he who gives you power to get wealth; that he may confirm his covenant which he swore to your fathers, as at this day. [19]And if you forget the Lord your God and go after other gods and serve them and worship them, I solemnly warn you this day that you shall surely perish. [20]Like the nations that the Lord makes to perish before you, so shall you perish, because you would not obey the voice of the Lord your God."

If verses 1-10 explored the possible effects of living in conditions of hardship, the rest of the chapter asks what effects prosperity is likely to have on the morals of a nation. It was a question to be posed by every generation of Israel in turn, living as they did in the settled conditions of Palestine. By modern western standards, it is true, the prosperity of ancient Palestine was limited and insecure: droughts, locusts, and invading marauders, were only three of the hazards. Even so, life in Palestine had infinitely more to offer than the desert with its much fiercer hazards (see v. 15)— once again the readers are reminded of their forefathers' wilderness experiences (Exod. 17:6; Num. 21:6). Besides which, in the desert it is impossible to create food or water out of nothing, but fertile soil always offers hope to those who are prepared to roll up their sleeves and do some hard work.

Prosperity may be only relative, but it has its dangers. The *first* is *complacency*, which arises from a contentment with things as they are, and a failure to look back and remember the lessons of the past. It amounts to living for the moment when one ignores the past and refuses to consider the future; and that is folly for any man. The *second* and more serious danger is *arrogance*. Hard work is a virtue, to be sure; but all too easily, the attitude of the man who works hard and achieves success, changes from a natural satisfaction to a sense of pride, and then to the sort of arrogance expressed in verse 17. Very similar is the sort of arrogance sometimes found in the upper levels of society—the attitude that the rich deserve to be prosperous and influential, while the poor deserve to be poor. Verse 18 gives the answer to all such attitudes; we are all ultimately dependent upon God alone for everything that we have. We cannot claim credit for our talents nor even for our ability to work hard.

The *third* danger mentioned in this passage is that of *rejecting God*. Verse 19 talks of forgetting God, but in fact idolatry was a deliberate, rather than a casual, neglect of the worship due to the God of Israel. The history of our modern world shows that affluence has led to far more atheism (to say nothing of strange cults, occult practices and the like) than poverty ever did. And yet it is not God's will that his people should be poor (v. 18)! This is the divine dilemma.

THE DANGER OF COMPLACENCY

Deuteronomy 9:1–5

¹"Hear, O Israel; you are to pass over the Jordan this day, to go in to dispossess nations greater and mightier than yourselves, cities great and fortified up to heaven, ²a people great and tall, the sons of the Anakim, whom you know, and of whom you have heard it said, 'Who can stand before the sons of Anak?' ³Know therefore this day that he who goes over before you as a devouring fire is the Lord your God; he will destroy them and subdue them before you; so you shall drive them out, and make them perish quickly, as the Lord has promised you.

⁴"Do not say in your heart, after the Lord your God has thrust them out before you, 'It is because of my righteousness that the Lord has brought me in to possess this land'; whereas it is because of the wickedness of these nations that the Lord is driving them out before you. ⁵Not because of your righteousness or the uprightness of your heart are you going in to possess their land; but because of the wickedness of these nations the Lord your God is driving them out from before you, and that he may confirm the word which the Lord swore to your fathers, to Abraham, to Isaac, and to Jacob."

In 7:17–24 the Israelites were encouraged to march boldly and fearlessly into battle against the Canaanites: "not a man shall be able to stand against you", they were told (7:24). Here the emphasis is quite different: "Who can stand before the sons of

Anak?" (v. 2). The promise is the same in both chapters—thanks to God's help, Israel's victory is assured—but the lesson to be learned is rather different. In chapter 7 the lesson was "you shall not be afraid" (7:18); a message for timid hearts who tended to magnify the imagined problems and obstacles. Here in chapter 9, the text itself magnifies the difficulties, singling out for mention the *Anakim*, a pre-Israelite group in Canaan, who were renowned for their tall stature and fighting qualities ("a people great and tall"). The purpose was not of course to frighten the Israelites, but to remind them that the victory was only possible by God's help. Deuteronomy contains several separate sermons (see Introduction, pp. 3, 4), and clearly they were not all intended for the same audience. Chapter 7 was meant for the fearful; these verses in chapter 9 for the arrogant.

Verses 4 and 5 provide a theological explanation for the Israelites' right to the Promised Land; or rather, it justifies the previous inhabitants' loss of the land. Two reasons are given: (1) those nations were guilty of *wickedness* (although this is not explained or detailed); (2) the Lord had long since promised the land to Israel. The fact that the Israelites are warned here not to pat themselves on the back and pride themselves on their own *righteousness*, suggests that once in Palestine, many Israelites compared their own moral standards as a nation with those of the Canaanites, and felt very virtuous as a result. We are all prone to the thought that other nations' customs and modes of conduct are inferior to our own; it seems to be a universal human failing to despise those who are *different* in any way. (It is a spirit which infects the Churches just as much, with one denomination despising the other.) The biblical retort is a sharp one: God's gifts have nothing to do with his people's uprightness or lack of it. It is very likely that this prevalent attitude among the Israelites caused the problem of complacency which the prophets struggled against, as they tried to convince one generation after another that their conduct stood condemned in God's sight. Jesus saw it as a permanent danger of the human spirit, in his well-known challenge to remove the plank from one's own eye before attending to the speck in someone else's (Matt. 7:3–5).

PRIEST OR PROPHET?

Deuteronomy 9:6–23

6"Know therefore, that the Lord your God is not giving you this good land to possess because of your righteousness; for you are a stubborn people. 7Remember and do not forget how you provoked the Lord your God to wrath in the wilderness; from the day you came out of the land of Egypt, until you came to this place, you have been rebellious against the Lord. 8Even at Horeb you provoked the Lord to wrath, and the Lord was so angry with you that he was ready to destroy you. 9When I went up the mountain to receive the tables of stone, the tables of the covenant which the Lord made with you, I remained on the mountain forty days and forty nights; I neither ate bread nor drank water. 10And the Lord gave me the two tables of stone written with the finger of God; and on them were all the words which the Lord had spoken with you on the mountain out of the midst of the fire on the day of the assembly. 11And at the end of forty days and forty nights the Lord gave me the two tables of stone, the tables of the covenant. 12Then the Lord said to me, 'Arise, go down quickly from here; for your people whom you have brought from Egypt have acted corruptly; they have turned aside quickly out of the way which I commanded them; they have made themselves a molten image.'

13"Furthermore the Lord said to me, 'I have seen this people, and behold, it is a stubborn people; 14let me alone, that I may destroy them and blot out their name from under heaven; and I will make of you a nation mightier and greater than they.' 15So I turned and came down from the mountain, and the mountain was burning with fire; and the two tables of the covenant were in my two hands. 16And I looked, and behold, you had sinned against the Lord your God; you had made yourselves a molten calf; you had turned aside quickly from the way which the Lord had commanded you. 17So I took hold of the two tables, and cast them out of my two hands, and broke them before your eyes. 18Then I lay prostrate before the Lord as before, forty days and forty nights; I neither ate bread nor drank water, because of all the sin which you had committed, in doing what was evil in the sight of the Lord, to provoke him to anger. 19For I was afraid of the anger and hot displeasure which the Lord bore against you, so that he was ready to destroy you. But the Lord hearkened to me that time also. 20And the Lord was so angry with Aaron that he was ready to destroy him; and I prayed for Aaron also at the same time. ²¹Then I took the sinful thing, the calf which you had made, and burned it with fire and crushed it, grinding it very small, until it was as fine as dust; and I threw the dust of it into the brook that descended out of the mountain.

²²"At Taberah also, and at Massah, and at Kibroth-hattaavah, you provoked the Lord to wrath. ²³And when the Lord sent you from Kadesh-barnea, saying, 'Go up and take possession of the land which I have given you,' then you rebelled against the commandment of the Lord your God, and did not believe him or obey his voice."

How do you jolt people out of their complacency and force them to examine their own behaviour and standards? Self-righteousness is a very difficult attitude to combat. This chapter finds quite an effective way to do it; listeners, or readers, were familiar with many traditions of their own history as a nation, and could not deny that certain episodes showed plainly that Israel had a very flawed background. One might have thought that Israel's most faithful and devout era, her honeymoon period in her relationship with Yahweh, would have been at the time of the covenant and law-giving at Sinai (or *Horeb*, v. 8). The truth was sadly very different. As Exodus 32 tells the story, no sooner was Moses' back turned, in order to commune alone with God and receive the *tables* or tablets of the law, than the Israelites turned to blatant idolatry. Even *Aaron*, from whom all Israel's priests were to be descended, was implicated (v. 20). While God himself was writing down the Ten Commandments (as the Israelites believed he had done, v. 10), his people were breaking one of them. The story indicated that God's anger was extreme; he all but decided to destroy Israel because of it. Moses' action in breaking the two tablets (v. 17) was a symbolic one: it was a public sign demonstrating that the covenant between God and Israel had been broken. (There is evidence that in the ancient Near East, treaty documents were publicly smashed as a sign that the treaty had been broken.)

The chief lesson of this whole episode was clear enough: no later generation of Israel dared to be complacent, when his people had such a checkered history behind them. Throughout the centuries of the Hebrew monarchy, moreover, there were all too many idols and images worshipped here and there among the Israelite people; their very existence was a challenge to complacency. Only the very rare king, like Josiah (2 Kings 23:4–25), ever took firm action against them. So any complacent Israelite of later times had only to look around him to see signs of national apostasy.

The passage contains an interesting contrast. As we have noted, Aaron was as guilty as anyone else; but Moses was not only innocent of it, he was also the man who, in a sense, saved Israel from destruction. He prayed to God for his people, and for Aaron too, and it was only because of his intercession that God relented (vv. 18–20). Although the story is told in personal terms, it is important to realize that Moses is the symbol of Israel's prophets and Aaron is the symbol of Israel's priests. In other words, Israelites in later epochs would be wise to listen to Israel's prophets, and should not turn deaf ears to them and put all their faith in the priesthood. Just by being there and superintending the system of sacrifices and offerings, the priests could cause complacency; provided that they had paid their tithes and offered their sacrificial animals, ordinary citizens could suppose that they stood in a perfectly good relationship with God. Many ordinary churchgoers have shown exactly the same sort of complacency, based on carrying out the right forms of religious observance. It was the prophets who challenged the conscience of the nation; but there were all too many deaf ears. Then, as now, the offering-plate was more popular than the sermon.

LESSONS FROM HISTORY

Deuteronomy 9:24–10:5

[24]"You have been rebellious against the Lord from the day that I knew you.

[25]"So I lay prostrate before the Lord for these forty days and forty nights, because the Lord had said he would destroy you. [26]And I prayed to the Lord, 'O Lord God, destroy not thy people and thy heritage, whom thou hast redeemed through thy greatness, whom thou hast brought out of Egypt with a mighty hand. [27]Remember thy

servants, Abraham, Isaac, and Jacob; do not regard the stubbornness of this people, or their wickedness, or their sin, 28lest the land from which thou didst bring us say, "Because the Lord was not able to bring them into the land which he promised them, and because he hated them, he has brought them out to slay them in the wilderness." 29For they are thy people and thy heritage, whom thou didst bring out by thy great power and by thy outstretched arm.'

"At that time the Lord said to me, 'Hew two tables of stone like the first, and come up to me on the mountain, and make an ark of wood. 2And I will write on the tables the words that were on the first tables which you broke, and you shall put them in the ark.' 3So I made an ark of acacia wood, and hewed two tables of stone like the first, and went up the mountain with the two tables in my hand. 4And he wrote on the tables, as at the first writing, the ten commandments which the Lord had spoken to you on the mountain out of the midst of the fire on the day of the assembly; and the Lord gave them to me. 5Then I turned and came down from the mountain, and put the tables in the ark which I had made; and there they are, as the Lord commanded me."

Perhaps a good many readers of this little commentary are unfamiliar with the placenames listed in verse 22, and would find it difficult to say what happened at each of them; but it is obvious that the author of Deuteronomy fully expected *his* readers to know immediately what he meant. He was referring to well-known events. At *Taberah* (cf. Num. 11:1–6) the Israelites had complained bitterly about the hardships of the wilderness and remembered the luxuries—not the slavery!—in Egypt. At *Massah* (Exod. 17:1–7) they had shown a similar spirit of revolt against Moses when water ran short. At *Kibroth-hattaavah* (Num. 11:7–34) they had in effect rejected God's gift of the mysterious but satisfying manna. What happened at *Kadesh-barnea* (v. 23) has already been told in more detail in 1:19–46. Without elaborating, then, this Deuteronomic sermon was able to show that the Israelite attitude towards God displayed at Sinai–Horeb itself was not some youthful immaturity which they had rapidly abandoned, but a deep-seated and continuous spirit of rebellion (v. 24). In the New Testament, a long speech by Stephen (Acts 7), reviewing many centuries of Israel's history, presents a similar disturbing picture of a *stiff-necked* people.

Are such reviews of history fair? After all, history is complex and multi-faceted, and every nation can point to some proud moments, victories and achievements, however limited the list. Yes, but the fact is that nations typically remember *only* the high points; few national monuments commemorate defeats! So a review of this kind helps to fill the gaps in a people's all-too-selective memory. Also, the more important question is, which events in a nation's history are the *typical* ones? Was Israel characterized by loyalty to Yahweh or by rebellion against him? Deuteronomy, at least, is in no doubt as to the answer! One can only wonder what events in Church history this biblical writer would have selected as typical of Christian conduct—the blood of the martyrs, say, or the cruel religious wars of the Reformation era?

Of course, the real point of the sermon is not to find the right category in which to place ancient Israel; it is rather to call the contemporary generation to an examination of themselves, not their ancestors. Provided that God's people are jolted out of any complacency, and are willing to face unpleasant facts about themselves, there is always a way back—or rather, a way forward. In this passage, in fact, nothing is said about any repentance on Israel's part. The emphasis is rather on the good offices of Moses as an intercessor, and the willingness of God to bless his own people in spite of everything.

The section ends with the re-making of the *two tables* of the law (10:1–5), to symbolize the re-making of the covenant. There is a double-edged lesson in this paragraph. On the one hand, Israelites can take heart that God's covenant with them, and his love for them, are secure—"there they are" (v. 5). On the other hand, the very symbols of the covenant contained *the ten commandments* (v. 4), and they too must be taken to heart—*there they are*, to be heeded and obeyed by the covenant people.

THE COVENANT BOX

Deuteronomy 10:6–11

[6](The people of Israel journeyed from Be-eroth Bene-jaakan to

Moserah. There Aaron died, and there he was buried; and his son Eleazar ministered as priest in his stead. [7]From there they journeyed to Gudgodah, and from Gudgodah to Jotbathah, a land with brooks of water. [8]At that time the Lord set apart the tribe of Levi to carry the ark of the covenant of the Lord, to stand before the Lord to minister to him and to bless in his name, to this day. [9]Therefore Levi has no portion or inheritance with his brothers; the Lord is his inheritance, as the Lord your God said to him.)

[10]"I stayed on the mountain, as at the first time, forty days and forty nights, and the Lord hearkened to me that time also; the Lord was unwilling to destroy you. [11]And the Lord said to me, 'Arise, go on your journey at the head of the people, that they may go in and possess the land, which I swore to their fathers to give them.'"

The chief purpose of 10:1–11 is to describe the renewal of the covenant at Sinai, following the sin of Israel and the intercession of Moses, outlined in chapter 9. Into this section is set a brief paragraph (vv. 6–9) which seems to interrupt the flow of the narrative; the RSV has sensibly placed these verses between brackets. There is a connecting theme, however, which we may denote as *priestly arrangements*. The tables of the law, so important because of what they contained and what they stood for, were solid physical objects and had to be preserved and cared for, and also transported (until they finally came to rest in Solomon's temple, presumably). So verses 1–9 give a brief account of the arrangements made for these supremely sacred objects: verses 1–5 describe their container—a box made of acacia (a hard and durable wood) which is usually known in the Old Testament as the *ark of the covenant* (v. 8); and verses 6–9 refer to the sacred officials appointed as curators of both the ark and the stone tablets. The details given in verses 6–9 are drawn, with some slight modifications, from Numbers 20:22–29 and Numbers 33:31–33. Both the priesthood—Aaron's descendants—and the Levites, who between them fulfilled the priestly functions in Israel for many centuries, had divine sanction for their rôle: the sacred ark too was ordained by God himself (v. 1). Nothing was left to chance or to casual *ad hoc* arrangements. (See 18:1–8 for further discussion of the Levites.)

It is clear that these verses emphasize the outstanding importance of the tablets of the law; by comparison, the sacred box and the priestly personnel occupy a subsidiary position. In fact, of course, the priests and Levites had many other duties; and the ark of the covenant also had its own special rôle in Israelite religion. It symbolized the throne of Yahweh, and served as the visible symbol of God's invisible presence; and Exodus 25:10–22 describes the rich ornamentation of it. (It is widely supposed that the ark carried hither and thither in the wilderness was very much less elaborate than the ark which later resided in Solomon's temple.) There has been much discussion among scholars as to the original function and purpose of this sacred object, which was certainly the most treasured article in the Israelites' sanctuary. It is, at any rate, very likely that Deuteronomy wanted the Israelites to pay less attention to the ark and more attention to the divine words which it contained. The ark could readily become a sort of magic object, attracting superstitious worship; indeed it could become a substitute idol. But the covenant was all about obeying God's recorded wishes, not about paying reverence to boxes.

The whole danger of ritual (and all Churches have their rituals!) is that the symbol may become a substitute for God—or worse, that we may become so devoted to the symbols that we have no time or inclination to listen to what God *says*.

GOD'S REQUIREMENTS

Deuteronomy 10:12–22

[12]"And now, Israel, what does the Lord your God require of you, but to fear the Lord your God, to walk in all his ways, to love him, to serve the Lord your God with all your heart and with all your soul, [13]and to keep the commandments and statutes of the Lord, which I command you this day for your good? [14]Behold, to the Lord your God belong heaven and the heaven of heavens, the earth with all that is in it; [15]yet the Lord set his heart in love upon your fathers and chose their descendants after them, you above all peoples, as at this day. [16]Circumcise therefore the foreskin of your heart, and be no longer stub-

born. [17]For the Lord your God is God of gods and Lord of lords, the great, the mighty, and the terrible God, who is not partial and takes no bribe. [18]He executes justice for the fatherless and the widow, and loves the sojourner, giving him food and clothing. [19]Love the sojourner therefore; for you were sojourners in the land of Egypt. [20]You shall fear the Lord your God; you shall serve him and cleave to him, and by his name you shall swear. [21]He is your praise; he is your God, who has done for you these great and terrible things which your eyes have seen. [22]Your fathers went down to Egypt seventy persons; and now the Lord your God has made you as the stars of heaven for multitude."

After considering a number of past events, especially those surrounding the Sinai law-giving, the writer turns abruptly to his own day and generation: "And now, Israel, what does the Lord your God require of you?" It was (and is) a reasonable question, but the answers are provided. Five requirements are given in verses 12 and 13: God's people should *fear, love* and *serve* him, and they should "walk in all his ways" and *keep* his *commandments*. The first of the five—*fear*—means primarily an attitude of reverence, not of terror, because God loves Israel (v. 15) and wishes to do them no harm. Reverence and love, then, are the attitudes God looks for; they best show themselves in service (*ie* worship) and obedience. To walk in God's ways is a comprehensive idea, which really includes all the other demands. Verses 20 and 21 endorse these demands in different words; "He is your praise" really means "He is to be the object of your praise", and is a further call not to neglect the worship of him.

God's awesome greatness is highlighted in verses 14 and 17, not in order to terrify his people, but to induce their wonder that the Almighty Creator should have "set his heart in love" upon Israel, and, in particular, the generation hearing or reading these words (v. 15). Verse 17 emphasizes God's impartiality; this makes it clear that Israel did not understand God's choice of them to be his people as in any sense favouritism. The writer is thinking here, however, of the individual rather than the nation; God cares for rich and poor alike. Orphans and widows usually fared badly in the ancient Near East, and foreign settlers (*sojourners*) still tend to be second-class citizens throughout the world. Now we find another demand: the Israelites are to imitate their God in their conduct towards the needy in society (vv. 18ff.). There is a double motive, in fact: they have an obligation to the weak and the needy not only because of God's example, but also because of their own previous experience in *Egypt*. It is surprising how often those who have risen in society (or in prosperity) forget or even despise those who have been less fortunate. Jesus had a message for such people: the parable in Matthew 18:23–35 is relevant to more than the question of forgiveness.

One further challenge in this paragraph must not be overlooked, namely the call to *circumcise* the *heart* in verse 16. Circumcision was already an ancient custom in the time of Moses (see Gen. 17:9–14), and it was probably scrupulously followed, but devoid of meaning, in later centuries. Deuteronomy seems to interpret it as representing humble submission to a painful operation (performed, it is true, on very young babies); the devout Jew, says verse 16, is not satisfied to have been circumcised as a baby boy, but will make humble submission to God's wishes a characteristic of his life, even at some cost or discomfort to himself.

DEPENDENCE ON GOD

Deuteronomy 11:1–17

[1]"You shall therefore love the Lord your God, and keep his charge, his statutes, his ordinances, and his commandments always. [2]And consider this day (since I am not speaking to your children who have not known or seen it), consider the discipline of the Lord your God, his greatness, his mighty hand and his outstretched arm, [3]his signs and his deeds which he did in Egypt to Pharaoh the king of Egypt and to all his land; [4]and what he did to the army of Egypt, to their horses and to their chariots; how he made the water of the Red Sea overflow them as they pursued after you, and how the Lord has destroyed them to this day; [5]and what he did to you in the wilderness, until you came to this place; [6]and what he did to Dathan and Abiram the sons of Eliab, son of Reuben; how the earth opened its mouth and swallowed them up, with their households, their tents, and every living thing that followed

them, in the midst of all Israel; [7]for your eyes have seen all the great work of the Lord which he did.

[8]"You shall therefore keep all the commandment which I command you this day, that you may be strong, and go in and take possession of the land which you are going over to possess, [9]and that you may live long in the land which the Lord swore to your fathers to give to them and to their descendants, a land flowing with milk and honey. [10]For the land which you are entering to take possession of it is not like the land of Egypt, from which you have come, where you sowed your seed and watered it with your feet, like a garden of vegetables; [11]but the land which you are going over to possess is a land of hills and valleys, which drinks water by the rain from heaven, [12]a land which the Lord your God cares for; the eyes of the Lord your God are always upon it, from the beginning of the year to the end of the year.

[13]"And if you will obey my commandments which I command you this day, to love the Lord your God, and to serve him with all your heart and with all your soul, [14]he will give the rain for your land in its season, the early rain and the later rain, that you may gather in your grain and your wine and your oil. [15]And he will give grass in your fields for your cattle, and you shall eat and be full. [16]Take heed lest your heart be deceived, and you turn aside and serve other gods and worship them, [17]and the anger of the Lord be kindled against you, and he shut up the heavens, so that there be no rain, and the land yield no fruit, and you perish quickly off the good land which the Lord gives you."

This last chapter of exhortation, before the laws are set out in chapters 12–26, is explicitly addressed (v. 2) to people who had first-hand experience of the Exodus from Egypt and all that had occurred during the wilderness wanderings; but of course the lessons were intended for all succeeding generations (cf. v. 19). Verses 1–17 contain a history lesson and a geography lesson; a careful look at Israel's recent history and at Palestine's geography would amount to *instruction* (v. 2, RSV footnote) from God himself. The lesson drawn from history is the sheer power of God, which had been demonstrated in destructive acts. The Egyptians had suffered when they tried to oppose Israel; the reference is to the plagues (Exod. 7–12) and to the Exodus itself (Exod. 13–14). *Dathan* and *Abiram*, whose story (coupled with the story of a

Levite called Korah) is told in Numbers 16, were men who re-belled against the authority of Moses and wanted to lead Israel in the opposite direction—away from Palestine and back to Egypt. They too, then, like Pharaoh, tried to thwart God's plans for his people. There was reassurance in the history lesson; nothing and nobody could stop God's plans for Israel in the Promised Land.

The mention of *the land* (v. 8) leads on to a description of its geography, or rather to a contrast between it and Egypt (vv. 10–14). Egypt consists mainly of the long, flat Nile valley, and its rainfall is negligible; so irrigation, using the Nile waters, is the method of agriculture. (The obscure phrase "watered it with your feet" must refer to irrigation, cf. GNB.) The hilly terrain of Palestine, by contrast, has few rivers or streams, and its fertility is wholly dependent on rainfall; verse 14 indicates the typical pattern of rainfall, with *the early rain* in the autumn and *the later rain* in the spring. In Egypt, it is implied, a farmer could always get more produce from the soil by harder work and more thorough irrigation; but in Palestine, the farmer had no alternative but faith in God to give rain. However, the farmer's one alternative was to turn to the fertility gods and fertility rituals of the Canaanites, and that is precisely the danger that this passage warns against (v. 16).

The passage is not making a general statement that God gives rain to devout people and withholds it from the wicked (indeed, Matt. 5:45 refutes any such idea); the good and the evil are mingled in any nation. The lesson is rather that Israel's whole future is dependent upon the God who controls both history and climate; and the well-being of God's people in turn depends upon their response to him. The passage therefore repeats the call for love and obedience towards God (v. 1), and warns against lack of belief in his love or in his power.

In our modern world, the general attitude to history is that it is ambiguous and meaningless, while we are inclined to view weather and climatic conditions as purely the product of natural forces and mechanisms. Unless we can find a place for God's activity in both, we are far from sharing the faith of the writers of either the Old Testament or the New Testament.

GEOGRAPHICAL DETAILS

Deuteronomy 11:18–32

18"You shall therefore lay up these words of mine in your heart and in your soul; and you shall bind them as a sign upon your hand, and they shall be as frontlets between your eyes. 19And you shall teach them to your children, talking of them when you are sitting in your house, and when you are walking by the way, and when you lie down, and when you rise. 20And you shall write them upon the doorposts of your house and upon your gates, 21that your days and the days of your children may be multiplied in the land which the Lord swore to your fathers to give them, as long as the heavens are above the earth. 22For if you will be careful to do all this commandment which I command you to do, loving the Lord your God, walking in all his ways, and cleaving to him, 23then the Lord will drive out all these nations before you, and you will dispossess nations greater and mightier than yourselves. 24Every place on which the sole of your foot treads shall be yours; your territory shall be from the wilderness and Lebanon and from the River, the river Eu-phrates, to the western sea. 25No man shall be able to stand against you; the Lord your God will lay the fear of you and the dread of you upon all the land that you shall tread, as he promised you.

26"Behold, I set before you this day a blessing and a curse: 27the blessing, if you obey the commandments of the Lord your God, which I command you this day, 28and the curse, if you do not obey the commandments of the Lord your God, but turn aside from the way which I command you this day, to go after other gods which you have not known. 29And when the Lord your God brings you into the land which you are entering to take possession of it, you shall set the blessing on Mount Gerizim and the curse on Mount Ebal. 30Are they not beyond the Jordan, west of the road, toward the going down of the sun, in the land of the Canaanites who live in the Arabah, over against Gilgal, beside the oak of Moreh? 31For you are to pass over the Jordan to go in to take possession of the land which the Lord your God gives you; and when you possess it and live in it, 32you shall be careful to do all the statutes and the ordinances which I set before you this day."

In this final part of the preface to the detailed law code, there is little that is completely new. For the most part, earlier themes are repeated and re-emphasized, so that no reader should fail to appreciate the importance of the laws. The laws must become part of the Israelites' life, indeed in the very forefront of it, never forgotten and never neglected, faithfully transmitted from one generation to the next. Again it is stressed that success and well-being in the Holy Land are dependent upon faithfulness to the laws of God. The geographical details in verse 24 are new, however; the potential frontiers mentioned are very much wider than those of the land of Israel itself (see map, p. xii). The frontiers are in fact major geographical barriers: the barren terrain to the south and to the east; the Mediterranean to the west; the mountains of Lebanon to the north; and the northern part of the Euphrates (in Syria, not Mesopotamia) to the north-east. So the verse is saying that, within these natural limits, nothing is impossible of achievement. In actual history, David in the tenth century achieved an empire approaching these dimensions, but it did not last very long. The real thrust of the message was no doubt for the returning exiles of the sixth century, who came back to a tiny, weak, humiliated land of Judah; but if they were now obedient to God's laws, the future could be transformed. The New Testament translates such territorial promises into a spiritual inheritance (cf. 1 Pet. 1:4), described by such phrases as "the kingdom of God" and "eternal life".

The final paragraph of the chapter also mentions new geographical details, in its reference to two neighbouring mountains in the very heart of Israel, *Gerizim* and *Ebal* (v. 29). The detailed map reference provided for them in verse 30 is a little obscure to us, but we know their location exactly; one on each side of the important ancient city of Shechem. They are mentioned in connection with a ritual which was carried out regularly there: one occasion when the ritual was carried out is described in Joshua 8:30–35. It was a ceremony of covenant renewal, and one feature of it was to read to the Israelite assembly "all that is written in the book of the law" (Josh. 8:34). The fertile slopes of Mount Gerizim were used symbolically to depict *the blessing* (v. 27) merited by those who would obey the law, while the barren Mount Ebal represented *the curse* (v. 28) which would fall upon the disobedient. The covenant between God and Israel in many ways resembled ancient treaties between nations (or to be more precise, between their kings), and a list of blessings and curses was a regular part of such treaties. God demands no less fidelity from his people than the loyalty and trustworthiness that one nation has a right to expect from another.

The two mountains, together with a considerable list of specific curses and blessings, are discussed again in chapters 27 and 28 of Deuteronomy.

ONE SHRINE

Deuteronomy 12:1–14

[1]"These are the statutes and ordinances which you shall be careful to do in the land which the Lord, the God of your fathers, has given you to possess, all the days that you live upon the earth. [2]You shall surely destroy all the places where the nations whom you shall dispossess served their gods, upon the high mountains and upon the hills and under every green tree; [3]you shall tear down their altars, and dash in pieces their pillars, and burn their Asherim with fire; you shall hew down the graven images of their gods, and destroy their name out of that place. [4]You shall not do so to the Lord your God. [5]But you shall seek the place which the Lord your God will choose out of all your tribes to put his name and make his habitation there; thither you shall go, [6]and thither you shall bring your burnt offerings and your sacrifices, your tithes and the offering that you present, your votive offerings, your freewill offerings, and the firstlings of your herd and of your flock; [7]and there you shall eat before the Lord your God, and you shall rejoice, you and your households, in all that you undertake, in which the Lord your God has blessed you. [8]You shall not do according to all that we are doing here this day, every man doing whatever is right in his own eyes; [9]for you have not as yet come to the rest and to the inheritance which the Lord your God gives you. [10]But when you go over the Jordan, and live in the land which the Lord your God gives you to inherit, and when he gives you rest from all your enemies round about, so that you live in safety, [11]then to the place which the Lord your God will choose, to make his name dwell there, thither you shall bring all that I command you: your burnt offerings and your sacrifices, your tithes and the offering that you present, and all your votive

offerings which you vow to the Lord. [12]And you shall rejoice before the Lord your God, you and your sons and your daughters, your menservants and your maidservants, and the Levite that is within your towns, since he has no portion or inheritance with you. [13]Take heed that you do not offer your burnt offerings at every place that you see; [14]but at the place which the Lord will choose in one of your tribes, there you shall offer your burnt offerings, and there you shall do all that I am commanding you."

(i)

The first two of the Ten Commandments ordained the exclusive worship of Yahweh and prohibited idols of any sort (5:7ff.). So it is quite appropriate that the detailed law code of Deuteronomy should begin by giving some directions about worship. A true relationship with God is the only basis for living under his covenant. The chief concern of this passage is to clarify *where* God could properly be worshipped; and the answer given, a rather startling idea, is that there was to be only one acceptable sanctuary in the whole of the Holy Land (v. 14). The contrast with Canaanite worship, with its multitude of temples and open-air shrines (v. 2), is enormous. It is a very common pattern for conquerors and invaders of a country to take over old shrines for their own forms of worship: the most famous case is probably the Byzantine Cathedral of Saint Sophia, which was turned into a mosque after Constantinople (Istanbul) fell to the Muslims in 1453.

There is no doubt at all that the Israelites did in practice adopt, for their own use, many a Canaanite shrine. Special importance, however, was given to some of their own shrines, and probably central importance was given to the shrine which housed the ark of the covenant: this was of course Jerusalem, from the time of David onwards (cf. 2 Sam. 5ff.). It is not unlikely that the concept of a single sanctuary went back to the wilderness period, for evidently the Israelites then possessed only one portable shrine; but in Palestine, there seems to have been no serious attempt to centralize worship in one place until the reign of Josiah in the late seventh century (the details of his reforms are given in 2 Kings 23). No doubt Deuteronomy 12 was a powerful factor in persuading the Jews after the Exile to make Jerusalem's rebuilt temple their one and only place of worship.

In one sense, synagogues later came to replace the rural sanctuaries of earlier times; the big difference was that synagogues have never been places of animal sacrifice. By New Testament times, then, there was one temple but a vast number of synagogues; in A.D. 70 the Temple was destroyed by the Romans, and has never been rebuilt, so that for many centuries Judaism has had neither temple nor animal sacrifices. The *Torah*—the law of Moses and of God—has become the central institution in Jewish worship, displacing the old sacrificial system. The whole system of worship of the Israelite and Jewish people has thus been transformed over the centuries; and Deuteronomy 12 could be called the pivot, the radical law which dictated the direction of the transformation.

John 4:19–24 is the basic text for the Christian view of the place of worship. Although we may choose to consecrate and to beautify our churches, chapels and cathedrals, the true centre of worship is not *Jerusalem*—nor Rome, Canterbury, Geneva, and so on—but the shrine of the heart. Bunyan and Bonhoeffer, for example, held the deepest communion with God in prison cells.

... AND ONLY ONE!

Deuteronomy 12:1–14 (*cont'd*)

(ii)

We may well believe that the gradual transformation of worship has been Providential, but we need to ask why Deuteronomy was so insistent that a single sanctuary was God's will. After all, this law deprived many people of frequent opportunities for joining in corporate worship; Jerusalem became a centre of pilgrimage for all who lived at any distance. Verse 3 hints at the danger; all the trappings of Canaanite worship—*altars, pillars*, sacred poles (*Asherim*), and of course, *idols*—evidently attracted the Israelites throughout the land, who fell into religious practices of very varied kinds. Verse 8 suggests that a sort of "do-it-yourself" religion emerged. The real danger was not so much pagan worship (although it too was a danger) as what is technically known as "syncretism"; the blending of two religions. We do not possess a full, objective description of Canaanite religious practices, but we know at least that they tended to promote sexual immorality, and that—if only rarely—they included human sacrifice (see v. 31). Since in both Israelite and Canaanite worship animals were sacrificed, one can readily see how ordinary folk might confuse the two faiths and drift unawares into Canaanite practices. It was chiefly in order to safeguard against any corruption of the true faith that the law of the single sanctuary was decreed. It was much easier to regulate religious practices in one central shrine, which was under the control of the royal court or the senior priest, than in a multitude of places throughout the land.

The dangers of syncretism are still with us. There are those who would teach us, for example, that obedience to their particular recipes for Christian practice and conduct will automatically bring us material blessings—large houses, large cars and large bank-balances. Whether they realize it or not, the apostles of this creed have confused the worship of God with the worship of Mammon; and since Jesus said it is impossible to serve both (Matt. 6:24), the truth is that they are worshipping only Mammon. The Way of the Cross and the path of self-denial have been lost sight of.

Within the Protestant tradition, indeed, there is an ever-present danger of putting "freedom" (of belief and practice) on a pedestal. Whatever the gains, this at least has been a marked disadvantage arising from the loss of centralized control in the wake of the Reformation. "Every man doing whatever is right in his own eyes" (v. 8) is never the best recipe for worship or for society.

WORSHIP AT THE SHRINE

Deuteronomy 12:1–14 (*cont'd*)

(iii)

Much of Deuteronomy 12:1–14, then, adds up to a prohibition:

there should be no organized worship except in the place of God's choice. However, we must not overlook the positive aspects of the passage. The reader is instructed that it is his duty to make his way to the authorized sanctuary (v. 5), and there is a brief description given of what Israelite worship should consist of (vv. 6, 7, 11, 12). However distant the sanctuary, worship must certainly not be neglected. A variety of sacrifices and offerings are listed; some of these were *freewill offerings*, others were in payment of vows previously made (*votive offerings*), and others again were obligatory, part of the regular sacrificial ceremonies. Not only animals, but such items as grain, wine, and olive oil were given. Apart from the *burnt offerings*, which were completely burned, the priests and Levites and the worshippers themselves would all get their share of each offering; hence the joyful feasting mentioned in verse 7.

The various sacrifices and offerings had a number of differing values and purposes in the ritual of Israel. In general, in the ancient world, sacrifices were thought to please the gods, whether as gifts, or as food for them; sacrifices might placate them when they were angry, and by sacrifices to the gods, humans could enter into communion with them. Sacrifices were costly—as our modern phrase "to make sacrifices" still implies. Now much of this symbolism of sacrifice could be, and was, shared by Israel. Her God demanded nothing *less* of his people, even although, in course of time, these animal and vegetable offerings were replaced by different modes of worship.

In its day, therefore, Deuteronomy did not reject or alter the sacrificial system; but it gives an emphasis to its brief description of the system which is worth noting. It does not dwell on sin or guilt—indeed, they are not even mentioned here. Nor is anything said of placating an angry God, even although God's anger with Israel has been a theme present in Deuteronomy. All the emphasis is given here to joyful communion, expressed especially in the feasting which then followed the offering of sacrifices. Families were to worship together and then feast together (v. 7) in gratitude for all God's gifts to them. Nor must such worship be self-centred; *servants* were to share with the family (v. 12). Verse 12 also takes into account the Levites who would lose both their rôle in society and their source of income once shrines outside Jerusalem were shut down. Although the mode of worship is very different now, there is a model here for any Christian Church to follow—joy, gratitude, sharing and communion, into which other people are drawn without stint.

THE PROVISION OF MEAT

Deuteronomy 12:15–32

15"However, you may slaughter and eat flesh within any of your towns, as much as you desire, according to the blessing of the Lord your God which he has given you; the unclean and the clean may eat of it, as of the gazelle and as of the hart. 16Only you shall not eat the blood; you shall pour it out upon the earth like water. 17You may not eat within your towns the tithe of your grain or of your wine or of your oil, or the firstlings of your herd or of your flock, or any of your votive offerings which you vow, or your freewill offerings, or the offering that you present; 18but you shall eat them before the Lord your God in the place which the Lord your God will choose, you and your son and your daughter, your manservant and your maidservant, and the Levite who is within your towns; and you shall rejoice before the Lord your God in all that you undertake. 19Take heed that you do not forsake the Levite as long as you live in your land.

20"When the Lord your God enlarges your territory, as he has promised you, and you say, 'I will eat flesh,' because you crave flesh, you may eat as much flesh as you desire. 21If the place which the Lord your God will choose to put his name there is too far from you, then you may kill any of your herd or your flock, which the Lord has given you, as I have commanded you; and you may eat within your towns as much as you desire. 22Just as the gazelle or the hart is eaten, so you may eat of it; the unclean and the clean alike may eat of it. 23Only be sure that you do not eat the blood; for the blood is the life, and you shall not eat the life with the flesh. 24You shall not eat it; you shall pour it out upon the earth like water. 25You shall not eat it; that all may go well with you and with your children after you, when you do what is right in the sight of the Lord. 26But the holy things which are due from you, and your votive offerings, you shall take, and you shall go to the place which the Lord will choose, [27]and offer your burnt offerings, the flesh and the blood, on the altar of the Lord your God; the blood of your sacrifices shall be poured out on the altar of the Lord your God, but the flesh you may eat. [28]Be careful to heed all these words which I command you, that it may go well with you and with your children after you for ever, when you do what is good and right in the sight of the Lord your God.

[29]"When the Lord your God cuts off before you the nations whom you go in to dispossess, and you dispossess them and dwell in their land, [30]take heed that you be not ensnared to follow them, after they have been destroyed before you, and that you do not inquire about their gods, saying, 'How did these nations serve their gods?—that I also may do likewise.' [31]You shall not do so to the Lord your God; for every abominable thing which the Lord hates they have done for their gods; for they even burn their sons and their daughters in the fire to their gods.

[32]"Everything that I command you you shall be careful to do; you shall not add to it or take from it."

The whole discussion in this passage concerns the eating of meat. There were three categories of animals, from the ritual point of view, which we may class as *unclean, secular* and *sacrificial*. The first category was absolutely forbidden as food (see the list in Lev. 11), so they need no discussion in this chapter. *Secular* animals were primarily those caught by hunters: game animals like the "gazelle" and "hart" (v. 15). *Sacrificial* animals were typically farm animals, such as cattle and sheep. We may reasonably assume that the general practice in Palestine, observed by the Canaanites and also by the Israelites when they entered the land, was to eat the flesh of the secular animals in their homes, as and when it was available; but they would not eat beef or mutton except at sacrificial feasts. In other words, they treated the sacrificial class of beasts as *sacred* animals, which could only be eaten on sacred occasions.

Given this cultural setting, it is easy to see the reason for this passage. The radical law of verses 13 and 14, which closed down all sanctuaries but one, would have reduced the meat consumption of the Israelites drastically, unless permission was given to eat beef and mutton in the same way as the game animals. So we find here not a prohibition, like so many laws (of all nations), but a law which gave greater freedom. Cattle and sheep became *secular* animals for most purposes—except that of course they still remained the correct animals for sacrificial usage and for sacrificial feasts, as before. (Jesus went a step further when "he declared all foods clean", Mark 7:19.)

There are two concerns in this section. The *first* is clearly humane, the desire to ensure that God's people were not deprived and would be properly fed. The *second* is to urge that the relaxation being granted should not affect proper sacrificial and ritual procedures. There must have been the danger that with meat freely available on Israelite farms, many people would begin to neglect to visit the sanctuary and to offer their sacrifices there. Verses 26–28 urge the Israelites to make the necessary journey (that is to Jerusalem, at festival times) and to *be careful* to do everything properly. A very real danger of the new arrangements was that everything in the home would become viewed as secular, while *religion* was isolated at the sanctuaries. The law about *blood* (vv. 16, 23)—in itself a very ancient law (cf. Gen. 9:4)—went some way to avoid the development of any such idea, as did all the food restrictions of other kinds (see chapter 14). Christians may wonder about the value of all the dietary laws observed by Jewish people; but at least they give the home a sacred dimension. It is all too easy for Christians to act as if *religion* belonged only to church buildings and to Sundays.

THE DANGERS OF TOLERANCE

Deuteronomy 13:1–18

[1]"If a prophet arises among you, or a dreamer of dreams, and gives you a sign or a wonder, [2]and the sign or wonder which he tells you comes to pass, and if he says, 'Let us go after other gods,' which you have not known, 'and let us serve them,' [3]you shall not listen to the words of that prophet or to that dreamer of dreams; for the Lord your God is testing you, to know whether you love the Lord your God with all your heart and with all your soul. [4]You shall walk after the Lord your God and

fear him, and keep his commandments and obey his voice, and you shall serve him and cleave to him. ⁵But that prophet or that dreamer of dreams shall be put to death, because he has taught rebellion against the Lord your God, who brought you out of the land of Egypt and redeemed you out of the house of bondage, to make you leave the way in which the Lord your God commanded you to walk. So you shall purge the evil from the midst of you.

⁶"If your brother, the son of your mother, or your son, or your daughter, or the wife of your bosom, or your friend who is as your own soul, entices you secretly, saying, 'Let us go and serve other gods,' which neither you nor your fathers have known, ⁷some of the gods of the peoples that are round about you, whether near you or far off from you, from the one end of the earth to the other, ⁸you shall not yield to him or listen to him, nor shall your eye pity him, nor shall you spare him, nor shall you conceal him; ⁹but you shall kill him; your hand shall be first against him to put him to death, and afterwards the hand of all the people. ¹⁰You shall stone him to death with stones, because he sought to draw you away from the Lord your God, who brought you out of the land of Egypt, out of the house of bondage. ¹¹And all Israel shall hear, and fear, and never again do any such wickedness as this among you.

¹²"If you hear in one of your cities, which the Lord your God gives you to dwell there, ¹³that certain base fellows have gone out among you and have drawn away the inhabitants of the city, saying, 'Let us go and serve other gods,' which you have not known, ¹⁴then you shall inquire and make search and ask diligently; and behold, if it be true and certain that such an abominable thing has been done among you, ¹⁵you shall surely put the inhabitants of that city to the sword, destroying it utterly, all who are in it and its cattle, with the edge of the sword. ¹⁶You shall gather all its spoil into the midst of its open square, and burn the city and all its spoil with fire, as a whole burnt offering to the Lord your God; it shall be a heap for ever, it shall not be built again. ¹⁷None of the devoted things shall cleave to your hand; that the Lord may turn from the fierceness of his anger, and show you mercy, and have compassion on you, and multiply you, as he swore to your fathers, ¹⁸if you obey the voice of the Lord your God, keeping all his commandments which I command you this day, and doing what is right in the sight of the Lord your God."

Chapter 12 has dealt with the insidious danger to the Israelite faith posed by the existence of pagan or semi-pagan shrines throughout the country. This chapter finds just as insidious a danger lying inside the minds of certain Israelites; people who would persuade others to abandon the true faith for the worship of other gods. Three types of situation are envisaged, and in each case capital punishment is prescribed for the offenders. In the Western world today, our laws are quite the reverse, protecting the right of the individual to believe and practise any religion he chooses, and enshrining toleration; and none of us would wish to see a return to the harsh laws of yesteryear. We must remember that harsh laws were commonplace even in the West until a century or so ago; and that the idea of toleration is a very recent development.

Moreover, it is important to realize that toleration is not nearly so easy to practise in relatively unstable political situations. Many countries of the world still fear dissidents, minority religious groups, political opponents, and so on, particularly if they are outspoken. Deuteronomy 13 was very much concerned with the social and political well-being of Israel; we are not reading here about some purely religious issue. The enemies of society, as the writer of Deuteronomy saw the matter, were fully comparable with today's traitors or spies, whom our societies still punish with considerable severity.

The *first* danger is that of the *prophet* or visionary (vv. 1–5), standing outside organized religion (very probably), and proving very persuasive to ordinary folk. The demagogue, with a magnetic personality and a glib tongue, can very easily gain a following: Adolf Hitler was able to dominate a whole nation, we recall. Nowadays many self-made religious leaders spring to mind. The test is clear: does their message promote true worship, or detract from it?

(a) Moreover, as with 7:1–3, it is best to read this passage as a reflection on the past and condemnation of its laxity and apostasy, not as a viable programme for the future.

(b) The second paragraph (vv. 6–11) notes that in many cases the temptation to turn from true worship arises in the family circle; the conversation at the family meal-table may well prove a corrupting influence. A *second* danger arises here; family solidarity could easily protect traitors. Firm action in defence of the truth is called for.

(c) Verses 12–18 take note of a special danger in the cities, where it is much easier to act anonymously, and where the whole population could be drawn away from true worship. It is a well-known fact that cities are more irreligious, and, at the same time, more attracted by exotic cults and creeds, than rural areas. The harsh remedy prescribed (vv. 15–16) reminds us of Jesus' startling words to the individual in Matthew 5:29–30; neither Deuteronomy 13 nor Matthew 5 are to be applied literally, but both indicate that there are limits to toleration—not least in the toleration of our own sinful tendencies.

PROHIBITED FOOD ITEMS

Deuteronomy 14:1–21

[1]"You are the sons of the Lord your God; you shall not cut yourselves or make any baldness on your foreheads for the dead. [2]For you are a people holy to the Lord your God, and the Lord has chosen you to be a people for his own possession, out of all the peoples that are on the face of the earth.

[3]"You shall not eat any abominable thing. [4]These are the animals you may eat: the ox, the sheep, the goat, [5]the hart, the gazelle, the roebuck, the wild goat, the ibex, the antelope, and the mountain-sheep. [6]Every animal that parts the hoof and has the hoof cloven in two, and chews the cud, among the animals, you may eat. [7]Yet of those that chew the cud or have the hoof cloven you shall not eat these: the camel, the hare, and the rock badger, because they chew the cud but do not part the hoof, are unclean for you. [8]And the swine, because it parts the hoof but does not chew the cud, is unclean for you. Their flesh you shall not eat, and their carcasses you shall not touch.

[9]"Of all that are in the waters you may eat these: whatever has fins and scales you may eat. [10]And whatever does not have fins and scales you shall not eat; it is unclean for you.

[11]"You may eat all clean birds. [12]But these are the ones which you shall not eat: the eagle, the vulture, the osprey, [13]the buzzard, the kite, after their kinds; [14]every raven after its kind; [15]the ostrich, the night-hawk, the sea gull, the hawk, after their kinds; [16]the little owl and the

great owl, the water hen [17]and the pelican, the carrion vulture and the cormorant, [18]the stork, the heron, after their kinds; the hoopoe and the bat. [19]And all winged insects are unclean for you; they shall not be eaten. [20]All clean winged things you may eat.

[21]"You shall not eat anything that dies of itself; you may give it to the alien who is within your towns, that he may eat it, or you may sell it to a foreigner; for you are a people holy to the Lord your God.

"You shall not boil a kid in its mother's milk.''

The chapter begins by prohibiting certain customs *for the dead*; in other words, customs associated with mourning. The reason given—that Israel, in contrast to other *peoples*, belongs to Yahweh—gives a sufficient clue to the purpose behind the law of verse 1. The prohibited rites must have featured in Canaanite religious practice; to perform them would be, not a sign of respect for the dead, but a sign of involvement in pagan worship. The Canaanites, like many other ancient peoples, believed in deities of the underworld.

Very probably the same sort of consideration goes a long way to explaining the list of unclean creatures in verses 3–21. It is a very comprehensive list (cf. Lev. 11), giving clear guidance to the Israelites on how to distinguish clean animals from unclean; once the laws on eating meat were relaxed (see commentary on Deut. 12:15–32), it became important for the layman to know some of the rules previously administered by the priests, to prevent ordinary farmers from killing and eating creatures considered to be unclean. Since it would be difficult to memorize such a long list, some general principles are incorporated (vv. 6, 7, 9, 10, 19, 20).

For some types of meat no doubt a natural aversion was felt; any creature that was a scavenger is prohibited, for instance, and so best avoided at all times. We must also remember that in Israel's world many creatures were held to be sacred, and it is likely that a major factor in compiling this list was the desire to keep Israel at a safe distance from Canaanite religious practices. The final law in verse 21 certainly looks like a ban on a specific fertility ritual practised by the Canaanites.

If the reasons for specific prohibitions were varied, the overall purpose is stated plainly in verse 2: Israel as *a people* must be *holy*. Our modern concept of holiness would not involve matters of diet, but to the Israelites, holiness included the ideas of discrimination and orderliness: God as Creator had put all things in their proper categories, and it was man's duty to observe important distinctions.

Israel is viewed as a family, "the sons of the Lord" (v. 1), and as a family they are to be distinctive—for that is the chief value of the word *holy* in this context. In Israel's world, that distinctiveness showed itself in separation from everything that in any way had to do with false religion. In the course of time, the strict Jewish adherence to these laws has undoubtedly made the Jews a distinctive people, and often puts up a social barrier, since orthodox Jews will not eat in a Gentile home. That is the primary reason why the New Testament repealed these laws for the Church (see Mark 7:14–19 and Acts 15); no barriers must prevent the fellowship of Christians. Yet the Christian family is meant to be distinctive: St. Paul, for example, provides his own list of what we might call "clean" and "unclean" behaviour, in Galatians 5:16–26.

THE PURPOSE OF TITHES

Deuteronomy 14:22–29

22"You shall tithe all the yield of your seed, which comes forth from the field year by year. 23And before the Lord your God, in the place which he will choose, to make his name dwell there, you shall eat the tithe of your grain, of your wine, and of your oil, and the firstlings of your herd and flock; that you may learn to fear the Lord your God always. 24And if the way is too long for you, so that you are not able to bring the tithe, when the Lord your God blesses you, because the place is too far from you, which the Lord your God chooses, to set his name there, 25then you shall turn it into money, and bind up the money in your hand, and go to the place which the Lord your God chooses, 26and spend the money for whatever you desire, oxen, or sheep, or wine or strong drink, whatever your appetite craves; and you shall eat there before the Lord your God and rejoice, you and your household. 27And you shall not forsake the Levite who is within your towns, for he has no portion or inheritance with you.

²⁸"At the end of every three years you shall bring forth all the tithe of your produce in the same year, and lay it up within your towns; ²⁹and the Levite, because he has no portion or inheritance with you, and the sojourner, the fatherless, and the widow, who are within your towns, shall come and eat and be filled; that the Lord your God may bless you in all the work of your hands that you do."

In Old English, "tithe" and *tenth* were the same word, and very probably (although we cannot be absolutely certain) we can make the same equation for the Hebrew terms: hence the Good News Bible reads, "Set aside a tithe—a tenth of all that your fields produce each year" (v. 22). The custom was a very old one, both in the Old Testament (cf. Gen. 28:22) and outside Israel. Tithing had two values: (1) it represented a gift to God, recognizing that farm produce and livestock came from him—indeed, a tithe was a token repayment to him; (2) it provided a large part of the resources needed to maintain temples and temple personnel, such as priests and Levites. So a tithe was a combination of a sacrificial offering and a religious tax, and Deuteronomy reinforces here the importance of obeying this older law and custom. No doubt tithes were usually paid to the nearest shrine; and one can readily suppose that once sanctuaries and temples outside Jerusalem were closed down, country folk became far less scrupulous and careful about paying tithes—the more so when practical problems arose, such as driving farm animals for many miles.

There are some puzzling differences between Deuteronomy 14 and the other sections which set out laws about tithing: Leviticus 27 and Numbers 18. Probably the laws in Leviticus and Numbers are to be set against different situations. At any rate, we must take this passage in its own right, and observe how closely it is connected with the law of the single sanctuary in chapter 12. The law insists that it is still the Israelite's duty to go to the sanctuary (v. 23), but if Jerusalem is too far away, then money may be taken in lieu of farm produce (vv. 24–25). (Probably an annual visit to Jerusalem is implied.) Since, however, the Levites, who had lost their livelihood when rural shrines were shut, had no farms and were now in need, then every third year tithes were to go to local towns instead of Jerusalem, in order to support these Levites and other needy people (vv. 27–29). Here we see very clearly displayed the social conscience of Deuteronomy; Israel was seen to need a social welfare system.

The tithe could have been a mechanical and joyless thing, treated much as the average citizen today views the payment of income tax. Deuteronomy took this ancient and universal law and instead made it a thing of joy as well as generosity. The Israelite paying this tax did not do so at a remote distance; he and his family gave a feast in Jerusalem, in which of course they fully shared (v. 26). (Self-evidently, they did not spend the whole tithe feeding themselves!) As St. Paul says, "God loves a cheerful giver" (2 Cor. 9:7). The Christian Church makes the same sort of appeal to individual Christians and their families; the upkeep of the Churches and the social needs of the world require our voluntary self-denial. The New Testament exhortation to give hospitality (*eg* Heb. 13:2) may also derive ultimately from these verses in Deuteronomy.

HELP FOR THE POOR

Deuteronomy 15:1–11

¹"At the end of every seven years you shall grant a release. ²And this is the manner of the release: every creditor shall release what he has lent to his neighbour; he shall not exact it of his neighbour, his brother, because the Lord's release has been proclaimed. ³Of a foreigner you may exact it; but whatever of yours is with your brother your hand shall release. ⁴But there will be no poor among you (for the Lord will bless you in the land which the Lord your God gives you for an inheritance to possess), ⁵if only you will obey the voice of the Lord your God, being careful to do all this commandment which I command you this day. ⁶For the Lord your God will bless you, as he promised you, and you shall lend to many nations, but you shall not borrow; and you shall rule over many nations, but they shall not rule over you.

⁷"If there is among you a poor man, one of your brethren, in any of your towns within your land which the Lord your God gives you, you shall not harden your heart or shut your hand against your poor brother, ⁸but you shall open your hand to him, and lend him sufficient

for his need, whatever it may be. [9]Take heed lest there be a base thought in your heart, and you say, 'The seventh year, the year of release is near,' and your eye be hostile to your poor brother, and you give him nothing, and he cry to the Lord against you, and it be sin in you. [10]You shall give to him freely, and your heart shall not be grudging when you give to him; because for this the Lord your God will bless you in all your work and in all that you undertake. [11]For the poor will never cease out of the land; therefore I command you, You shall open wide your hand to your brother, to the needy and to the poor, in the land."

Poverty and debts are a universal problem (as v. 11 ruefully admits), and many societies throughout history have made some attempt to deal with them. Here Deuteronomy tackles the problem of debts by legislating that every seventh year should be a year of *release*, when all debts should be cancelled. Obviously the number seven links up with the concept of the sabbath, and we must note that an old law in Israel decreed that the land should lie fallow every seventh year (Lev. 25:1–7). Deuteronomy does not mention this old law, but the fallow year may well be connected with this year of cancellation of all debts. Some commentators suggest that debts were merely suspended, not cancelled, in the fallow year, when peasants would get no harvest and would be simply unable to pay; but the whole tenor of this passage strongly supports the view that permanent cancellation is meant. The law is not extended to aliens (v. 3), very likely because foreign traders are envisaged, not foreign residents who, like most Israelites, would live off the land. The passage is very much concerned with Israel as a family; that is why foreigners are not included, and why international debts are prohibited (v. 6). Rich Israelites are to recognize and treat poor Israelites as brothers (v. 7), and treat them with generosity and kindness. The year of release must have been a fixed year, known to all, otherwise the exhortation of verse 9 would make no sense.

It is one thing to make a law enforcing the cancellation of debts at a specific time; it is quite impossible though to force richer citizens to make loans, and we can see that the passage is an appeal, a plea for generosity. The basis is the covenant; the covenant bound Israelites together in unity as the people of God. Israelites therefore had moral obligations towards each other; and if moreover as a nation they fulfilled their obligations towards God, then his blessing could eliminate poverty (vv. 4–5). The elimination of poverty is of course an ideal (as v. 11 realistically acknowledges), but the point is that it is an ideal worth pursuing.

Here we see at its clearest that Deuteronomy's "laws" are not just fixed decrees but a "design for life". The climax of the passage is not the law about the cancellation of debts but the appeal to the heart in verse 11. The opposite of law is "crime"; the opposite of God's moral laws is "sin". Matthew Henry aptly comments that what we might call simple prudence can be sin. In our world the structures and laws regarding debts and relating to poverty are very different, and a year of release would not be practical; but the principle expressed in verse 11 is of permanent validity. Within the Christian family, the national family and the world family, our obligations have not changed in the sight of God.

REGULATING SLAVERY

Deuteronomy 15:12–23

12"If your brother, a Hebrew man, or a Hebrew woman, is sold to you, he shall serve you six years, and in the seventh year you shall let him go free from you. 13And when you let him go free from you, you shall not let him go empty-handed; 14you shall furnish him liberally out of your flock, out of your threshing floor, and out of your wine press; as the Lord your God has blessed you, you shall give to him. 15You shall remember that you were a slave in the land of Egypt, and the Lord your God redeemed you; therefore I command you this today. 16But if he says to you, 'I will not go out from you,' because he loves you and your household, since he fares well with you, 17then you shall take an awl, and thrust it through his ear into the door, and he shall be your bondman for ever. And to your bondwoman you shall do likewise. 18It shall not seem hard to you, when you let him go free from you; for at half the cost of a hired servant he has served you six years. So the Lord your God will bless you in all that you do.

¹⁹"All the firstling males that are born of your herd and flock you shall consecrate to the Lord your God; you shall do no work with the firstling of your herd, nor shear the firstling of your flock. ²⁰You shall eat it, you and your household, before the Lord your God year by year at the place which the Lord will choose. ²¹But if it has any blemish, if it is lame or blind, or has any serious blemish whatever, you shall not sacrifice it to the Lord your God. ²²You shall eat it within your towns; the unclean and the clean alike may eat it, as though it were a gazelle or a hart. ²³Only you shall not eat its blood; you shall pour it out on the ground like water."

One of the chief effects of large debts in the ancient Near East was that debtors could be forced to sell themselves into slavery. Other slaves in society were foreigners, in fact prisoners of war, but this passage is concerned only with Israelite (*ie Hebrew*) slaves. Approximately the same law of release contained in verses 1–11 is applied to them too, except that *the seventh year* was no longer a fixed calendar year, since all such slaves were bound to *six years* in servitude (v. 12).

The RSV terms "bondman" and "bondwoman" (v. 17) do not have the same overtones in English as *slave* (v. 15), but in Hebrew there is no difference. We must be careful not to draw our concept of slavery from memories of reading *Uncle Tom's Cabin*; Uncle Tom was certainly not released with a "golden handshake" after six years' service. Slaves in Israel clearly did have some rights—which is of course the whole point of verses 12–18. All the same, slavery was a humiliating position; and the tone of verse 18 suggests that not all slave-owners in practice proved willing to release valuable slaves and cheap labour.

The basic law is in Exodus 21:2–6. The big difference here is the exhortation—scarcely a law—in verses 13–14, to give the slave a generous parting gift. This injunction was not only humane, but might help to prevent the released man or woman from falling into debt and slavery once again. Thus Deuteronomy here in principle moves towards the prevention of slavery, but without upsetting the whole fabric of society. The logic behind verse 15 is "freely you have received, freely give" (Matt. 10:8, NIV).

Like Exodus 21, verse 16 recognizes that some slaves felt at home and secure as they were, and provides that they may voluntarily accept permanent slave-status. The old custom of verse 17 produced a permanent visible badge of slave-status. The permanence of this status was double-edged; it not only bound the slave to his master, but equally prevented the master from throwing the slave out once he became old or incapacitated.

The final paragraph adjusts the old law, concerning first-born farm animals (cf. Exod. 13:2), to conform with the single-sanctuary law. All first-born animals were still to be dedicated to God, and taken to Jerusalem for sacrifice and the sacrificial banquet; but if they were in any way defective they were not sacrificed, and could be eaten locally. This law is linked with 12:1–19. The basic principle involved is the recognition that all life belongs to God (as v. 23 also testifies, with a different symbolism); the farmer was to acknowledge that for all his own hard work, it is God who gives the harvest.

THE PASSOVER

Deuteronomy 16:1–8

[1]"Observe the month of Abib, and keep the passover to the Lord your God; for in the month of Abib the Lord your God brought you out of Egypt by night. [2]And you shall offer the passover sacrifice to the Lord your God, from the flock or the herd, at the place which the Lord will choose, to make his name dwell there. [3]You shall eat no leavened bread with it; seven days you shall eat it with unleavened bread, the bread of affliction—for you came out of the land of Egypt in hurried flight—that all the days of your life you may remember the day when you came out of the land of Egypt. [4]No leaven shall be seen with you in all your territory for seven days; nor shall any of the flesh which you sacrifice on the evening of the first day remain all night until morning. [5]You may not offer the passover sacrifice within any of your towns which the Lord your God gives you; [6]but at the place which the Lord your God will choose, to make his name dwell in it, there you shall offer the passover sacrifice, in the evening at the going down of the sun, at the time you came out of Egypt. [7]And you shall boil it and eat it at

the place which the Lord your God will choose; and in the morning you shall turn and go to your tents. [8]For six days you shall eat unleavened bread; and on the seventh day there shall be a solemn assembly to the Lord your God; you shall do no work on it.''

Laws governing the observance of the three major festivals of ancient Israel are to be found in a number of Old Testament passages (Exod. 23:14–17; Lev. 23). These festivals were clearly considered to be of very great importance, and Deuteronomy's law concerning a single sanctuary enhanced them, since it made all three obligatory pilgrimages (v. 16). The Gospels record how Jesus, among others, journeyed regularly to Jerusalem for these festivals. The three (plus some other festivals of later origin) are still important in Jewish practice today, but the destruction of the Temple in A.D. 70 changed their character again, and they are now celebrated in the home and in the local synagogue.

There has been a great deal of debate and discussion regarding the origins of the festivals; and much controversy also surrounds the interrelationship of the various relevant Old Testament passages, listed above. The issues are particularly complex in the case of *the passover*, and interested readers may pursue them in larger commentaries or in Bible dictionaries.

The chief point of academic interest is that this spring festival (celebrated in *Abib*, otherwise called Nisan, which falls in March–April by our calendar) has two rituals to it and two names associated with it: it is both *the passover* (v. 1) and "the feast of unleavened bread" (v. 16). The former was basically a *sacrifice* (v. 2) made on one particular *evening* (v. 4) each year, with subsequent feasting (v. 7); while the eating of *unleavened bread* was a ritual that lasted *six days*, followed by *a solemn assembly* on the following day (v. 8). Opinions are divided concerning whether or not these two rituals were originally quite separate and unrelated. Whatever the case, in Deuteronomy the two belong together, and one runs on from the other. In this connection it should be observed that the injunction—go to your tents the morning after the passover—may include both homes and tents (or lodgings), since the journey back from Jerusalem could take many days for Israelites who lived a far distance away.

Very likely this spring festival linked several themes, one of which was undoubtedly agricultural: note that both the other festivals were of agricultural significance (vv. 9–15). With good reason, however, the emphasis is laid not on God's annual blessings (of springtime growth and the promise of a harvest), but on his greatest benefit to Israel—their deliverance from Egypt, which had allowed them to become a nation in the first place. The passover feast recalled their last meal in Egypt and all that was associated with it (cf. Exod. 12). Unleavened bread was clearly not eaten with any pleasure, since it was called "the bread of affliction" (or "bread of suffering", GNB, v. 3). It too linked up with the Exodus (cf. Exod. 12:8); and no doubt it was also a reminder of Israel's wilderness wanderings, when bread containing yeast would have been an unobtainable luxury.

The purpose in keeping this annual feast is set out briefly but plainly in verse 3: God's greatest gifts to his people must never be forgotten.

(ii)

The English word "passover" derives from Exodus 12:13, and the phrase "I will pass over you": that is, "I [God] will spare your lives [the Israelites]", at the time of the passover celebration in Egypt. The Hebrew word for the feast is *pesach* (compare our word "paschal"), and the related verb *pasach* means "pass over", or "spare", in Exodus 12:13. The sacrificial animal was originally a lamb (Exod. 12), although Deuteronomy 16:2 widens the options; the animal thus killed was naturally seen as a substitute for the Israelites whose lives were *passed over* while Egyptians were dying. The lamb was therefore a symbol; and so too was the leaven or yeast. The absence of leaven signified haste of preparation, according to verse 3. However, verse 4 goes further and bans even the possession of leaven during the festival; this instruction is still applied very vigorously in Jewish households, and children will join in the hunt to make sure every last crumb of it is thrown out. (Jewish mothers will often hide a little of it, for their children to discover and throw out.) It is not surprising then, that leaven came to stand as a symbol for evil, especially as leaven is something that works powerfully unseen, and affects the whole substance into which it is put.

The crucifixion of Jesus was precisely at the passover season, and naturally enough the early Christians saw that this was no coincidence. Just as the ancient Israelites had been saved from death through the sacrifice of a lamb in each household, so now Christians had been delivered from sin and death and hell by the once-and-for-all sacrifice of Christ. As St. Paul puts it, "Christ, our paschal lamb, has been sacrificed" (1 Cor. 5:7). The Christian Easter has replaced the Jewish passover, although unlike the passover, Easter commemorates resurrection as well as death. The Jewish passover, enhanced in this way, still holds great meaning for the church.

The New Testament uses the symbol of leaven several times: for example, when Jesus warned his disciples against the evils to be found even in religious men (Matt. 16:6). Continuing his comments on Christ as our "paschal lamb", Paul urges Christians to "celebrate the festival" not by any annual rituals, however moving, but by rooting out the leaven of such things as boasting and malice (1 Cor. 5:6–8). In general, Paul was far more interested in the everyday lives of his converts, than in the celebration of sacred days.

JOY AND GENEROSITY

Deuteronomy 16:9–17

9"You shall count seven weeks; begin to count the seven weeks from the time you first put the sickle to the standing grain. 10Then you shall keep the feast of weeks to the Lord your God with the tribute of a freewill offering from your hand, which you shall give as the Lord your God blesses you; 11and you shall rejoice before the Lord your God, you and your son and your daughter, your manservant and your maidservant, the Levite who is within your towns, the sojourner, the fatherless, and the widow who are among you, at the place which the Lord your God will choose, to make his name dwell there. 12You shall remember that you were a slave in Egypt; and you shall be careful to observe these statutes.

¹³"You shall keep the feast of booths seven days, when you make your ingathering from your threshing floor and your wine press; ¹⁴you shall rejoice in your feast, you and your son and your daughter, your manservant and your maidservant, the Levite, the sojourner, the fatherless, and the widow who are within your towns. ¹⁵For seven days you shall keep the feast to the Lord your God at the place which the Lord will choose; because the Lord your God will bless you in all your produce and in all the work of your hands, so that you will be altogether joyful.

¹⁶"Three times a year all your males shall appear before the Lord your God at the place which he will choose: at the feast of unleavened bread, at the feast of weeks, and at the feast of booths. They shall not appear before the Lord empty-handed; ¹⁷every man shall give as he is able, according to the blessing of the Lord your God which he has given you."

The second festival, some *seven weeks* after passover, was called the "feast of weeks"; it is better known to us as *Pentecost* or *Whitsun*. The rough-and-ready system of calculating it was to suit an agricultural community with no fixed calendar. Undoubtedly this was an agricultural festival, marking the end of the barley harvest; it must have been well enough known and understood to need no explanation. In later times it became linked with the lawgiving at Mount Sinai.

The "feast of booths" (v. 13) was an autumn harvest festival, also known as "the feast of tabernacles" (or *Succoth*). The *booths* were made of branches and boughs, and Israelites were instructed to live in them for the seven festal days (cf. Lev. 23:39–43). Once again Deuteronomy saw no need to elaborate on the details or purpose of the festival.

The primary purpose of both of these festivals was clearly to give thanks to God for his generous provision to his people in the annual harvests. That unstated fact supplies the logic for the exhortations of this passage, to be equally generous and openhanded both towards God and towards fellow-Israelites. Nobody should come to Jerusalem *empty-handed* (v. 16); Deuteronomy does not stipulate fixed donations, but asks that "every man shall give as he is able" (v. 17). The responsibility falls upon the males

(v. 16)—that is, the heads of families—but everyone is to benefit: the family and the farm workers, resident foreigners (*the sojourner*), *Levites* (who were now very dependent on charity), and orphans and *widows* too (vv. 11, 14). So the *whole* community was to benefit from the three pilgrimages each year.

Apart from the plea to be generous, the passage calls upon the worshippers to be *joyful* (vv. 11, 14, 15). The service of God was not intended to be some cheerless ritual, demanding great self-sacrifice, to say nothing of the nuisance of having to make the journey up to Jerusalem. On the contrary, it was something to be enjoyed by everyone in the national family. In Islam, it is well known that the annual pilgrimage to Mecca creates a great sense of joy and brotherhood. The destruction of the Jewish Temple in A.D. 70 destroyed the centre of pilgrimage for Jews everywhere; but many of their festivals retain the sense of joy, and reinforce the unity of the local community, at least. For Christians, Christmas is probably the most joyful festival; but how easily the generosity can be restricted to the immediate family, and the sense of Christian brotherhood quite forgotten. Generosity and joy can be stimulated by actively remembering what God's blessings to us have really been (cf. vv. 12, 17).

JUSTICE

Deuteronomy 16:18-20

18"You shall appoint judges and officers in all your towns which the Lord your God gives you, according to your tribes; and they shall judge the people with righteous judgment. 19You shall not pervert justice; you shall not show partiality; and you shall not take a bribe, for a bribe blinds the eyes of the wise and subverts the cause of the righteous. 20Justice, and only justice, you shall follow, that you may live and inherit the land which the Lord your God gives you."

To Western readers, these three verses appear to change the subject, interrupting various passages about religious observances in order to discuss legal practices briefly. But in the ancient world, law and religion were very closely linked—as of course the whole book of Deuteronomy demonstrates. In fact, this short paragraph tackles yet another side-effect of the law of the single sanctuary. Local temples were not only places of worship but also the law courts; when Deuteronomy closed down all the shrines outside Jerusalem, the result could have been to deprive ordinary citizens of *justice* (the key term of v. 20): it would have been difficult and expensive to make a long journey to Jerusalem in pursuit of some legal right or claim, or to defend oneself against a charge. So *judges* and court *officers* were to be appointed in *all* the towns where sanctuaries had been. Once again we see how Deuteronomy never forgets the welfare of the man in the street. It may be that this reallocation of legal duties also lessened the rôle of the royal court in lawsuits.

Possibly this severing of law from religion (for the new officials were presumably secular appointments) seemed likely to diminish the quality of justice. Professional judges, whose income was entirely derived from their legal practice, could be more susceptible to bribery than sanctuary officials had been. (It is clear from some of the prophets that bribery and corruption in the law courts were a problem in Israel—cf. Isa. 5:23; Amos 2:6.) Verses 19 and 20 therefore set a standard to follow. Verse 19 is negative, warning against the chief ways in which it is possible to *pervert justice*. Verse 20 sets up *justice* as a goal, a target to achieve—addressed just as much to the whole nation as to the judges themselves—and rounds off with the implied threat that an unjust nation will lose its *land*. Even if law was to be divorced from sanctuaries, it was not to be divorced from God's standards; and he himself would in the end judge the judges.

It is all too easy to confuse what is legal and what is just. Modern governments create new laws at their own whims, some good and some bad. It is of course right and proper that a legal system should be free from corruption, as verse 19 insists; but laws themselves can be unjust at times, and it is important to bear in mind the distinction between legality and justice. Absolute justice is God's standard, not because of some theoretical desirability, but because he cares for individual people. God's people should care deeply about injustice wherever they perceive it.

PROHIBITED WORSHIP

Deuteronomy 16:21–17:7

> 21"You shall not plant any tree as an Asherah beside the altar of the Lord your God which you shall make. 22And you shall not set up a pillar, which the Lord your God hates.
>
> 1"You shall not sacrifice to the Lord your God an ox or a sheep in which is a blemish, any defect whatever; for that is an abomination to the Lord your God.
>
> 2"If there is found among you, within any of your towns which the Lord your God gives you, a man or woman who does what is evil in the sight of the Lord your God, in transgressing his covenant, 3and has gone and served other gods and worshipped them, or the sun or the moon or any of the host of heaven, which I have forbidden, 4and it is told you and you hear of it; then you shall inquire diligently, and if it is true and certain that such an abominable thing has been done in Israel, 5then you shall bring forth to your gates that man or woman who has done this evil thing, and you shall stone that man or woman to death with stones. 6On the evidence of two witnesses or of three witnesses he that is to die shall be put to death; a person shall not be put to death on the evidence of one witness. 7The hand of the witnesses shall be first against him to put him to death, and afterward the hand of all the people. So you shall purge the evil from the midst of you."

Here Deuteronomy reverts to the theme of wrongful worship, and prohibits three activities.

(a) *Corrupting true worship* (16:21–22). The *altar* is dedicated to Yahweh, Israel's God, but the *tree* (or sacred pole) and the sacred *pillar* were standard items in Canaanite religion. The pole was a symbol of the goddess *Asherah* (hence the name could be applied to the pole), and pillars represented the male deity. So the practice described was a deliberate mixing of two religions, while giving lip-service to the God of Israel. It really signified *lack* of faith, since it meant that the Israelites did not really trust their own God to give them fertility of the land and good harvests.

(b) *Defective sacrifices* (17:1). To offer God defective animals in sacrifice was to give him second best. It was also hypocrisy, since it gave the impressive appearance of a pious act, but was a ruse to save money, for obviously such animals would fetch low prices in the market. No punishment is mentioned, but the strong words about God's attitude to such conduct make their own point.

(c) *Deliberate apostasy* (17:2–7). In the case of the deliberate practice of pagan worship, a very severe punishment is named. Nowadays we are fully aware that religious freedom must be given to everyone, and we have no such laws on our statute books. Before we dismiss Deuteronomy's law as both bigoted and harsh, however, we need to see the deed in the perspective of the time and the situation. The chief hostility of verse 3 is reserved for the worship of sky-deities, with emphasis on star-worship ("the host of heaven"). This cult became prominent towards the end of the Israelite monarchy, and was not so much a native development as a borrowing from Mesopotamia. In other words, this form of worship was seen not just as a religious evil but as deliberate political treachery, turning to the gods of Israel's worst oppressors (Assyria, and then Babylon). Moreover, the cohesion and unity of Israel were clearly seen as a social and political necessity.

At the same time, however stern the penalty, verse 6 seeks to prevent any person being executed for a crime he did not commit. The *evidence* must be adequate and credible; and anyone ready to make a serious accusation must be prepared to be executioner as well as *witness*.

Our circumstances are very different, but the general principles stand the test of time. Above all, if we claim to worship God, then we must treat that worship seriously.

OFFICERS OF THE LAW

Deuteronomy 17:8–20

> [8]"If any case arises requiring decision between one kind of homicide and another, one kind of legal right and another, or one kind of assault and another, any case within your towns which is too difficult for you, then you shall arise and go up to the place which the Lord your God

will choose, ⁹and coming to the Levitical priests, and to the judge who is in office in those days, you shall consult them, and they shall declare to you the decision. ¹⁰Then you shall do according to what they declare to you from that place which the Lord will choose; and you shall be careful to do according to all that they direct you; ¹¹according to the instructions which they give you, and according to the decision which they pronounce to you, you shall do; you shall not turn aside from the verdict which they declare to you, either to the right hand or to the left. ¹²The man who acts presumptuously, by not obeying the priest who stands to minister there before the Lord your God, or the judge, that man shall die; so you shall purge the evil from Israel. ¹³And all the people shall hear, and fear, and not act presumptuously again.

¹⁴"When you come to the land which the Lord your God gives you, and you possess it and dwell in it, and then say, 'I will set a king over me, like all the nations that are round about me'; ¹⁵you may indeed set as king over you him whom the Lord your God will choose. One from among your brethren you shall set as king over you; you may not put a foreigner over you, who is not your brother. ¹⁶Only he must not multiply horses for himself, or cause the people to return to Egypt in order to multiply horses, since the Lord has said to you, 'You shall never return that way again.' ¹⁷And he shall not multiply wives for himself, lest his heart turn away; nor shall he greatly multiply for himself silver and gold.

¹⁸"And when he sits on the throne of his kingdom, he shall write for himself in a book a copy of this law, from that which is in charge of the Levitical priests; ¹⁹and it shall be with him, and he shall read in it all the days of his life, that he may learn to fear the Lord his God, by keeping all the words of this law and these statutes, and doing them; ²⁰that his heart may not be lifted up above his brethren, and that he may not turn aside from the commandment, either to the right hand or to the left; so that he may continue long in his kingdom, he and his children, in Israel."

This section of Deuteronomy is all about the institutions of Israel and especially the officials (including the king) who are to administer them. Local magistrates (as we would call them) have already been mentioned in 16:18, and now rules are laid down for a supreme court in Jerusalem (vv. 8–13). Again we note the reference to the single sanctuary (v. 8). It is not a court of appeal, but a superior court, set up to deal with particularly *difficult* cases of various kinds; in some of which the penalty could be the death sentence.

Two types of officials are mentioned—"Levitical priests" and "the judge who is in office" (v. 9); the wording may suggest a tribunal of several Levites and a single judge (although cf. v. 12). The exact form of the tribunal is not clear; the point of chief interest is that there is no place on the tribunal for the king. We know that the king did in fact play an important rôle in the administration of law (see, for example, 2 Sam. 12:1–6: the episode when David pronounced a verdict on himself; and also 2 Sam. 14); and we can well believe that the king's own vested interests sometimes caused injustices. (1 Kings 21 shows a legal situation in which the king had a clear interest, but in this case he did not preside at the trial, plainly.) By excluding the king, Deuteronomy is quietly, but firmly, indicating the principle that the supreme court should be impartial, since its decisions must be final and irrevocable (vv. 10–13). Verses 12 and 13 may suggest that the supreme court's decisions were flouted at times.

The monarchy is the subject of verses 14–20. The attitude taken towards the *king* could be described as grudging, but on the other hand Deuteronomy envisages no other arrangement for political control in Israel. These verses are more in the nature of an appeal to future kings, than legislation (except that v. 15 bans Israel from making any *foreigner* their king). Solomon in particular multiplied *horses* and *wives* (1 Kings 10:26, 11:1–3), and moved in the direction of creating a despotic oriental monarchy. Ideally the king ought to feel close kinship with all his subjects—he was their *brother* (v. 15)—and avoid ostentation and greed. It seems very difficult for any human being who reaches a position of high authority to avoid arrogance, and the Bible would not disagree with Acton's adage that "power corrupts"; verse 20 indeed says as much, but a remedy is offered in verses 18–19. The remedy is at the same time physical and spiritual: the king is to get hold of "a copy of this law" *ie* the Deuteronomic law code, and keep it beside him; and by constantly reading it, he is to master its contents and so "learn to fear the Lord". The RSV may well be right to say that the king is to "write for himself" his copy of

Deuteronomy, which would certainly imprint much of it on his mind; every student knows that writing is a better aid to memory than mere reading. However, possibly all that is meant is that he should have a copy made, no doubt by professional scribes (see NEB, GNB).

This law is for the king, because it is his responsibility to ensure that the whole law is observed throughout his realm; but the principle that the frequent reading of Scripture keeps God's will in our minds is valid for every Christian.

Verse 18 contains the phrase which indirectly gave Deuteronomy its name: see Introduction, page 1.

THE WELFARE OF THE LEVITES

Deuteronomy 18:1–8

[1]"The Levitical priests, that is, all the tribe of Levi, shall have no portion or inheritance with Israel; they shall eat the offerings by fire to the Lord, and his rightful dues. [2]They shall have no inheritance among their brethren; the Lord is their inheritance, as he promised them. [3]And this shall be the priests' due from the people, from those offering a sacrifice, whether it be ox or sheep: they shall give to the priest the shoulder and the two cheeks and the stomach. [4]The first fruits of your grain, of your wine and of your oil, and the first of the fleece of your sheep, you shall give him. [5]For the Lord your God has chosen him out of all your tribes, to stand and minister in the name of the Lord, him and his sons for ever.

[6]"And if a Levite comes from any of your towns out of all Israel, where he lives—and he may come when he desires—to the place which the Lord will choose, [7]then he may minister in the name of the Lord his God, like all his fellow-Levites who stand to minister there before the Lord. [8]They shall have equal portions to eat, besides what he receives from the sale of his patrimony."

The proper maintenance of the Jerusalem Temple must have been important for Deuteronomy, and this passage deals with the priestly personnel. It does not discuss their duties, however, but is solely concerned with their welfare. The whole "tribe of Levi" is mentioned in verse 1, and this is undoubtedly the scope of the author's interest, whether or not he equated the Levites with the priesthood, as is usually thought to be the case. (If so, the concept differs from that expressed in, for example, Numbers 18, which distinguishes the priesthood—the sons of Aaron—from the Levites. However, the whole question is a complex one, and interested readers should consult commentaries or Bible dictionaries for detailed discussion.) In any case, the Levites as a whole were sanctuary personnel; and the author was plainly concerned that none of them should be or become destitute, especially when the shrines outside Jerusalem were to be shut down (cf. 14:27–29).

The Levites were unique among the tribes which constituted Israel, in that they had no tribal holding, no *inheritance* in that sense (v. 2). Such a situation could not easily be changed, obviously, and verse 1 endorses it while urging that the Levites must be given all their "rightful dues". Verses 2–5 indicate what these were. It goes without saying that if the Israelites were ever lax in offering their sacrifices and first fruits, the Levites would fare badly. One option for the priestly personnel from sanctuaries that were no longer functioning was to go to Jerusalem, in the hope of joining the Temple staff there. Verses 6–8 maintain that rural Levites had every right to do so, and must be treated as equals by the Jerusalem priesthood; in practice, as we know from 2 Kings 23:9, in the time of King Josiah at least, they made no attempt to move to Jerusalem, and it is widely assumed that they were not welcome there.

The important principle laid down in verse 2 is that "the Lord is their inheritance". In other words, their income and livelihood came not from farming, for the Levites had no land, but from temple revenues, *ie* from the offerings brought by all Israelites to their God in worship. The principle is much the same in Matthew 10:10, where Jesus insists that "the [Christian] worker is worth his keep" (NIV). It was a position of great dignity to claim the Lord for one's *inheritance*: as the Good News Bible expresses it in verse 2, "their share is the privilege of being the Lord's priests". But it could all too easily be a position of awful poverty unless God's people—then and now—recognize their responsibilities to give the Lord and his ministers their *rightful dues*. In all too many local churches and denominations as a whole, minis-terial incomes are extraordinarily low.

PROPHETS TRUE AND FALSE

Deuteronomy 18:9–22

9"When you come into the land which the Lord your God gives you, you shall not learn to follow the abominable practices of those nations. 10There shall not be found among you any one who burns his son or his daughter as an offering, any one who practises divination, a soothsayer, or an augur, or a sorcerer, 11or a charmer, or a medium, or a wizard, or a necromancer. 12For whoever does these things is an abomination to the Lord; and because of these abominable practices the Lord your God is driving them out before you. 13You shall be blameless before the Lord your God. 14For these nations, which you are about to dispossess, give heed to soothsayers and to diviners; but as for you, the Lord your God has not allowed you so to do.

15"The Lord your God will raise up for you a prophet like me from among you, from your brethren—him you shall heed—16just as you desired of the Lord your God at Horeb on the day of the assembly, when you said, 'Let me not hear again the voice of the Lord my God, or see this great fire any more, lest I die.' 17And the Lord said to me, 'They have rightly said all that they have spoken. 18I will raise up for them a prophet like you from among their brethren; and I will put my words in his mouth, and he shall speak to them all that I command him. 19And whoever will not give heed to my words which he shall speak in my name, I myself will require it of him. 20But the prophet who presumes to speak a word in my name which I have not commanded him to speak, or who speaks in the name of other gods, that same prophet shall die.' 21And if you say in your heart, 'How may we know the word which the Lord has not spoken?'—22when a prophet speaks in the name of the Lord, if the word does not come to pass or come true, that is a word which the Lord has not spoken; the prophet has spoken it presumptuously, you need not be afraid of him."

(i)

Broadly speaking, there were two rather different types of re-ligious officials in the ancient world. In practice, in different nations and communities, the two were not always clearly distinguished, and the two categories may often have overlapped; but it may be helpful to try to make a broad distinction between them. For convenience, we may use the words "priest" for one type and "prophet" for the other. The two types were well known in Israel, and the English words, "priest" and "prophet", have long been used to translate the two main Old Testament Hebrew words, *kohen* and *nabi*. The priest's rôle was to organize, maintain and operate temples, and in particular, to present sacrifices and offerings according to the proper rituals. The Levites, discussed in verses 1–8, belonged to this category.

The chief purpose of the prophetic rôle, on the other hand, was to find out the will of one deity or another and transmit the message to the individual worshipper, to the nation, or to the king. In Israel, then, it was the prophet who spoke with authority in the name of God, to king and people alike, giving them God's guidance and directives. In doing so, prophets often spoke of the future, especially in the threats or promises that they voiced. Verses 15–22 discuss the *prophet* and give guidance about his rôle.

We know relatively little about the organizational structure of prophets in ancient Israel. There are many unanswered questions, but at least we may reasonably assume that prophetic status was then a well-understood and a recognizable rôle, not to be confused with a whole range of other religious "operators", listed in verses 10ff.. Israel is told sharply to have nothing to do with *soothsayers, diviners* (v. 14) and the rest. All of them belong to our general prophetic category, and that is why this chapter sweeps them to one side before discussing the true Israelite prophet. It is emphasized that they belonged to foreign, pagan nations; there was no place for them in Israelite religion. Like prophets, all these practitioners claimed to be able to ascertain the divine will, or to read the future. They used a wide variety of means, which explains why the list is so long. Some *read* the stars, some *read* the entrails of slaughtered animals, and so on—they were all specialists in their own way.

Why is the Old Testament so hostile towards them? Partly, to be sure, because of their association with other deities; and indeed this is the first, and a perfectly adequate, reason for rejecting them. God makes it abundantly clear that he will not reveal his mind nor give any guidance for the future to anyone who resorts to such false methods; and as for non-existent deities, they have no guidance to offer. So any resort to divination, astrology, and the like, is doomed to failure; the answers received will be false and likely to lead to wrong action.

(ii)

There are three other reasons for rejecting all the practices covered by verses 10–11.

(a) *They are mechanical and mindless.* There is no logical reason to believe that the colour of an animal's entrails, or the pattern of tea-leaves in a cup, or the relative positions of the planets, mean anything at all. Strangely enough, ancient man was a little more logical than his modern counterpart, since he at least believed that the stars, for instance, were controlled by distinct divine beings; but of course this belief too was misplaced.

(b) *They are amoral.* Since the supposed findings of these methods of divination are totally mechanical, questions of right and wrong do not come into consideration. Nothing could be more of a contrast with the prophets of Israel, who constantly urged their listeners to act righteously and morally, and indicated that the shape of their future depended upon their conduct, since God is himself a moral being.

(c) *They tend to be immoral.* It would plainly be an exaggeration to suggest that the average horoscope page in a magazine encourages immorality; most of their recommendations are obviously innocuous enough. (Even so, they may well encourage self-centredness, since they urge you to "do your own thing", "be true to yourself", "obey your stars", *etc.*) But divination shaded into what we might call black magic, and it sought to manipulate gods and unseen powers—often enough to cause the hurt of other human beings. At their worst, occult practices are undoubtedly demonic and downright evil.

There is no easy dividing line to be drawn between the innocuous, the selfish and the immoral, where all such superstitious practices are concerned. With their mixture of absurdity, falsity and evil, they are lumped together and repudiated by all the biblical writers who discuss them.

(iii)

Were the people of God then denied all glimpses of the future and all guidance concerning it? On the contrary: their God had promised one office in Israel through which his voice and his wishes would be made known—that of the *prophet*. His was not an elected office, nor did it come by birth (unlike the Levites), but by the direct choice of God (v. 15). The mark of the prophet was his call (see, for example, Isa. 6); an experience which set him apart from his countrymen and fitted him to be God's spokesman. The function of the prophet is described here in terms of Moses ("a prophet like me", *ie* like Moses, v. 15). Just as Moses had acted as God's spokesman at Horeb (v. 16), so a succession of prophets in Israel would continue to guide the nation in its affairs, giving it the authentic word of God (v. 18). Thus Israel would never be left rudderless.

In the context, this is the natural sense of verse 18—a promise that at no time would Israel be deprived of the prophetic voice. Taking a historical perspective, we can see that for many centuries after the time of Moses there was a succession of prophets active in Israel, north and south. Some time after the Exile, however, the office of prophet seemed to have died out, and the prophetic voice became limited to the written word, namely the prophetic books of the Old Testament. It remained a powerful and effective voice, for all that; but there were those who longed for the rise of new prophets, and so, in some circles, Deuteronomy 18:18 was taken to promise not a whole succession of prophets, but one specific future prophet; a second Moses, in fact a messianic figure. This common expectation among Jews of New Testament times explains why John the Baptist was asked, "Are you *the* prophet?" (John 1:21). The early Christians very naturally identified this expected prophet with Jesus of Nazareth, whom they saw as the fulfilment of so many Old Testament predictions and promises.

For the Christian reader of Deuteronomy, indeed, the two interpretations of 18:18 amount to much the same thing. Jesus was the perfect embodiment of the revelation of God, both eclipsing the prophets of earlier times and eliminating the need for any other prophetic figure in the future. (Christians can respect Muhammad and approve many of his teachings; however, they could never accept Islam's claim that he was "the seal of the prophets".) But Jesus is more than just a figure of history, a first century "second Moses": "he always lives", as Hebrews 7:25 expresses it, to be his people's constant guide throughout life. The prophetic voice is not silent.

THE PROTECTION OF LIFE

Deuteronomy 19:1–13

¹"When the Lord your God cuts off the nations whose land the Lord your God gives you, and you dispossess them and dwell in their cities and in their houses, ²you shall set apart three cities for you in the land which the Lord your God gives you to possess. ³You shall prepare the roads, and divide into three parts the area of the land which the Lord your God gives you as a possession, so that any manslayer can flee to them.

⁴"This is the provision for the manslayer, who by fleeing there may save his life. If any one kills his neighbour unintentionally without having been at enmity with him in time past—⁵as when a man goes into the forest with his neighbour to cut wood, and his hand swings the axe to cut down a tree, and the head slips from the handle and strikes his neighbour so that he dies—he may flee to one of these cities and save his life; ⁶lest the avenger of blood in hot anger pursue the manslayer and overtake him, because the way is long, and wound him mortally, though the man did not deserve to die, since he was not at enmity with his neighbour in time past. ⁷Therefore I command you, You shall set apart three cities. ⁸And if the Lord your God enlarges your border, as he has sworn to your fathers, and gives you all the land which he promised to give to your fathers—⁹provided you are careful to keep all this commandment, which I command you this day, by loving the Lord your God and by walking ever in his ways—then you shall add three other cities to these three, ¹⁰lest innocent blood be shed in your land

which the Lord your God gives you for an inheritance, and so the guilt of bloodshed be upon you.

¹¹"But if any man hates his neighbour, and lies in wait for him, and attacks him, and wounds him mortally so that he dies, and the man flees into one of these cities, ¹²then the elders of his city shall send and fetch him from there, and hand him over to the avenger of blood, so that he may die. ¹³Your eye shall not pity him, but you shall purge the guilt of innocent blood from Israel, so that it may be well with you."

The law codes of all societies have to make careful provision to protect the lives of their citizens, and Deuteronomy is no exception; the section of the book which begins here and ends at 21:9 is chiefly concerned with matters of life and death. Deliberate murder tends to pose few practical problems: "Your eye shall not pity him" was the guiding principle of Deuteronomy for dealing with a murderer (v. 13). Accidental killing, however, posed a problem in the ancient Near East which would not be considered as a difficulty in modern Western society. In communities based very much on the family or clan unit, very ancient conventions allowed, and indeed expected, the wronged family to avenge any murdered member; but the danger in such a system is of course that personal feelings will often prevent impartial judgment, and accidental killings may be punished as if they had been deliberate homicide. Aware of this danger, Israel's laws provided that an "innocent" killer—in other words, somebody claiming that an unnatural death had been accidental—could have a way of escape. (Deuteronomy exhibits both its humaneness and its preoccupation with justice; it is as concerned about the "innocent" killer's life as it is about his victim's, cf. v. 10.)

Israel's most basic law to provide for such a situation is given in Exodus 21:13. Deuteronomy 19 elaborates on the basic law by specifying that six cities, strategically located (v. 3), were to be recognized as *cities of refuge*. (Three of these cities have already been named in 4:41–43, and the later three, envisaged in v. 9 of this chapter, are named in Josh. 20.) It is disputed when exactly this institution came into being in Israel. It is also a matter of dispute whether the "avenger of blood" (v. 6) was a member of the wronged family, or some official with special responsibility for dealing with homicides; the reference to "hot anger" tends to support the former possibility. It is quite probable that the emphasis given here to these cities and their function is due to the law of centralization; if Jerusalem had become not only the exclusive sanctuary-city but also the only city of refuge, many individuals who caused accidental deaths could have forfeited their lives, unable to reach Jerusalem in time. So this passage insists that the six refuge-cities must continue to offer asylum.

Verses 11–13 were intended to make sure that cold-blooded murderers should not escape their due punishment.

Verses 5 and 11 mention extreme cases, by way of illustration. In practice, many cases must have arisen where it was by no means easy to decide on guilt or innocence. The passage leaves it to *the elders* of the accused man's city to decide, on the basis of the evidence open to them (v. 12); verse 11 puts some weight on the question of motive.

The chief interest, other than legal concerns, is in the emphasis put upon the value of each human life. This was remarkable in the ancient world, where so often life was held cheap; indeed, it is still in marked contrast to the conduct of both oppressive régimes and terrorist organizations in our modern world.

PERJURY

Deuteronomy 19:14–21

14"In the inheritance which you will hold in the land that the Lord your God gives you to possess, you shall not remove your neighbour's landmark, which the men of old have set.

15"A single witness shall not prevail against a man for any crime or for any wrong in connection with any offence that he has committed; only on the evidence of two witnesses, or of three witnesses, shall a charge be sustained. 16If a malicious witness rises against any man to accuse him of wrongdoing, 17then both parties to the dispute shall appear before the Lord, before the priests and the judges who are in office in those days; 18the judges shall inquire diligently, and if the witness is a false witness and has accused his brother falsely, 19then you shall do to him as he had meant to do to his brother; so you shall purge the evil from the midst of you. ²⁰And the rest shall hear, and fear, and shall never again commit any such evil among you. ²¹Your eye shall not pity; it shall be life for life, eye for eye, tooth for tooth, hand for hand, foot for foot."

With modern techniques in surveying, it is easily possible to define one's holding of land, although even today the surreptitious alteration of a boundary line (by moving a fence, for instance) might pass unnoticed for a very long time. There is plenty of evidence that in the ancient Near East there was a real problem over boundaries, and attempts were made to enforce ancient boundary-lines. There is even a proverb about the social problem caused by landowners who stole from their neighbours in this fashion (Prov. 22:28; cf. Hos. 5:10). Verse 14 is not concerned with the legitimate sale of land, although the ideal seems to have been that every Israelite should have a fixed allocation of ground, as his portion of the God-given Promised Land.

Verses 15–21 deal with a different form of cheating, in an amplification of the ninth Commandment (cf. 5:20). As in verses 1–13, the legislation of Deuteronomy is as concerned to protect the innocent victim of a lawsuit as it is to punish the guilty. Indeed, those who bring false charges *are* the guilty party, and the various legal officials (see 17:9) must do all in their power to establish the truth. False witness is to Deuteronomy an extremely serious crime, so much so that the penalty is defined (vv. 19–21) as the precise penalty which the falsely accused person would have suffered if found guilty. So a false accusation of murder, for instance, would—if discovered to be false—bring the penalty of execution upon the *malicious witness* (v. 16). The purpose of this extremely severe penalty was to deter the whole community from perjury of this sort (v. 20).

It is in this context that we meet the familiar law of verse 21; the *lex talionis*, as it is widely known. In Exodus 21:23–25 this law is applied to a totally different type of situation. In general, indeed, this law set a *maximum* penalty; human nature being what it is, an injured party is often tempted to overreact to a provocation—and demand two teeth for one! But in this case, the law of exact retribution is clearly intended to provide a very strong deterrent against perjury. The *lex talionis* is often contrasted with Christ's famous ethic of Matthew 5:38–42; but this verse of Deuteronomy is better set alongside the Christian emphasis on truth (cf. 1 Cor. 5:8; Eph. 4:25). The issue is not that of the limits of personal retaliation but that of the harm caused by malicious lies. Truth is so often a casualty in our modern society that even Christians may easily forget the serious hurt that lies can cause to other people.

THE CONDUCT OF WARFARE

Deuteronomy 20:1–20

[1]"When you go forth to war against your enemies, and see horses and chariots and an army larger than your own, you shall not be afraid of them; for the Lord your God is with you, who brought you up out of the land of Egypt. [2]And when you draw near to the battle, the priest shall come forward and speak to the people, [3]and shall say to them, 'Hear, O Israel, you draw near this day to battle against your enemies: let not your heart faint; do not fear, or tremble, or be in dread of them; [4]for the Lord your God is he that goes with you, to fight for you against your enemies, to give you the victory.' [5]Then the officers shall speak to the people, saying, 'What man is there that has built a new house and has not dedicated it? Let him go back to his house, lest he die in the battle and another man dedicate it. [6]And what man is there that has planted a vineyard and has not enjoyed its fruit? Let him go back to his house, lest he die in the battle and another man enjoy its fruit. [7]And what man is there that has betrothed a wife and has not taken her? Let him go back to his house, lest he die in the battle and another man take her.' [8]And the officers shall speak further to the people, and say, 'What man is there that is fearful and fainthearted? Let him go back to his house, lest the heart of his fellows melt as his heart.' [9]And when the officers have made an end of speaking to the people, then commanders shall be appointed at the head of the people.

[10]"When you draw near to a city to fight against it, offer terms of peace to it. [11]And if its answer to you is peace and it opens to you, then all the people who are found in it shall do forced labour for you and shall serve you. [12]But if it makes no peace with you, but makes war

against you, then you shall besiege it; [13]and when the Lord your God gives it into your hand you shall put all its males to the sword, [14]but the women and the little ones, the cattle, and everything else in the city, all its spoil, you shall take as booty for yourselves; and you shall enjoy the spoil of your enemies, which the Lord your God has given you. [15]Thus you shall do to all the cities which are very far from you, which are not cities of the nations here. [16]But in the cities of these peoples that the Lord your God gives you for an inheritance, you shall save alive nothing that breathes, [17]but you shall utterly destroy them, the Hittites and the Amorites, the Canaanites and the Perizzites, the Hivites and the Jebusites, as the Lord your God has commanded; [18]that they may not teach you to do according to all their abominable practices which they have done in the service of their gods, and so to sin against the Lord your God.

[19]"When you besiege a city for a long time, making war against it in order to take it, you shall not destroy its trees by wielding an axe against them; for you may eat of them, but you shall not cut them down. Are the trees in the field men that they should be besieged by you? [20]Only the trees which you know are not trees for food you may destroy and cut down that you may build siegeworks against the city that makes war with you, until it falls."

Once again the topic is that of life and death, but here the situation is war, not accident and homicide, and the issues are quite different. The treatment is quite different, too: chapter 19 included actual laws and legal practices, but chapter 20 is not so much law as what we should call recommendations, and to that extent it represents an ideal, or rather a set of ideals. It is probably one of the sermons of Deuteronomy (see Introduction, pp. 3, 4). The recommendations it makes provide an interesting contrast (perhaps consciously so) to the practices of the Assyrian armies. There are three lessons to be learned.

(a) *Trust in God, not in big battalions* (vv. 1–9). The Assyrians were able to muster vast armies and crush small states with them. Israel and Judah were themselves small states, yet this paragraph recommends that their armies should be reduced, not built up! At the practical level, it is true that distracted, discontented or panicky soldiers are likely to sap the morale of the rest; but the real message is not that a more elite army is a better one, but that

God fights for his own people. We can readily assent to the truth of this if we apply the lesson outside the military sphere; a small congregation of dedicated and single-minded Christians is far more effective than a large congregation of half-hearted and discontented people.

(b) *Be reasonable and discriminating* (vv. 10–18). The Assyrian armies were notorious for their brutality, and they set out to terrorize all the countries around them. Israel is here counselled to adopt a peaceful approach, even in a war situation, and to avoid fighting as far as possible. The command to exterminate *the Canaanites* and other Palestinian peoples (vv. 16–18) makes a startling contrast to the eirenic note of verses 10–14, but we must again recall that Deuteronomy is not really setting out a programme, but looking *back*, dismayed at the idolatry Israel had picked up from these peoples. The general lesson of this paragraph, if we again remove it from the military sphere, is that we need to recognize who (or what) are the real enemies of faith. The gravest spiritual dangers are often the unrecognized ones on our own doorsteps. Perhaps the greatest danger to the Christian life is sheer complacency—the failure to recognize that spiritual dangers even exist. St. Paul was in no doubt that we need "the whole armour of God" (see Eph. 6:10–18). But on the other hand, those who are not against us are on our side (Mark 9:40); we must certainly not view non-Christians as automatically our enemies.

(c) *Beware of short-term advantages* (vv. 19–20). The Assyrians may be said to have raped the countries they invaded. Many centuries of warfare and careless depredations have robbed Palestine in particular of its ancient forests. So Deuteronomy here wisely counsels against what we should call total warfare. In the heat of battle it is all too easy to forget the needs of tomorrow. The practical lesson is obvious; but in the spiritual sphere, we may need reminding that even in "fighting the good fight", not all weapons and strategies are legitimate or prudent. It is surprising how often keen Christians can lose sight of moral principles when they are convinced that their cause is the Lord's; and if they are guilty of this, it will appear later that they have damaged Christ's cause.

UNSOLVED MURDERS

Deuteronomy 21:1–9

> [1]"If in the land which the Lord your God gives you to possess, any one is found slain, lying in the open country, and it is not known who killed him, [2]then your elders and your judges shall come forth, and they shall measure the distance to the cities which are around him that is slain; [3]and the elders of the city which is nearest to the slain man shall take a heifer which has never been worked and which has not pulled in the yoke. [4]And the elders of that city shall bring the heifer down to a valley with running water, which is neither ploughed nor sown, and shall break the heifer's neck there in the valley. [5]And the priests the sons of Levi shall come forward, for the Lord your God has chosen them to minister to him and to bless in the name of the Lord, and by their word every dispute and every assault shall be settled. [6]And all the elders of that city nearest to the slain man shall wash their hands over the heifer whose neck was broken in the valley; [7]and they shall testify, 'Our hands did not shed this blood, neither did our eyes see it shed. [8]Forgive, O Lord, thy people Israel, whom thou hast redeemed, and set not the guilt of innocent blood in the midst of thy people Israel; but let the guilt of blood be forgiven them.' [9]So you shall purge the guilt of innocent blood from your midst, when you do what is right in the sight of the Lord."

All societies take seriously the discovery of a body murdered "by person or persons unknown". We fully expect our police forces to do all they can to trace and apprehend the killer. In other words, we recognize the responsibility of the community in such matters—even if the dead person has no next of kin and no belongings. Ancient societies were also keenly aware of a similar communal responsibility, but with two differences. In the *first* place, they had no detective forces and few techniques for detection, so that many a murder no doubt went unsolved. *Second*, they felt strongly that an unsolved death and an unidentified and unpunished murderer brought, not only shame, but indeed corruption upon the whole community. Outside Israel, magical and superstitious rites were commonplace in such circumstances, for fear that bad luck would fall upon the community. Israel too, as this passage indicates, felt obliged to carry out a carefully organized religious ceremony. The *heifer's* death was thought, in some unexplained way, to purify the community. Without some such ceremony in the name of Yahweh, we may be sure ordinary citizens would have turned to pagan rites simply to ward off any bad luck.

The ritual described here probably incorporates very ancient and primitive elements, but at least part of the symbolism and the value of the actions performed can be assessed. (1) The whole community, represented by its *elders* and *Levites*, acknowledged their responsibility. By taking a solemn oath (v. 7) they indicated that the murder had not been suborned by the community as a whole. (In effect, they outlawed the murderer, although they were unable to identify him.) (2) The death of the *heifer* signalled that a life ought to be forfeit for that of the dead person's: someone deserved to die. (3) The use of water (v. 6) was a well known and solemn public ritual for declaring one's innocence; cf. the actions of Pilate, Matthew 27:24. (4) Lastly, in a situation where human beings were helpless to bring about justice, the community in its own way handed the problem over to God. It is interesting to notice that their prayer was not that God would identify or punish the guilty person for them, but that God would *forgive* the community. It was a true insight that the welfare of the whole society is important. While we may reject the communist view that society as a whole is far more important than the individual, we need to be careful not to go to the other extreme and neglect the needs of the community. The existence of awful poverty, for instance, is not only a tragedy for the destitute individuals, it is an indictment of the whole society that permits such a situation.

The New Testament Churches recognized themselves as communities, and not only expressed the mutual love and care that were necessary but also exercised a certain discipline to maintain the moral well-being of each local congregation: see, for example, 1 Corinthians 5:9–13. A Church is far more than a random collocation of individuals whose conduct affects nobody but themselves.

SOME RIGHTS AND DUTIES

Deuteronomy 21:10–23

10"When you go forth to war against your enemies, and the Lord your God gives them into your hands, and you take them captive, 11and see among the captives a beautiful woman, and you have desire for her and would take her for yourself as wife, 12then you shall bring her home to your house, and she shall shave her head and pare her nails. 13And she shall put off her captive's garb, and shall remain in your house and bewail her father and her mother a full month; after that you may go in to her, and be her husband, and she shall be your wife. 14Then, if you have no delight in her, you shall let her go where she will; but you shall not sell her for money, you shall not treat her as a slave, since you have humiliated her.

15"If a man has two wives, the one loved and the other disliked, and they have borne him children, both the loved and the disliked, and if the first-born son is hers that is disliked, 16then on the day when he assigns his possessions as an inheritance to his sons, he may not treat the son of the loved as the first-born in preference to the son of the disliked, who is the first-born, 17but he shall acknowledge the first-born, the son of the disliked, by giving him a double portion of all that he has, for he is the first issue of his strength; the right of the first-born is his.

18"If a man has a stubborn and rebellious son, who will not obey the voice of his father or the voice of his mother, and, though they chastise him, will not give heed to them, 19then his father and his mother shall take hold of him and bring him out to the elders of his city at the gate of the place where he lives, 20and they shall say to the elders of his city, 'This our son is stubborn and rebellious, he will not obey our voice; he is a glutton and a drunkard.' 21Then all the men of the city shall stone him to death with stones; so you shall purge the evil from your midst; and all Israel shall hear, and fear.

22"And if a man has committed a crime punishable by death and he is put to death, and you hang him on a tree, 23his body shall not remain all night upon the tree, but you shall bury him the same day, for a hanged man is accursed by God; you shall not defile your land which the Lord your God gives you for an inheritance."

The laws in chapters 21–25 deal with a miscellany of topics, but a common theme in chapter 21 is *respect*; a theme very appropriate after the topics of murder and warfare in chapters 19 and 20. In verses 10–14 it is emphasized that prisoners-of-war had their rights; a female captive had few enough rights in the context of the ancient world, but she must at least be treated with respect. Verses 15–17 deal with the rights of the *first-born* son in a polygamous household. Personal feelings must not be allowed to interfere with his rights; his status entitled him to this degree of respect.

These situations seem very foreign to us today, and the legislation provided by Deuteronomy is evidently based on customs and conventions of a bygone age. The same is true of verses 22–23, which relate to the public execution of a criminal, and the public display of his corpse (on a tree, *ie* a gibbet, cf. NEB). The reason for the burial of the corpse on *the same day* as the execution is not respect for the dead man, but respect for the *land*. The argument is that it is God's land, and the very sight of a criminal guilty of a capital crime offends God's eyes. In less literal terms, we might say that God's community is not benefited by such public displays, whatever their deterrent effect. Most modern societies seem to have accepted that public executions do much more harm than the good that former eras saw in them.

Verses 18–21 deal with what seems a much more commonplace problem, that of a *rebellious son* in a household; but the penalty is horrifyingly extreme by modern standards. We must recognize that the words "stubborn and rebellious" are extremely strong; the situation envisaged is certainly not an everyday one. We may be sure that loving parents would never have put such a savage law into operation merely because of a few disagreements and angry words. The accusation of gluttony and drunkenness (the sort of accusation which could be proved or disproved by *the elders*, who had the power to reject it) points to the sort of rebellious conduct Deuteronomy saw as deeply harmful to the whole community. The typical domestic situation in Israel was a smallholding, in which all the family had a vital part to play; here "a glutton and a drunkard" represented a parasite, someone who contributed nothing and took everything. In a peasant economy, few households could possibly afford such a son; hence the very severe penalty, which was no doubt meant as a warning, not as an inflexible or frequently applied ruling. The basic principle is the Commandment to honour one's father and mother (5:16); it is endorsed too by the New Testament, cf. Ephesians 6:1–3. The wider principle is that, in a divinely ordered society, all must work together, for the good of all, as the description of the Church as the "body" of Christ makes clear (1 Cor. 12:12–27; Eph. 4:12–16).

DISTINCTIVE FEATURES

Deuteronomy 22:1–12

[1]"You shall not see your brother's ox or his sheep go astray, and withhold your help from them; you shall take them back to your brother. [2]And if he is not near you, or if you do not know him, you shall bring it home to your house, and it shall be with you until your brother seeks it; then you shall restore it to him. [3]And so you shall do with his ass; so you shall do with his garment; so you shall do with any lost thing of your brother's, which he loses and you find; you may not withhold your help. [4]You shall not see your brother's ass or his ox fallen down by the way, and withhold your help from them; you shall help him to lift them up again.

[5]"A woman shall not wear anything that pertains to a man, nor shall a man put on a woman's garment; for whoever does these things is an abomination to the Lord your God.

[6]"If you chance to come upon a bird's nest, in any tree or on the ground, with young ones or eggs and the mother sitting upon the young or upon the eggs, you shall not take the mother with the young; [7]you shall let the mother go, but the young you may take to yourself; that it may go well with you, and that you may live long.

[8]"When you build a new house, you shall make a parapet for your roof, that you may not bring the guilt of blood upon your house, if any one fall from it.

[9]"You shall not sow your vineyard with two kinds of seed, lest the whole yield be forfeited to the sanctuary, the crop which you have sown and the yield of the vineyard. [10]You shall not plough with an ox and an ass together. [11]You shall not wear a mingled stuff, wool and linen together.

¹²"You shall make yourself tassels on the four corners of your cloak with which you cover yourself."

This passage contains a miscellany of short laws. From the legal point of view, they are more in the nature of recommendations, because they apply to the home situation, either indoors or on the farm, and they would have been very difficult to enforce. Sacred laws, however, are not like secular codes, and those who adhere to any faith are expected to obey the rules of that faith, in private as well as in public. Deuteronomy therefore has no hesitation in issuing laws of this domestic kind; it is no surprise, however, to find that no punishments are specified.

The reasons for these laws are not explained, and not all of them are very obvious to us today. Verse 8 is self-explanatory—an obvious safety measure. The rule about preserving the life and freedom of mother birds (vv. 6–7) is not so much humanitarian as prudent, a matter of food conservation from which others too would benefit. It is possible that the strange prohibitions of verses 9–11 represent a hostile reaction to certain Egyptian practices; clearly such laws have no bearing today on Christian conduct. There is good reason to suppose that the law of verse 5 is not concerned with the mild sexual aberration known as transvestism, but is a repudiation of certain pagan religious practices of that era; so this law is no more a fashion guide for today than is the law about *tassels* in verse 12. These tassels, whatever their origin, were intended as a visible reminder to every Israelite of his duty to obey God's laws (cf. Num. 15:37–41). In effect, they made Israelites distinctive in their dress.

Two lessons for Christian conduct can legitimately be drawn from this passage. *First*, Christians ought to be as distinctive in society as Israelites had to be, but not of course by the same means. Indeed, distinctive Jewish dress was one of the many things abandoned by the early Church which imposed no more than one or two Jewish customs upon Gentile Christians (cf. Acts 15:19–21). The distinctive characteristics of a Christian should be internal rather than external. There is something wrong, however, if such inward characteristics are not visible to other people.

The *second* lesson is embodied in the first paragraph, verses 1–4. Deuteronomy insists that there is a higher law than the negative one of refraining from harming other people: "you may not withhold your help". In farming communities one often finds a degree of the good-neighbourliness demanded here; but in urban societies there is a well-entrenched custom of "passing by on the other side". The Christian ethic, taught by Jesus himself (Luke 10:29–37), endorses the principle of these verses, not just towards one's *brother* or neighbour, but towards all men. To fulfil it requires not only the right attitude of mind and the willingness to take positive steps to give help, but first and foremost, the mental readiness to observe and perceive the difficulties and problems of other people. There are none so blind as those who do not wish to see.

SEXUAL MORALITY

Deuteronomy 22:13–30

[13]"If any man takes a wife, and goes in to her, and then spurns her, [14]and charges her with shameful conduct, and brings an evil name upon her, saying, 'I took this woman, and when I came near her, I did not find in her the tokens of virginity,' [15]then the father of the young woman and her mother shall take and bring out the tokens of her virginity to the elders of the city in the gate; [16]and the father of the young woman shall say to the elders, 'I gave my daughter to this man to wife, and he spurns her; [17]and lo, he has made shameful charges against her, saying, "I did not find in your daughter the tokens of virginity." And yet these are the tokens of my daughter's virginity.' And they shall spread the garment before the elders of the city. [18]Then the elders of that city shall take the man and whip him; [19]and they shall fine him a hundred shekels of silver, and give them to the father of the young woman, because he has brought an evil name upon a virgin of Israel; and she shall be his wife; he may not put her away all his days. [20]But if the thing is true, that the tokens of virginity were not found in the young woman, [21]then they shall bring out the young woman to the door of her father's house, and the men of her city shall stone her to death with stones, because she has wrought folly in Israel by playing

the harlot in her father's house; so you shall purge the evil from the midst of you.

²²"If a man is found lying with the wife of another man, both of them shall die, the man who lay with the woman, and the woman; so you shall purge the evil from Israel.

²³"If there is a betrothed virgin, and a man meets her in the city and lies with her, ²⁴then you shall bring them both out to the gate of that city, and you shall stone them to death with stones, the young woman because she did not cry for help though she was in the city, and the man because he violated his neighbour's wife; so you shall purge the evil from the midst of you.

²⁵"But if in the open country a man meets a young woman who is betrothed, and the man seizes her and lies with her, then only the man who lay with her shall die. ²⁶But to the young woman you shall do nothing; in the young woman there is no offence punishable by death, for this case is like that of a man attacking and murdering his neighbour; ²⁷because he came upon her in the open country, and though the betrothed young woman cried for help there was no one to rescue her.

²⁸"If a man meets a virgin who is not betrothed, and seizes her and lies with her, and they are found, ²⁹then the man who lay with her shall give to the father of the young woman fifty shekels of silver, and she shall be his wife, because he has violated her; he may not put her away all his days.

³⁰"A man shall not take his father's wife, nor shall he uncover her who is his father's."

The next topic is that of sexual relationships. Once again we find very severe punishments laid down for infringements of the law. The first and longest section (vv. 13–21) deals with the situation which occurs when a man had accused his wife of premarital infidelity or promiscuity. Such a charge was an extremely serious one—the penalty was death—so the legislation takes pains to establish the rules of evidence. Existing conventions already supplied evidence that could be tested; namely *the tokens* of a woman's *virginity* held by her parents since her marriage. This proof is usually thought to have consisted of the bed-sheet stained by the blood during the first intercourse in marriage; another possibility is that it was a *garment* stained with menstrual blood, a sign that the woman had not been pregnant on her wedding day. Such a proof would seem highly unsatisfactory today, and one wonders if there was some form of notarization. In any case, clearly promiscuity was a criminal offence, and so was adultery (v. 22); and verses 22–27 make the crime of adultery apply to *betrothed* as well as married women. Verses 28–29 insist that a man who rapes an unmarried, unbetrothed girl must pay for it; he must undertake to maintain her as his wife for life (v. 29) and pay her father the full bride-price that all bridegrooms paid in those days.

Verse 30 prohibits an older custom; it is not attacking immoral behaviour as such.

It is quite clear from these laws that Israel had very high standards of sexual morality. Casual sexual relationships outside marriage were outlawed, and marriage between certain degrees of relationship were banned (see Lev. 18:6–18 for a thorough list of prohibited degrees). All societies have some such rules, although they vary widely; while it is true that in modern Western countries the laws allow a great deal of liberty and latitude, every state tries in its own fashion to maintain the good order of society and to preserve and uphold the institution of marriage. In ancient Israel we may see two additional motives behind such legislation. (1) The marriage relationship was seen as a God-given institution—God's own plan for human relationships. It must therefore be treated with complete seriousness and solemnity. To undermine the value of marriage was to undermine the fabric of the covenant-society. (2) Sexual immorality was, in the eyes of the Old Testament writers, the hallmark of the Canaanites, and it was closely intertwined with their religious practices. Israel must therefore set visibly higher standards.

Both of these motives receive New Testament support. Jesus deplored divorce as utterly contrary to the divine plan (Mark 10:2–12); and Paul deplored the sexual immorality that was typical of the culture of a pagan city like Corinth, cf. 1 Corinthians 5–6. In our twentieth century we shall hardly wish for legislation enacting harsh penalties for sexual misdemeanours; but in all spheres of life, we should seek to establish standards which are visibly higher than those of people who make no religious commitment. We have both a goal and an example that they do not share.

THE NATIONAL ASSEMBLY

Deuteronomy 23:1–8

[1]"He whose testicles are crushed or whose male member is cut off shall not enter the assembly of the Lord.

[2]"No bastard shall enter the assembly of the Lord; even to the tenth generation none of his descendants shall enter the assembly of the Lord.

[3]"No Ammonite or Moabite shall enter the assembly of the Lord; even to the tenth generation none belonging to them shall enter the assembly of the Lord for ever; [4]because they did not meet you with bread and with water on the way, when you came forth out of Egypt, and because they hired against you Balaam the son of Beor from Pethor of Mesopotamia, to curse you. [5]Nevertheless the Lord your God would not hearken to Balaam; but the Lord your God turned the curse into a blessing for you, because the Lord your God loved you. [6]You shall not seek their peace or their prosperity all your days for ever.

[7]"You shall not abhor an Edomite, for he is your brother; you shall not abhor an Egyptian, because you were a sojourner in his land. [8]The children of the third generation that are born to them may enter the assembly of the Lord."

Verses 1–8 seem very strange to us: they are something of a cross between immigration laws and rules for church membership! The "assembly of the Lord" was not a local congregation, but the national gathering of the people of Israel for special purposes including worship and warfare, so it is not surprising that the rules for membership of it are partly secular, partly sacred. One can readily see why Ammonites and Moabites were excluded (vv. 3–6); the reason was not religious bigotry or racism, but what we should call national security, in view of the persistent hostility these two states had shown to Israel. The passage recalls past events in proof of this enmity; cf. 2:29, Numbers 22:5–6. From our historical perspective we are puzzled by the different attitude shown towards Edomites and Egyptians (vv. 7–8); but clearly at the time, the recommendations of Deuteronomy made perfectly good sense to the readers.

On the other hand, the reasons for excluding the man with *crushed testicles*, and the *bastard* and his descendants, must have been purely religious. As verses 12–14 show, the Israelites had a keen view of God's abhorrence of anything "indecent", but it is quite likely that there is more to verses 1 and 2 than appears on the surface. The physical defects mentioned may not have been due to simple accidents, but rather to pagan rites. Similarly the category, *bastard*, must have included the offspring of Canaanite temple prostitutes. The general intention of the legislation then, was to keep the national assembly free of any potentially contaminating influence, from any person who might betray either the national or the religious interests of Israel. There is no question of depriving individual residents of Israel of all opportunity to worship God. Other Old Testament passages show that these rules were not of permanent validity. Isaiah 56:3–8 brings all foreigners, and eunuchs (a general term for men with genital defects and deficiencies), within the range of the covenant of Israel. The criterion is no longer simply racial or physical, but a test of their religious convictions.

It is important then to recognize that the nature and function of the assembly of Israel were political. The Christian Church is quite different, and it is fully appropriate that its membership tests are purely those of faith and of moral conduct.

SOME VARIED LAWS

Deuteronomy 23:9–25

9"When you go forth against your enemies and are in camp, then you shall keep yourself from every evil thing.

10"If there is among you any man who is not clean by reason of what chances to him by night, then he shall go outside the camp, he shall not come within the camp; 11but when evening comes on, he shall bathe himself in water, and when the sun is down, he may come within the camp.

12"You shall have a place outside the camp and you shall go out to it; 13and you shall have a stick with your weapons; and when you sit down outside, you shall dig a hole with it, and turn back and cover up your excrement. ¹⁴Because the Lord your God walks in the midst of your camp, to save you and to give up your enemies before you, therefore your camp must be holy, that he may not see anything indecent among you, and turn away from you.

¹⁵"You shall not give up to his master a slave who has escaped from his master to you; ¹⁶he shall dwell with you, in your midst, in the place which he shall choose within one of your towns, where it pleases him best; you shall not oppress him.

¹⁷"There shall be no cult prostitute of the daughters of Israel, neither shall there be a cult prostitute of the sons of Israel. ¹⁸You shall not bring the hire of a harlot, or the wages of a dog, into the house of the Lord your God in payment for any vow; for both of these are an abomination to the Lord your God.

¹⁹"You shall not lend upon interest to your brother, interest on money, interest on victuals, interest on anything that is lent for interest. ²⁰To a foreigner you may lend upon interest, but to your brother you shall not lend upon interest; that the Lord your God may bless you in all that you undertake in the land which you are entering to take possession of it.

²¹"When you make a vow to the Lord your God, you shall not be slack to pay it; for the Lord your God will surely require it of you, and it would be sin in you. ²²But if you refrain from vowing, it shall be no sin in you. ²³You shall be careful to perform what has passed your lips, for you have voluntarily vowed to the Lord your God what you have promised with your mouth.

²⁴"When you go into your neighbour's vineyard, you may eat your fill of grapes, as many as you wish, but you shall not put any in your vessel. ²⁵When you go into your neighbour's standing grain, you may pluck the ears with your hand, but you shall not put a sickle to your neighbour's standing grain."

As in 22:1–12, we have a miscellany of short laws. There is little direct connection between the brief paragraphs. We should consider the law of verses 12–13 a matter of simple hygiene, but to the Israelite lawgiver, not only was "cleanliness next to godliness", cleanliness was *part* of "godliness". A seminal emission overnight (v. 10) was also considered unclean; but we must not confuse uncleanliness with sin. No guilt was attached to the man concerned—provided that he obeyed the rules here laid down.

Verses 15–16 pronounce a humane law. Probably the runaway slave envisaged is a foreigner; the law prohibits his extradition—in contrast to 1 Kings 2:39–40. Deuteronomy constantly gives humane rulings, in a world that was far more callous than ours. There is the basis here for the abolition of slavery, although that would have been unthinkable in the ancient world.

Verses 17–18 turn to the practice of religious rites, and prohibit the practice of religious prostitution in the name of Yahweh. (The word "dog" is thought to mean a male sanctuary prostitute, familiar in Canaanite religion.)

Verses 19–20 express a law very much at odds with modern commercial practices. Nowadays we should be very surprised if loans were not available for all sorts of purposes; and we should be even more surprised if no *interest* was payable on the loans. The Old Testament world, however, knew nothing of such routine commercial loans, which are intended for the mutual benefit of lender and borrower. Deuteronomy had in mind people in desperate poverty, forced to borrow from wealthier neighbours simply to survive; and the evidence shows that ancient rates of interest were exorbitant. This law, then, is another example of Deuteronomy's deep concern for human welfare. It was equally concerned to see the Sinai covenant binding Israelites together in mutual consideration: this is yet another instance of loving one's neighbour as oneself. The *foreigner* was outside the covenant; most foreigners would in practice have been traders, not destitute farmers, so the imposition of interest is permitted in their case.

The chapter ends with a commonsense law (vv. 24–25) to discourage meanness and greediness on the part of farmers, and theft on the part of passers-by. The situation is a specific one, but it could well illustrate the sort of mature attitudes which ought to be seen in any true brotherhood. Under the Sinai covenant, all Israelites were meant to be brothers.

Enclosed between these last two humane demands is a quite different law, or rather an exhortation, in verses 21–23. It exhorts Israelites to keep their promises to God. It was common to *vow* to offer him sacrifices when seeking some benefit, such as healing from illness; but the existence of this law suggests that it was not

uncommon for Israelites to forget all about such vows subsequently. Forgetfulness and ingratitude are all too frequent
human failings, but the Bible takes oaths and promises very
seriously. God is never deceived by insincere human promises; it
is far better to make him no promises at all (v. 22).

SOME PROBLEMS IN SOCIETY

Deuteronomy 24:1–9

[1]"When a man takes a wife and marries her, if then she finds no favour
in his eyes because he has found some indecency in her, and he writes
her a bill of divorce and puts it in her hand and sends her out of his
house, and she departs out of his house, [2]and if she goes and becomes
another man's wife, [3]and the latter husband dislikes her and writes her
a bill of divorce and puts it in her hand and sends her out of his house,
or if the latter husband dies, who took her to be his wife, [4]then her
former husband, who sent her away, may not take her again to be his
wife, after she has been defiled; for that is an abomination before the
Lord, and you shall not bring guilt upon the land which the Lord your
God gives you for an inheritance.

[5]"When a man is newly married, he shall not go out with the army or
be charged with any business; he shall be free at home one year, to be
happy with his wife whom he has taken.

[6]"No man shall take a mill or an upper millstone in pledge; for he
would be taking a life in pledge.

[7]"If a man is found stealing one of his brethren, the people of Israel,
and if he treats him as a slave or sells him, then that thief shall die; so
you shall purge the evil from the midst of you.

[8]"Take heed, in an attack of leprosy, to be very careful to do
according to all that the Levitical priests shall direct you; as I commanded them, so you shall be careful to do. [9]Remember what the Lord
your God did to Miriam on the way as you came forth out of Egypt."

In modern society, marriage and divorce are not only regulated
by law, but are invalid unless conducted or decreed by accredited
officials in accredited places (churches and register offices, or law-
courts in the case of divorce). In Israel, however, both were
purely domestic matters, with no officials and scarcely any docu-

ments involved; the *bill of divorce* was the exception, and it was essential, to protect the divorced woman from any charge of adultery, which was punishable by death (cf. 22:22). We may guess from verses 1–4 that in Canaanite circles, divorce and remarriage was freely permitted; but once again, Israel set herself higher standards. And Jesus set an even higher standard in this matter, cf. Mark 10:2–12.

Although verse 5 also concerns marriage, it belongs with the rest of the chapter in showing a concern for human welfare. Modern armies do not show the same consideration for newly-weds; but it must be remembered that Deuteronomy was thinking not of professional soldiers, but of farmers and peasants who might be called to arms if a national emergency arose. Such a law as 24:5 makes it clear that God's design for humankind unashamedly includes marriage and marital love.

Verse 6 begins to deal with the subject of pledges; a topic continued in verses 10–12. A *pledge* would be made as a guarantee against a loan, so we are concerned here with desperately poor people. Presumably the creditor could name the article he wished to take as a pledge. The *mill* (consisting of two stones; a heavy lower one and a more portable *upper millstone*) was perhaps a tempting object to take away, because it was such an essential article in every household, and the debtor would soon be desperate to retrieve it. So Deuteronomy here bans such a practice totally, in order to protect the poor.

Verse 7 prohibits kidnapping and enslavement. If theft of any kind was outlawed by God—as the eighth Commandment declares—then kidnapping was all the more abhorrent to him.

Verses 8–9 turn to a matter of hygiene, as we would term it. *Leprosy* was not limited to the disease we know today by that name, but included a wide variety of skin diseases, and the chief fear was of major epidemics such as plague. In a society without doctors and with very primitive medical knowledge, it was important that any apparently serious skin complaint should be referred to the only people with any competence to handle the situation, namely *the Levitical priests*. (Lev. 13 and 14 give some of their detailed instructions.) The mention of Moses' own sister,

Miriam, may be intended as a reminder that not even the highest people in society are immune from disease, and they could just as easily start an epidemic unless the regulations were complied with. Miriam's leprosy is discussed in Numbers 12:9–15.

Primitive societies typically see disease as a religious matter. Obviously nowadays we should go to the surgery, not to the manse or vicarage, if afflicted by some illness. It does us no harm to be reminded, however, that sickness and health, indeed life and death themselves, are ultimately in the hands of God.

THE UNDERPRIVILEGED

Deuteronomy 24:10–22

[10]"When you make your neighbour a loan of any sort, you shall not go into his house to fetch his pledge. [11]You shall stand outside, and the man to whom you make the loan shall bring the pledge out to you. [12]And if he is a poor man, you shall not sleep in his pledge; [13]when the sun goes down, you shall restore to him the pledge that he may sleep in his cloak and bless you; and it shall be righteousness to you before the Lord your God.

[14]"You shall not oppress a hired servant who is poor and needy, whether he is one of your brethren or one of the sojourners who are in your land within your towns; [15]you shall give him his hire on the day he earns it, before the sun goes down (for he is poor, and sets his heart upon it); lest he cry against you to the Lord, and it be sin in you.

[16]"The fathers shall not be put to death for the children, nor shall the children be put to death for the fathers; every man shall be put to death for his own sin.

[17]"You shall not pervert the justice due to the sojourner or to the fatherless, or take a widow's garment in pledge; [18]but you shall remember that you were a slave in Egypt and the Lord your God redeemed you from there; therefore I command you to do this.

[19]"When you reap your harvest in your field, and have forgotten a sheaf in the field, you shall not go back to get it; it shall be for the sojourner, the fatherless, and the widow; that the Lord your God may bless you in all the work of your hands. [20]When you beat your olive trees, you shall not go over the boughs again; it shall be for the sojourner, the fatherless, and the widow. [21]When you gather the

grapes of your vineyard, you shall not glean it afterward; it shall be for the sojourner, the fatherless, and the widow. ²²You shall remember that you were a slave in the land of Egypt; therefore I command you to do this."

The rest of chapter 24 is wholly concerned with the protection of the underprivileged. In a mainly agricultural society, the loss by death of the man in any family would deprive it of its chief breadwinner, and the *widow* and the *fatherless* (mentioned in several verses) were usually in great poverty. The *sojourner* is bracketed with them; many foreigners who came to reside in Israel must have done so because of debts, injustice or oppression elsewhere, so they too were poor. Besides which, history reveals all too clearly that foreigners and immigrants are ready targets for prejudice, ill-treatment and general social injustice.

In various respects, then, Deuteronomy here tries to protect such people. The rulings it gives cannot easily have been endorsed by laws: for instance, as far as the law goes, any farmer has the right to take his full harvest, but verse 19 recommends otherwise. Some of the rulings are precise, but it is very improbable that the victims of any breaches could have taken law-breakers to court. Other rulings are more general: to "oppress a hired servant" (v. 14) seems a matter of interpretation, and to "pervert . . . justice" (v. 17) covers a whole range of possible abuses of law and legal procedure. It is clear from some of the Old Testament prophets that abuses in the legal system proved to be a serious problem at times (cf. Isa. 1:23; Mic. 7:13). So we can read this section as a plea from the heart rather than as a list of laws.

In this context, verse 16 may be prohibiting a particularly serious breach of law. It is reinforcing the older law that protected a family from sharing the penalty imposed on one particular member of it who had committed a crime. Perhaps unscrupulous rich farmers misused the legal system to wipe out whole families on neighbouring properties, in order to increase their own holdings. The section as a whole, however, is not addressed to rich people only; it is just as relevant to people who had something, however little, they could lend to, or share with, their poorer fellow-countrymen. Wealth is a very relative concept.

Clearly the appeal of Deuteronomy 24 was a necessary one at the time. Why should anyone have listened to it? Two good reasons are supplied: (1) God himself would reward generosity (v. 19) and also punish disobedience to these laws (v. 15 implies); (2) Israel's own past experience should lead all Israelites to wish to ease the lot of the underprivileged (vv. 18 and 22). But beyond these stated arguments there is a hidden one: the very mention of the problems, by drawing attention to the needs of society, ought to stir active consciences. Very often human callousness is not deliberate or intentional, but due to forgetfulness and thought-lessness. These verses of Deuteronomy can still move forgetful consciences to remember the less fortunate—whether in the Third World or in the next street—and to take some positive steps on their behalf.

CONCERN FOR HUMANS AND ANIMALS

Deuteronomy 25:1–10

[1]"If there is a dispute between men, and they come into court, and the judges decide between them, acquitting the innocent and condemning the guilty, [2]then if the guilty man deserves to be beaten, the judge shall cause him to lie down and be beaten in his presence with a number of stripes in proportion to his offence. [3]Forty stripes may be given him, but not more; lest, if one should go on to beat him with more stripes than these, your brother be degraded in your sight.

[4]"You shall not muzzle an ox when it treads out the grain.

[5]"If brothers dwell together, and one of them dies and has no son, the wife of the dead shall not be married outside the family to a stranger; her husband's brother shall go in to her, and take her as his wife, and perform the duty of a husband's brother to her. [6]And the first son whom she bears shall succeed to the name of his brother who is dead, that his name may not be blotted out of Israel. [7]And if the man does not wish to take his brother's wife, then his brother's wife shall go up to the gate to the elders, and say, 'My husband's brother refuses to perpetuate his brother's name in Israel; he will not perform the duty of a husband's brother to me.' [8]Then the elders of the city shall call him, and speak to him: and if he persists, saying, 'I do not wish to take her,'

⁹then his brother's wife shall go up to him in the presence of the elders, and pull his sandal off his foot, and spit in his face; and she shall answer and say, 'So shall it be done to the man who does not build up his brother's house.' ¹⁰And the name of his house shall be called in Israel, The house of him that had his sandal pulled off."

This passage contains three more miscellaneous laws, quite unconnected with each other; a common theme is, once again, concern for the welfare and dignity of others. The recipients of this concern may surprise us in some ways. We have observed before that Deuteronomy's punishments were, by our standards, harsh; yet verses 1–3 show a concern for the dignity of a man condemned to be flogged. We also tend to assume that interest in the welfare of animals is a modern idea; but verse 4 reveals exactly such a concept, long before the time of Christ. The longest paragraph, verses 5–10, deals with the question of a woman left not only widowed, but childless (or rather, without a son). Today our only concern could well be the financial welfare of such a woman, but Deuteronomy 25 is equally concerned about the dignity of the family, and indeed of the dead man. (The conventions strike us as very peculiar, but they were perfectly normal in certain societies in the ancient world.) The birth of a son to the widow, fathered by the dead man's brother, would ensure her financial welfare in the long term—when the boy grew old enough to be the breadwinner—and would preserve the family identity too. Note the disgrace which was attached to any brother who refused to obey this old custom. At a later date the practice of daughters inheriting property became widespread (cf. Num. 27:1–11), and this old custom of the brother fathering a son died out. The custom (known technically as *levirate marriage*) was so ancient and obsolete by New Testament times that the Sadducees used it as a means of ridiculing Jesus' teachings about resurrection, cf. Mark 12:18–27.

The law of verses 1–3 shows a humane approach to a punishment that was extremely common in many societies until quite recently (and is by no means disused throughout the world yet). The *forty* strokes set an absolute limit, which was later reduced to thirty-nine, to err on the safe side; Paul suffered such a flogging more than once, no doubt for breach of the peace (2 Cor. 11:24). It is part of human nature, it seems, to feel vindictive towards law-breakers. It is surprising, for instance, how many sincere and devout Christians today wish to preserve, or to bring back, the death penalty. Deuteronomy, without concerning itself with the nature of the punishment, at least insists that even a law-breaker has moral rights that society must protect. How this should be done will vary from one era to another, and from society to society.

Finally, verse 4 should not be overlooked. In the New Testament, Paul quotes this precept and makes it a general principle, that the labourer is worthy of his hire (1 Cor. 9:8–14). The point is well taken, but we should not extend the principle to human situations without applying it first as it was intended by Deuteronomy. It has been called an animal lover's law. There is no doubt at all that while the Bible permits the killing of animals (for example, for food and for sacrifices), it certainly lends support to today's efforts to instil belatedly into brutish human beings, their moral responsibilities towards the animal kingdom and indeed towards the whole of God's creation.

SOME DANGERS TO SOCIETY

Deuteronomy 25:11–19

11"When men fight with one another, and the wife of the one draws near to rescue her husband from the hand of him who is beating him, and puts out her hand and seizes him by the private parts, 12then you shall cut off her hand; your eye shall have no pity.

13"You shall not have in your bag two kinds of weights, a large and a small. 14You shall not have in your house two kinds of measures, a large and a small. 15A full and just weight you shall have, a full and just measure you shall have; that your days may be prolonged in the land which the Lord your God gives you. 16For all who do such things, all who act dishonestly, are an abomination to the Lord your God.

17"Remember what Amalek did to you on the way as you came out of Egypt, 18how he attacked you on the way, when you were faint and weary, and cut off at your rear all who lagged behind you; and he did not fear God. [19]Therefore when the Lord your God has given you rest from all your enemies round about, in the land which the Lord your God gives you for an inheritance to possess, you shall blot out the remembrance of Amalek from under heaven; you shall not forget."

The law of verses 11–12 strikes us initially as harsh and punitive; a startling contrast to the humanitarian concern of the earlier part of the chapter. By Israelite conventions, to be sure, the action described here would have been an act of gross indecency; and all societies have laws to protect their citizens from offensive behaviour. But there seems to be more to it than that; the implication is probably that such an action could easily prevent the victim from having children—a very serious matter in Israel, as verses 5–10 have already indicated. Any action which might cause permanent harm to another family is obviously extremely serious.

Verses 13–16, without any ambiguity, set out to protect society. Again, all societies today insist on a fixed standard of weights and measures, and have inspectors to uphold such laws. Fixed standards were much more difficult to define in the ancient world, so that deliberate cheating was all too easy. The Old Testament prophets knew it as a serious social problem (Mic. 6:11; Prov. 11:1).

After these many laws to protect ordinary men and women, the last paragraph of chapter 25 may strike us as shocking—a sudden, vindictive attack on a neighbouring people. We have to recognize, first of all, that the general concern of verses 17–19 is the welfare of the Israelites, not the destruction of *Amalek* for its own sake. This small nomadic tribe, on the southern borders of Israel, plainly never relented from its hatred towards Israel. Quite apart from the ancient event described in verse 18, the Amalekites were a persistent threat to the settled population in Palestine. They were very mobile raiders, who could strike without warning (see 1 Sam. 30 for a vivid account of one of their raids). They must have been as terrifying to farmers in border areas as the Vikings were to the coastal residents of much of northern Europe a thousand years or so ago. It may be that Deuteronomy names them as a reminder to the central government of Israel that it had an on-going duty and responsibility to its citizens in every part of the land, for governments have a well-known tendency to neglect "the provinces". Seen in these terms, the content and tone of verses 17–19 can be understood. The trouble is that all too easily such passages can be used indiscriminately to justify racism, violence and vindictiveness. It is imperative that we recast such passages in the light of New Testament teachings. As Christians, we do indeed have enemies; against one category of enemy—the powers of evil in this world—we have a duty to fight vigorously (Eph. 6:10–12), but where the human category is concerned, our duty is to love them, pray for them, and turn the other cheek (Matt. 5:38–45).

FIRST FRUITS

Deuteronomy 26:1–11

¹"When you come into the land which the Lord your God gives you for an inheritance, and have taken possession of it, and live in it, ²you shall take some of the first of all the fruit of the ground, which you harvest from your land that the Lord your God gives you, and you shall put it in a basket, and you shall go to the place which the Lord your God will choose, to make his name to dwell there. ³And you shall go to the priest who is in office at that time, and say to him, 'I declare this day to the Lord your God that I have come into the land which the Lord swore to our fathers to give us.' ⁴Then the priest shall take the basket from your hand, and set it down before the altar of the Lord your God.

⁵"And you shall make response before the Lord your God, 'A wandering Aramean was my father; and he went down into Egypt and sojourned there, few in number; and there he became a nation, great, mighty, and populous. ⁶And the Egyptians treated us harshly, and afflicted us, and laid upon us hard bondage. ⁷Then we cried to the Lord the God of our fathers, and the Lord heard our voice, and saw our affliction, our toil, and our oppression; ⁸and the Lord brought us out of Egypt with a mighty hand and an outstretched arm, with great terror, with signs and wonders; ⁹and he brought us into this place and gave us this land, a land flowing with milk and honey. ¹⁰And behold, now I bring the first of the fruit of the ground, which thou, O Lord, hast given me.' And you shall set it down before the Lord your God, and worship

before the Lord your God; [11]and you shall rejoice in all the good which the Lord your God has given to you and to your house, you, and the Levite, and the sojourner who is among you."

The first fruits to be given to God may be the same as the "tithe" already discussed in 14:22–27, or it may have been an additional requirement. In either case, the emphasis here falls on the form of the religious service which must accompany the offering. The first fruits, *ie* "the first of all the fruit of the ground", were considered especially sacred in the ancient world. Even today a keen gardener takes a special pleasure in the first crop of the season, but perhaps in this scientific age, we have rather lost the wonder of it. Ancient man, however, still felt awe at the workings of nature, and was quick to show his gratitude to the divine powers he believed were responsible. Israelites were no different in this respect—and that is precisely where the danger lay. Awe can easily be misdirected and end up as sheer superstition; and many an Israelite was attracted to the special rites and rituals of the Canaanites which were dedicated to the fertility of the soil.

Against such a background, this section of Deuteronomy insists on three things: (1) that the worship must be directed to the true God; (2) that the worship must be conducted properly, and in the proper sanctuary (Jerusalem is meant); (3) that the Israelites should be *intelligently* grateful—not merely feeling a sense of awe at the new season's produce, but recognizing exactly what God's benefits amounted to.

The *first* of these points is underlined by the repetition of the name Yahweh, *the Lord*, and by the reminder that he (and no-one else) was their own God and the God of their ancestors. The *second* point is made by directing the worshippers to Jerusalem and the priesthood there (vv. 2 and 4). The *third* lesson is inculcated by teaching a *response* (v. 5); in other words, a confession which every Israelite should memorize and repeat in the priest's hearing whenever the first fruits were offered.

This ancient confession (vv. 5–10) gives a fascinating glimpse into the Israelite "prayer-book". It reminds the worshipper of past history, going back to his ancestor Jacob, "a wandering

Aramean" (*ie* someone who had left his home in Aram for an unsettled existence in Canaan). Jacob's wanderings and the hardships of servitude in Egypt were the unhappy past from which Israel had been rescued; the first fruits themselves demonstrated that God had given Israel a rich territorial heritage. The worshipper would then not only feel a sense of awe at the "magic" of natural growth; he would also perceive, in a much wider measure, the wealth of God's goodness—without forgetting to share the benefits with the less fortunate in society (v. 11).

In many Protestant Churches today we are apt to pride ourselves on our "freedom" from liturgy. This passage would remind us that forms of worship are not unimportant; they can lead and they can mislead. It is certainly important that our modes of worship should constantly lead us to a full appreciation of God, and at the same time a full awareness of the needs of others.

WALKING IN GOD'S WAYS

Deuteronomy 26:12–19

[12]"When you have finished paying all the tithe of your produce in the third year, which is the year of tithing, giving it to the Levite, the sojourner, the fatherless, and the widow, that they may eat within your towns and be filled, [13]then you shall say before the Lord your God, 'I have removed the sacred portion out of my house, and moreover I have given it to the Levite, the sojourner, the fatherless, and the widow, according to all thy commandment which thou hast commanded me; I have not transgressed any of thy commandments, neither have I forgotten them; [14]I have not eaten of the tithe while I was mourning, or removed any of it while I was unclean, or offered any of it to the dead; I have obeyed the voice of the Lord my God, I have done according to all that thou hast commanded me. [15]Look down from thy holy habitation, from heaven, and bless thy people Israel and the ground which thou hast given us, as thou didst swear to our fathers, a land flowing with milk and honey.'

[16]"This day the Lord your God commands you to do these statutes and ordinances; you shall therefore be careful to do them with all your heart and with all your soul. [17]You have declared this day concerning

the Lord that he is your God, and that you will walk in his ways, and keep his statutes and his commandments and his ordinances, and will obey his voice; [18]and the Lord has declared this day concerning you that you are a people for his own possession, as he has promised you, and that you are to keep all his commandments, [19]that he will set you high above all nations that he has made, in praise and in fame and in honour, and that you shall be a people holy to the Lord your God, as he has spoken."

Verses 12–15 prescribe a second religious service, yet with some interesting differences from the first. This service relates to the presentation of the *tithe* every *third year* (v. 12), already discussed in 14:28–29. Unlike the first fruits, this offering was not to be taken to Jerusalem and handled ceremonially by the priests there, but was given directly to the *Levites* and the poor. So no shrine or temple was involved—the sanctuary was, so to speak, the sky above (v. 15). We should no doubt label such an action as "charity", and we should probably treat it as something outside the religious sphere, even if done in the name of Christ. Yet Deuteronomy prescribes a spoken confession to accompany the gift; a solemn declaration to God above.

This declaration combines two things. *First*, the worshipper asserts that his gift is the full tithe, not a miserly portion of it. Nobody could easily check the truth of this declaration, but a solemn statement *before the Lord* would invite divine retribution if deliberately untrue. So this service had the useful effect of protecting the gifts to the Levites and the underprivileged. One wonders how much more generous Christian giving would be if we were asked to make such solemn declarations nowadays. *Second*, the worshipper declared that he had observed the regulations for giving his tithe to the poor *just as if he were going to offer sacrifice* (v. 14). Thus the gift to the poor was transformed into a symbolic sacrifice; a genuine form of worship to God. The thought is not unlike that expressed by Jesus in Matthew 25:31–46, "as you did it to one of the least of these my brethren, you did it to me". We simply cannot divorce the two great commandments of the law: to love God and to love our neighbour (Matt. 22:34–40). It is no accident that the offertory in Christian churches is part of the worship.

This chapter brings to an end the law code of Deuteronomy, which began with chapter 12. Verses 16–19 remind the readers that all the many laws in this central part of Deuteronomy were God's own "statutes and ordinances", designed for his own special *people*. We do not attach such reverence to the secular law codes in our countries, however much respect we may have for law and order; but for Israel, careful obedience to these laws amounted to *walking* in God's *ways*. This is a metaphor that has virtually become a cliché, so it may be worth recalling the degree to which it is used in the Bible. The most vivid usage is in Jesus' picture of the two ways (Matt. 7:13–14). The early Christians did not use the term "Christianity": they called it "the Way" (for example, in Acts 9:2). Our progress through life is a "walk" along a chosen—or ill-chosen—route, and leads to a specific destination. We do well to ask ourselves from time to time what our destination really is, and whether our route is the one indicated in the Holy Scriptures.

"KEEP SILENCE AND HEAR"

Deuteronomy 27:1–10

[1]"Now Moses and the elders of Israel commanded the people, saying, "Keep all the commandment which I command you this day. [2]And on the day you pass over the Jordan to the land which the Lord your God gives you, you shall set up large stones, and plaster them with plaster; [3]and you shall write upon them all the words of this law, when you pass over to enter the land which the Lord your God gives you, a land flowing with milk and honey, as the Lord, the God of your fathers, has promised you. [4]And when you have passed over the Jordan, you shall set up these stones, concerning which I command you this day, on Mount Ebal, and you shall plaster them with plaster. [5]And there you shall build an altar to the Lord your God, an altar of stones; you shall lift up no iron tool upon them. [6]You shall build an altar to the Lord your God of unhewn stones; and you shall offer burnt offerings on it to the Lord your God; [7]and you shall sacrifice peace offerings, and shall eat there; and you shall rejoice before the Lord your God. [8]And you shall write upon the stones all the words of this law very plainly."

⁹And Moses and the Levitical priests said to all Israel, "Keep silence and hear, O Israel: this day you have become the people of the Lord your God. ¹⁰You shall therefore obey the voice of the Lord your God, keeping his commandments and his statutes, which I command you this day."

Chapter 27 begins with a passing reminder to the reader that *Moses* has been the speaker for many chapters (cf. 5:1). Chapters 27 and 28 together set out instructions for a special ceremonial to ratify the covenant between God and Israel; 29:1 describes it as a covenant additional to the earlier one at Sinai (Horeb). It was important that Israel should obey the covenant laws no less in the Promised Land than in the Sinai wilderness; and of course it was vital to Deuteronomy's purpose that every generation of Israel should be obedient to God's commands. Many scholars believe that a covenant-renewal ceremony or festival was a regular part of Israel's religious calendar, and if so, Deuteronomy 27–28 outlines some of the aspects and component parts of it. Plainly a ceremony at *Mount Ebal* (v. 4), near the northern city of Shechem, cannot have served the people of Judah and Jerusalem once the Israelite kingdom split into two at the end of the tenth century B.C. We note, too, that the *altar* of verse 5 appears to conflict with chapter 12's instructions for one single sanctuary, *ie* at Jerusalem, unless perhaps a single, once-and-for-all ceremony is envisaged. Probably the logic of the book as a whole is that this early authorized altar, shortly after the Conquest of Canaan, was rightly at Mount Ebal, but that subsequently, it was meant to give way to the Jerusalem sanctuary. (In practice, many altars and shrines persisted until the reforms under Josiah, at the end of the seventh century B.C.: see Introduction p. 2.)

There is some uncertainty, moreover, about whether the altar was on Mount Ebal or the neighbouring Mount Gerizim; the latter is mentioned in verse 12, and replaces "Mount Ebal" in verse 4 in an important Old Testament manuscript.

Despite some questions and problems such as these, Deuteronomy 27 is clear enough in its basic instructions. Israel is defined as "the people of the Lord" (v. 9), with a duty to "obey the voice of the Lord" (v. 10). The ceremony underlines these points in two ways. (1) The sacrifices and *offerings* with their accompanying joyful meal (vv. 6–7) draw the two parties of the covenant—God and Israel—into the closest possible communion. For Christians, the Holy Communion "feast" serves a very similar function. (2) The people are summoned to *keep silence* while they listen to God's *voice* (vv. 9–10). For practical reasons we are silent in our churches while we listen to the sermon, but this silence is symbolic. In the covenant relationship, the two parties were by no means equal: God issued the commands and set the pattern, but Israel could not command him in any way. In worship they were not silent (Ps. 150, for instance, describes a full orchestra active in the praise of God), but where God's law is concerned, the worshipper can only humbly acknowledge that it is not for man to argue or to contradict. We sometimes accuse preachers of being "six feet above criticism"; but if they do indeed channel the message of God to us, there can be no criticism.

A LIST OF CURSES

Deuteronomy 27:11–26

[11]And Moses charged the people the same day, saying, [12]"When you have passed over the Jordan, these shall stand upon Mount Gerizim to bless the people: Simeon, Levi, Judah, Issachar, Joseph, and Benjamin. [13]And these shall stand upon Mount Ebal for the curse: Reuben, Gad, Asher, Zebulun, Dan and Naphtali. [14]And the Levites shall declare to all the men of Israel with a loud voice:

[15]"'Cursed be the man who makes a graven or molten image, an abomination to the Lord, a thing made by the hands of a craftsman, and sets it up in secret.' And all the people shall answer and say, 'Amen.'

[16]"'Cursed be he who dishonours his father or his mother.' And all the people shall say, 'Amen.'

[17]"'Cursed be he who removes his neighbour's landmark.' And all the people shall say, 'Amen.'

[18]"'Cursed be he who misleads a blind man on the road.' And all the people shall say, 'Amen.'

¹⁹"'Cursed be he who perverts the justice due to the sojourner, the fatherless, and the widow.' And all the people shall say, 'Amen.'

²⁰"'Cursed be he who lies with his father's wife, because he has uncovered her who is his father's.' And all the people shall say, 'Amen.'

²¹"'Cursed be he who lies with any kind of beast.' And all the people shall say, 'Amen.'

²²"'Cursed be he who lies with his sister, whether the daughter of his father or the daughter of his mother.' And all the people shall say, 'Amen.'

²³"'Cursed be he who lies with his mother-in-law.' And all the people shall say, 'Amen.'

²⁴"'Cursed be he who slays his neighbour in secret.' And all the people shall say, 'Amen.'

²⁵"'Cursed be he who takes a bribe to slay an innocent person.' And all the people shall say, 'Amen.'

²⁶"'Cursed be he who does not confirm the words of this law by doing them.' And all the people shall say, 'Amen.'"

The ceremony of blessing and cursing was briefly mentioned in 11:29. More detail is now given, with an indication of the location of the people in their twelve tribal groupings (vv. 12–13). The division seems to be roughly geographical, with the more northerly tribes stationed on the more northerly of the two mountains—*Ebal*. We can only guess at the precise form the ceremony took but there can have been no suggestion that the six tribes associated with Ebal were under *the curse*. On the contrary, all twelve tribes had been favoured by God with the gift of the land. The curses are pronounced not on tribes, but on individuals who break God's laws—in other words, who break their own promises to keep those laws.

A ceremony of cursing seems very strange to us. In Israel's world, however, solemn curses were common enough. For instance, when the kings of two nations drew up a treaty, the text of the treaty incorporated a number of curses; so if subsequently one of them broke his treaty obligations, he would be inviting the gods to punish him. The Hebrew word meaning "covenant" was the same as the word for treaty, and the Old Testament covenant between God and Israel had many similarities to political treaties of the time. The list of curses, then, was completely natural to the Israelites. In a sense, the curses are simply another way of expressing solemn promises to God, with the understanding that any breach of them would merit his punishment.

The curses pick up a selection of the laws. The first two (vv. 15–16) refer back to two of the Ten Commandments (5:8, 16), but verse 18 has no exact parallel in the earlier laws of Deuteronomy (the nearest parallel is in Lev. 19:14). We may speculate that the ceremony itself contained a much more comprehensive list of curses, and that this fairly short list was intended to be memorized, to serve as a guide to everyday conduct and as a reminder of the scope of God's laws. The final curse (v. 26) is in itself a very comprehensive pronouncement, as Paul pointed out in Galatians 3:10. It was perfectly true that the breach of one single law would place a man or a woman under a curse. *The Levites* (v. 14) recited the words of the curses, but *all the people* declared *Amen* to each of them, indicating their assent to each and every law. A law-breaker was therefore without any excuse. It is in this sense that the law was a burden to the tender conscience, an endless striving to obey a very large array of commands and demands; God's standards are of frightening dimensions, and it is easier to give intellectual assent to them than to obey them fully in day-to-day living. That is why Paul, in Galatians 3, without the slightest disrespect for the law of Moses, put it to one side as having been superseded by the Christian Gospel; but that is not to say that God's standards are obsolete, nor did Paul mean to imply that.

THE LOGIC OF THE COVENANT

Deuteronomy 28:1–14

¹"And if you obey the voice of the Lord your God, being careful to do all his commandments which I command you this day, the Lord your God will set you high above all the nations of the earth. ²And all these blessings shall come upon you and overtake you, if you obey the voice of the Lord your God. ³Blessed shall you be in the city, and blessed

shall you be in the field. ⁴Blessed shall be the fruit of your body, and the fruit of your ground, and the fruit of your beasts, the increase of your cattle, and the young of your flock. ⁵Blessed shall be your basket and your kneading-trough. ⁶Blessed shall you be when you come in, and blessed shall you be when you go out.

⁷"The Lord will cause your enemies who rise against you to be defeated before you; they shall come out against you one way, and flee before you seven ways. ⁸The Lord will command the blessing upon you in your barns, and in all that you undertake; and he will bless you in the land which the Lord your God gives you. ⁹The Lord will establish you as a people holy to himself, as he has sworn to you, if you keep the commandments of the Lord your God, and walk in his ways. ¹⁰And all the peoples of the earth shall see that you are called by the name of the Lord; and they shall be afraid of you. ¹¹And the Lord will make you abound in prosperity, in the fruit of your body, and in the fruit of your cattle, and in the fruit of your ground, within the land which the Lord swore to your fathers to give you. ¹²The Lord will open to you his good treasury the heavens, to give the rain of your land in its season and to bless all the work of your hands; and you shall lend to many nations, but you shall not borrow. ¹³And the Lord will make you the head, and not the tail; and you shall tend upward only, and not downward; if you obey the commandments of the Lord your God, which I command you this day, being careful to do them, ¹⁴and if you do not turn aside from any of the words which I command you this day, to the right hand or to the left, to go after other gods to serve them."

This long chapter deals with the outworkings and the consequences of the covenant. If a king broke the clauses of a treaty made with another king, then he might expect to pay the penalty for it—the punishment of the gods as well as the hostility of the other king. If he kept the treaty, on the other hand, he could reasonably expect to receive favours and friendship and loyalty from the other party to the treaty. Israel had similarly bound itself to the "King of Kings", God himself, in a solemn covenant; and in the covenant ceremony the nation called down blessings and curses upon itself, as we have seen in chapter 27. The question, then, was what blessings loyalty to the covenant would bring, and what curses disloyalty and disobedience would result in. So chapter 28 spells it out; verses 1–14 explain the blessings and verses 15–68 indicate, in great detail, the curses.

The political treaties, of course, could make only limited promises for loyalty; one nation can offer another military aid, trade benefits and financial support, but little beyond that. The divine covenant, by contrast, could and did offer an enormous range of benefits. Verses 3–6 are comprehensive: both *the city* and the countryside (*the field*) are included (v. 3); fertility will be universal (vv. 4–5); and all human activities, in war and peace alike, will be prosperous (v. 6). God wants his people to have these things—fertility and prosperity—and he is only too willing to give them. This is the *logic* of the covenant: if God had indeed chosen Israel and entered into covenant with her people, then he had put himself under obligation to them. He could do no less than bless them (and vv. 7–14 express the nature of the blessings more precisely), provided that they were true to him and kept their side of the bargain.

In practice, needless to say, Israel's experience was very different from this idealistic portrait of what might have been. The nation that should have been *the head* (v. 13) was all too often just *the tail*; a weak, rather poor, minor people of antiquity. Are we to say that the rosy picture of verses 1–14 could never have happened? Is it just a pipe-dream, totally unrealistic wishful thinking? Far from it, if we are to give Deuteronomy any credence! And before we dismiss Deuteronomy's logic as primitive and untenable philosophy, let us take note of the fact that, in spite of everything, Israel has survived many centuries of checkered existence and is better known today than she ever was in antiquity; whereas mighty nations like Assyria and Babylon vanished from the map many centuries ago. Israel, it must be admitted, is in itself an ambiguous evidence of God's plans and actions; but if we give thought to the other partner in the covenant—the God of Israel—then we are forced to recognize that if he is truly the omnipotent and only God, and if he has indeed made covenant with human beings, then his control of their history is hard to deny. This is as true for the Church as it was for ancient Israel. We are rightly aware of the many complex factors that shape our world and its history; but we should not forget that God stands supreme above them all.

THE PENALTIES OF DISOBEDIENCE

Deuteronomy 28:15–68

15"But if you will not obey the voice of the Lord your God or be careful to do all his commandments and his statutes which I command you this day, then all these curses shall come upon you and overtake you. 16Cursed shall you be in the city, and cursed shall you be in the field. 17Cursed shall be your basket and your kneading-trough. 18Cursed shall be the fruit of your body, and the fruit of your ground, the increase of your cattle, and the young of your flock. 19Cursed shall you be when you come in, and cursed shall you be when you go out.

20"The Lord will send upon you curses, confusion, and frustration, in all that you undertake to do, until you are destroyed and perish quickly, on account of the evil of your doings, because you have forsaken me. 21The Lord will make the pestilence cleave to you until he has consumed you off the land which you are entering to take possession of it. 22The Lord will smite you with consumption, and with fever, inflammation, and fiery heat, and with drought, and with blasting, and with mildew; they shall pursue you until you perish. 23And the heavens over your head shall be brass, and the earth under you shall be iron. 24The Lord will make the rain of your land powder and dust; from heaven it shall come down upon you until you are destroyed.

25"The Lord will cause you to be defeated before your enemies; you shall go out one way against them, and flee seven ways before them; and you shall be a horror to all the kingdoms of the earth. 26And your dead body shall be food for all birds of the air, and for the beasts of the earth; and there shall be no one to frighten them away. 27The Lord will smite you with the boils of Egypt, and with the ulcers and the scurvy and the itch, of which you cannot be healed. 28The Lord will smite you with madness and blindness and confusion of mind; 29and you shall grope at noonday, as the blind grope in darkness, and you shall not prosper in your ways; and you shall be only oppressed and robbed continually, and there shall be no one to help you. 30You shall betroth a wife, and another man shall lie with her; you shall build a house, and you shall not dwell in it; you shall plant a vineyard, and you shall not use the fruit of it. 31Your ox shall be slain before your eyes, and you shall not eat of it; your ass shall be violently taken away before your face, and shall not be restored to you; your sheep shall be given to your enemies, and there shall be no one to help you. 32Your sons and your daughters shall be given to another people, while your eyes look on and fail with longing for them all the day; and it shall not be in the power of your hand to prevent it. [33]A nation which you have not known shall eat up the fruit of your ground and of all your labours; and you shall be only oppressed and crushed continually; [34]so that you shall be driven mad by the sight which your eyes shall see. [35]The Lord will smite you on the knees and on the legs with grievous boils of which you cannot be healed, from the sole of your foot to the crown of your head.

[36]"The Lord will bring you, and your king whom you set over you, to a nation that neither you nor you fathers have known; and there you shall serve other gods, of wood and stone. [37]And you shall become a horror, a proverb, and a byword, among all the peoples where the Lord will lead you away. [38]You shall carry much seed into the field, and shall gather little in; for the locust shall consume it. [39]You shall plant vineyards and dress them, but you shall neither drink of the wine nor gather the grapes; for the worm shall eat them. [40]You shall have olive trees throughout all your territory, but you shall not anoint yourself with the oil; for your olives shall drop off. [41]You shall beget sons and daughters, but they shall not be yours; for they shall go into captivity. [42]All your trees and the fruit of your ground the locust shall possess. [43]The sojourner who is among you shall mount above you higher and higher; and you shall come down lower and lower. [44]He shall lend to you, and you shall not lend to him; he shall be the head, and you shall be the tail. [45]All these curses shall come upon you and pursue you and overtake you, till you are destroyed, because you did not obey the voice of the Lord your God, to keep his commandments and his statutes which he commanded you. [46]They shall be upon you as a sign and a wonder, and upon your descendants for ever.

[47]"Because you did not serve the Lord your God with joyfulness and gladness of heart, by reason of the abundance of all things, [48]therefore you shall serve your enemies whom the Lord will send against you, in hunger and thirst, in nakedness, and in want of all things; and he will put a yoke of iron upon your neck, until he has destroyed you. [49]The Lord will bring a nation against you from afar, from the end of the earth, as swift as the eagle flies, a nation whose language you do not understand, [50]a nation of stern countenance, who shall not regard the person of the old or show favour to the young, [51]and shall eat the offspring of your cattle and the fruit of your ground, until you are destroyed; who also shall not leave you grain, wine, or oil, the increase of your cattle or

the young of your flock, until they have caused you to perish. ⁵²They shall besiege you in all your towns, until your high and fortified walls, in which you trusted, come down throughout all your land; and they shall besiege you in all your towns throughout all your land, which the Lord your God has given you. ⁵³And you shall eat the offspring of your own body, the flesh of your sons and daughters, whom the Lord your God has given you, in the siege and in the distress with which your enemies shall distress you. ⁵⁴The man who is the most tender and delicately bred among you will grudge food to his brother, to the wife of his bosom, and to the last of the children who remain to him; ⁵⁵so that he will not give to any of them any of the flesh of his children whom he is eating, because he has nothing left him, in the siege and in the distress with which your enemy shall distress you in all your towns. ⁵⁶The most tender and delicately bred woman among you, who would not venture to set the sole of her foot upon the ground because she is so delicate and tender will grudge to the husband of her bosom, to her son and to her daughter, ⁵⁷her afterbirth that comes out from between her feet and her children whom she bears, because she will eat them secretly, for want of all things, in the siege and in the distress with which your enemy shall distress you in your towns.

⁵⁸"If you are not careful to do all the words of this law which are written in this book, that you may fear this glorious and awful name, the Lord your God, ⁵⁹then the Lord will bring on you and your offspring extraordinary afflictions, afflictions severe and lasting, and sickness grievous and lasting. ⁶⁰And he will bring upon you again all the diseases of Egypt, which you were afraid of; and they shall cleave to you. ⁶¹Every sickness also, and every affliction which is not recorded in the book of this law, the Lord will bring upon you, until you are destroyed. ⁶²Whereas you were as the stars of heaven for multitude, you shall be left few in number; because you did not obey the voice of the Lord your God. ⁶³And as the Lord took delight in doing you good and multiplying you, so the Lord will take delight in bringing ruin upon you and destroying you; and you shall be plucked off the land which you are entering to take possession of it. ⁶⁴And the Lord will scatter you among all peoples, from one end of the earth to the other; and there you shall serve other gods, of wood and stone, which neither you nor your fathers have known. ⁶⁵And among these nations you shall find no ease, and there shall be no rest for the sole of your foot; but the Lord will give you there a trembling heart, and failing eyes, and a languishing soul; ⁶⁶your life shall hang in doubt before you;

night and day you shall be in dread, and have no assurance of your life. [67] In the morning you shall say, 'Would it were evening!' and at evening you shall say, 'Would it were morning!' because of the dread which your heart shall fear, and the sights which your eyes shall see. [68] And the Lord will bring you back in ships to Egypt, a journey which I promised that you should never make again; and there you shall offer yourselves for sale to your enemies as male and female slaves, but no man will buy you."

(i)

If verses 1–14 are a picture of what might have been, the rest of the chapter is largely a picture of what actually *did* happen to Israel, although expressed in this conditional form: "if you [as a nation] will not obey . . . then all these curses shall come upon you" (v. 15). Four of the books that follow Deuteronomy— Joshua, Judges, Samuel and Kings—tell a story of political ups and downs, to be sure, but include many unhappy experiences for Israel, and end with total disaster. So there is no question about the realism of the picture given here. The list of curses incorporates three types of penalty for disobedience. The *first* category is the completely general list in verses 16–19, which is obviously the exact counterpart to the blessings of verses 3–6. *Second*, a great many of the curses are typical of the political curses which have been found in treaty documents from the ancient Near East. *Third*, as we have seen, many more are precisely the experiences that befell Israel during the period of the Judges and the monarchy. (The latter two categories in fact overlap.)

We can also divide up the curses in terms of their content. The general ones come first (vv. 16–19). Verses 20–24 then deal with drought, *pestilence* and disasters to the land and its food supply. Verse 25 mentions defeat in battle, but the rest of the paragraph is about personal disasters such as illness, *madness*, and loss in the home and on the farm (very much the problems that afflicted Job, cf. Job 1:13–2:8). Verses 34–46 spell out the horrors of exile. Verses 47–57 describe in awful detail the even worse horrors of a siege. Finally verses 58–68 depict the hopeless misery of a scattered, homeless people, insecure and oppressed. *Egypt* is singled out for mention (v. 68) for two reasons: *first* because Egypt was always a very natural refuge for Palestinians, all the more so when invaders attacked Israel from the north; and *second* for an important symbolic reason—God had blessed Israel by rescuing the nation from slavery in Egypt at the beginning of its history, so it was only too appropriate that God's curse should have the effect of returning the Israelites to slavery in Egypt.

Most scholars are of the opinion that the curses in this chapter were gradually expanded in the light of history: obviously verse 58 relates to the *book* of Deuteronomy, rather than any earlier public address to the nation. In any case, we can see that this chapter would have its most powerful appeal to a generation which had some experience of the disasters listed here; the dying days of the Judaean monarchy, or the early days of the return from the Babylonian Exile, were periods when thoughtful people would have been ready to listen to the challenge of this passage. The real power of Deuteronomy, indeed, can perhaps be best seen in the fact that after the Exile, the Jewish people increasingly became more and more dedicated to keeping the Law enshrined in it. Generally speaking, it is a wise people, and they are wise individuals, who are thus ready to learn the lessons of their past history.

(ii)

We should read Deuteronomy 28 as, first and foremost, a heart-felt appeal to the Israelite people to be true to their covenant with God. Verse 63 may depict God as taking *delight* in punishing them for any disobedience, but such a sentiment was meant to startle and shock the reader, not to express literal truths. At the same time, the chapter does express a clear philosophy of history; a philosophy which has provided the framework for the major historical books of the Old Testament (Joshua–Kings). As so often, the Bible speaks here in black and white terms, and offers specific detail. We should want to recognize that there are many neutral greys in history, and that we all act from complex and mixed motives. Deuteronomy does not necessarily argue against such a viewpoint, but it is concerned to show the reader the best possibilities and the worst possibilities, and to demand that its readers should make a conscious choice. If one does not consciously decide to follow God's design for life, then one can all too easily fall unawares into outright disobedience. The black-and-white picture compels attention.

On the other hand, Deuteronomy is not the last word on the subject of a covenant between God and man. At the individual level, the book of Job provides a counterbalance, by showing a man who kept faith with God and yet suffered bereavement, loss, and ill-health. However, taken by itself, Deuteronomy can lead to two misconceptions about God and man. *First*, many people thought that if any person prospered, he must have been righteous; and conversely, that any man (like Job) who suffered personal tragedy, must automatically have been wicked and sinful. Such mechanical judgments are not only likely to be wrong, but also, more seriously, can lead to grave injustices towards the person alleged to be wicked. *Second*, the idea developed that one could, so to speak, buy God's favour, so that many people obeyed Old Testament laws not because they were God's good design for human conduct, but in the hope of getting something out of it.

People with more insight could see that if Israel's history showed anything at all, it showed a people who were, as a nation, incapable of keeping God's covenant. That is the truth to which Deuteronomy 28 pointed, and it was left to prophets like Jeremiah to spell it out. The old Sinai covenant failed in the sense that it set an admirable standard but left the people without the means to reach that standard. What was needed, says Jeremiah 31:33–34, was a different sort of covenant, one which would affect and change men's hearts and minds, and give them both the power and the wish to obey God. Deuteronomy 28 points forward to Jeremiah 31, and in turn, Jeremiah 31 points forward to the New Testament. Hebrews 8:6–13 quotes extensively from the Jeremiah passage, and emphasizes the great change in the situation brought about by the work of Christ.

UNIVERSAL OBLIGATIONS

Deuteronomy 29:1–15

¹These are the words of the covenant which the Lord commanded Moses to make with the people of Israel in the land of Moab, besides the covenant which he had made with them at Horeb.

²And Moses summoned all Israel and said to them: "You have seen all that the Lord did before your eyes in the land of Egypt, to Pharaoh and to all his servants and to all his land, ³the great trials which your eyes saw, the signs, and those great wonders; ⁴but to this day the Lord has not given you a mind to understand, or eyes to see, or ears to hear. ⁵I have led you forty years in the wilderness; your clothes have not worn out upon you, and your sandals have not worn off your feet; ⁶you have not eaten bread, and you have not drunk wine or strong drink; that you may know that I am the Lord your God. ⁷And when you came to this place, Sihon the king of Heshbon and Og the king of Bashan came out against us to battle, but we defeated them; ⁸we took their land, and gave it for an inheritance to the Reubenites, the Gadites, and the half-tribe of the Manassites. ⁹Therefore be careful to do the words of this covenant, that you may prosper in all that you do.

¹⁰"You stand this day all of you before the Lord your God; the heads of your tribes, your elders, and your officers, all the men of Israel, ¹¹your little ones, your wives, and the sojourner who is in your camp, both he who hews your wood and he who draws your water, ¹²that you may enter into the sworn covenant of the Lord your God, which the Lord your God makes with you this day; ¹³that he may establish you this day as his people, and that he may be your God, as he promised you, and as he swore to your fathers, to Abraham, to Isaac, and to Jacob. ¹⁴Nor is it with you only that I make this sworn covenant, ¹⁵but with him who is not here with us this day as well as with him who stands here with us this day before the Lord our God."

Suddenly we find ourselves reading about yet another *covenant*! It seems fairly certain that Israel became accustomed to frequent, perhaps annual, ceremonies to renew their covenant with God, so this recurring motif will not have surprised ancient readers. We must also bear in mind the literary nature of Deuteronomy; the author undoubtedly meant to emphasize the central importance of Israel's covenant obligations to God, and he achieved this emphasis partly by repetition. So, as in earlier passages, he begins this new covenant section (chapters 29 and 30) with a detailed reminder of past events. The geographical setting, *Moab*, is broadly the same as the one at the start of the book (1:1); it was from Moabite territory that the Israelites crossed the Jordan and invaded the Promised Land (see map, p. xiii).

The flashback to earlier events concentrates on three things: the plagues suffered by the Egyptians (vv. 2–3); Israel's wilderness experiences (vv. 5–6); and her first conquests, in Transjordan (vv. 7–8). All three demonstrated God's power and goodness. The plagues had been God's miraculous way of rescuing his people from *Egypt*. In *the wilderness*, they could easily have perished from starvation and deprivation, but for his miraculous provision and care. In Transjordan they had been given victory over two powerful attackers who might easily have overwhelmed them. Verse 4 suggests that the Israelites tended to take pride in these achievements instead of crediting them to God. The proper lesson to learn was that unless God kept covenant with them, they were doomed to weakness and loss and defeat; but this covenant depended on *them* (v. 9). It is a feature of human nature to take the past for granted; things seen as miraculous at the time, soon seem commonplace in retrospect. Besides which, prosperity easily promotes complacency.

The new covenant ceremony then, seemed a psychological necessity. It was as comprehensive as possible, attended even by young children and foreign residents (v. 11). To fetch *wood* and *water* was the most lowly task, but even the humblest folk were part of the covenant people, and they too were to attend the ceremony. There was no elitism about the covenant. Verses 14–15 even draw attention to those who could not attend; by this, the writer means later generations. So nobody was to escape from the obligations of the covenant.

With our emphasis in Christianity on the priority of faith (over law and works) we can easily forget our personal and individual responsibilities to God. And with our present-day Western emphasis on the individual, we may need to remind ourselves that (in both Testaments) God's plans are "to establish . . . his people" (v. 13): together we are promoting his will (see 1 Peter 2:9–10).

THE SOURCE OF DISASTER

Deuteronomy 29:16–28

[16]"You know how we dwelt in the land of Egypt, and how we came through the midst of the nations through which you passed; [17]and you have seen their detestable things, their idols of wood and stone, of silver and gold, which were among them. [18]Beware lest there be among you a man or woman or family or tribe, whose heart turns away this day from the Lord our God to go and serve the gods of those nations; lest there be among you a root bearing poisonous and bitter fruit, [19]one who, when he hears the words of this sworn covenant, blesses himself in his heart, saying, 'I shall be safe, though I walk in the stubbornness of my heart.' This would lead to the sweeping away of moist and dry alike. [20]The Lord would not pardon him, but rather the anger of the Lord and his jealousy would smoke against that man, and the curses written in this book would settle upon him, and the Lord would blot out his name from under heaven. [21]And the Lord would single him out from all the tribes of Israel for calamity, in accordance with all the curses of the covenant written in this book of the law. [22]And the generation to come, your children who rise up after you, and the foreigner who comes from a far land, would say, when they see the afflictions of that land and the sicknesses with which the Lord has made it sick—[23]the whole land brimstone and salt, and a burnt-out waste, unsown, and growing nothing, where no grass can sprout, an overthrow like that of Sodom and Gomorrah, Admah and Zeboiim, which the Lord overthrew in his anger and wrath—[24]yea, all the nations would say, 'Why has the Lord done thus to this land? What means the heat of this great anger?' [25]Then men would say, 'It is because they forsook the covenant of the Lord, the God of their fathers, which he made with them when he brought them out of the land of Egypt, [26]and went and served other gods and worshipped them, gods whom they had not known and whom he had not allotted to them; [27]therefore the anger of the Lord was kindled against this land, bringing upon it all the curses written in this book; [28]and the Lord uprooted them from their land in anger and fury and great wrath, and cast them into another land, as at this day.'"

This section is an impassioned plea to the individual, the family and the nation to avoid idolatry at all costs. Idolatry is seen as the most insidious and urgent danger to Israel, and the precise cause of the Exile to Babylon (v. 28). It is emphasized that to worship idols was, in a literal sense, "foreign" to Israel; idolatry was something they had seen in evidence in *Egypt* to begin with (v. 16). To worship foreign gods was, by definition, utter treachery to Israel's own God. Verse 17 seems to contrast Israel's invisible God with the visible, tangible images of other nations.

Why would idolatry attract anyone? For one thing, because of the deliberate act of a warped mind (v. 18); the sort of mind which would today turn to Eastern cults or to occult sects, for no better reason than to be "different". The result, says verse 18, is "poisonous and bitter". Stubborn complacency is the next attitude that is reproved (v. 19); an attitude which would end in the loss of everything—"moist and dry" was a saying which meant *absolutely everything*. Stubborn refusal to keep faith with God is, for Deuteronomy, the unforgivable sin (v. 20).

False religion is catching, this passage implied: verses 16–21 are a warning to the individual, but verse 21 moves abruptly to the desolation of the whole country which would follow national apostasy. Verse 23 gives a vivid picture of desolation; the earliest readers were very familiar with the story of the fall of *Sodom and Gomorrah* (Gen. 19:24–25), and some of them probably knew for themselves how hard and forbidding the terrain was, around the aptly-named Dead Sea, where these cities had once been. What God had done to Sodom and Gomorrah, he could do to a sinful Israel as a whole.

We could consider this passage from another point of view. This picture of desolation might well remind us of the consequences of a nuclear holocaust. If a nuclear disaster occurs one day, any survivors who give thought to the matter, would surely not blame God for it, but blame instead the stupidity and viciousness of mankind. Wilful human failings, in other words, would have brought about their own punishment. That is, in one sense, what this section of Deuteronomy is saying: if the horrors of invasion and rampaging by brutal soldiery one day bring Israel to its knees, then Israel would be wholly responsible for it. We, in our situation, often shrug helplessly at the potential dangers in our world, as if we can do nothing about them. Verses 16–21 are a salutary reminder that the sins and defects of any community begin with the individual, and in the family. If we cannot change the world, we can at least influence our own society—our circle of friends, our work-mates, our neighbourhood.

SECRETS AND PLAIN LANGUAGE

Deuteronomy 29:29

> 29"The secret things belong to the Lord our God; but the things that are revealed belong to us and to our children for ever, that we may do all the words of this law."

The chapter ends with a challenging contrast between what is visible and what is invisible. Israel of old could not read the future; and neither can we. Mankind has always resented this limitation placed upon us; we saw in 18:10–11 the many devices by which ancient men tried (in vain) to gain a glimpse into the future. The same chapter indicated, it is true, that God gave his people prophets who were themselves given a measure of insight into the future; but not even a prophet has total forward vision. Some matters are always "secret things". The first lesson in this is *humility*, and the frank recognition of our limitations. Another lesson is *reassurance*, because the hidden future *belongs to the Lord*, who is not some impersonal fate but *our God*. The man with a serene faith in God does not need to know what tomorrow will bring; tomorrow is in the hands of a loving Father.

This verse is not primarily concerned with either humbling us or reassuring us, however. Its chief point is that we can see quite enough! God of course kept many things secret from ancient Israel, but his will was expressed perfectly clearly and plainly, embodied in the many laws set out in Deuteronomy. God's will was no secret. So the Israelites' eyes were directed not towards tomorrow's surprises, but towards today's responsibilities. The

Christian is not subject to the law code of Deuteronomy, but he too finds God's will fully laid out, in the pages of the New Testament. The psalmist rightly acknowledged that "Thy word is a lamp to my feet and a light to my path" (Ps. 119:105): the future may be dark and hidden, but we carry a torch as we move forward into it.

The verse also reminds the reader of another dimension to the future. Mankind has always tended to view the future as predetermined, governed by an inexorable fate; and both ancient Israelites and modern Christians can be tempted to think in the same way. But the Bible does not, in general, depict the future in any such way; rather, it suggests that we ourselves mould our own futures by our own actions. Deuteronomy certainly takes this standpoint, not least in this chapter: obedience to God's laws creates a happy future, while disobedience brings eventual disaster. If so, it makes no sense to worry about what "fate" might bring our way; instead, we should concern ourselves with the question of the fate we are inviting.

HOPE FOR DARK DAYS

Deuteronomy 30:1–10

[1]"And when all these things come upon you, the blessing and the curse, which I have set before you, and you call them to mind among all the nations where the Lord your God has driven you, [2]and return to the Lord your God, you and your children, and obey his voice in all that I command you this day, with all your heart and with all your soul; [3]then the Lord your God will restore your fortunes, and have compassion upon you, and he will gather you again from all the peoples where the Lord your God has scattered you. [4]If your outcasts are in the uttermost parts of heaven, from there the Lord your God will gather you, and from there he will fetch you; [5]and the Lord your God will bring you into the land which your fathers possessed, that you may possess it; and he will make you more prosperous and numerous than your fathers. [6]And the Lord your God will circumcise your heart and the heart of your offspring, so that you will love the Lord your God with all your heart and with all your soul, that you may live. [7]And the

Lord your God will put all these curses upon your foes and enemies who persecuted you. [8]And you shall again obey the voice of the Lord, and keep all his commandments which I command you this day. [9]The Lord your God will make you abundantly prosperous in all the work of your hand, in the fruit of your body, and in the fruit of your cattle, and in the fruit of your ground; for the Lord will again take delight in prospering you, as he took delight in your fathers, [10]if you obey the voice of the Lord your God, to keep his commandments and his statutes which are written in this book of the law, if you turn to the Lord your God with all your heart and with all your soul."

The last few chapters have pointed out, and emphasized by repetition, the two roads that lay before Israel—what Jesus was later to call *the broad way* and *the narrow way* (Matt. 7:13–14). The path of disobedience could bring curses down on the nation, while loyalty and obedience would mean blessing in the years ahead. Of course, real history is not so black and white as this challenging picture might suggest, and verse 1 realistically envisages both "the blessing and the curse" as Israel's experience-to-be as the generations come and go. As a whole, however, this section is discussing just one option: supposing the worst happens, and Israel is so disobedient that many of the disasters foreseen in chapter 28 actually happen—what then? Must that be the end of the story? Is cursing God's last word? The historical books that follow Deuteronomy in the Old Testament, from Joshua to 2 Kings, in themselves paint just such a picture, for the story ends with Jerusalem in ruins, the Temple destroyed, the monarchy swept away, hundreds and thousands of casualties, and the cream of the survivors exiled to far-away Babylon.

The generation that experienced the Exile must have reacted to it in several ways. No doubt some people, in stoicism or despair, simply endured the situation, without giving it much thought. Others must have been drawn to worship the gods of Babylon, who seemed to them stronger than the God of Israel. Others again were more loyal to Yahweh in their thinking, and tried to learn lessons from the recent disasters. It is to this third group that Deuteronomy 30 is addressed. If the people of Judah as a whole would even now mend their ways and "return to the Lord"

(v. 2), then there would be nothing final about even the most dreadful curses and calamities. The past cannot be undone, but the present can be changed, out of all recognition. So verses 3–10 are like the rewind effect on a video-recorder: the exiles can be brought back (vv. 3–4); the Promised Land can be re-entered; prosperity regained (vv. 5 and 9); and even the strongest enemies can be defeated (v. 7).

What would it mean, in practical terms, to "return to the Lord"? The consistent message of Deuteronomy is emphasized yet again: what God wants to see is *love* in the *heart* and *soul* of his people; a love expressed in willingness to "obey . . . all his commandments" (vv. 6 and 8). Verse 10 (like 29:27) belongs not to the sermon but to the *book*, Deuteronomy itself, which incorporates all the laws of earlier chapters and so stands as a permanent, referable reminder of God's wishes.

Two aspects of this passage are worth highlighting, not least for their continuing relevance. One is the basically optimistic look at a grim period of history. Our age seems deeply pessimistic, with many fatalistic voices about the "inevitability" of a nuclear holocaust. Both the Old and the New Testament realistically expect dreadful wars and attendant evils, but both insist that God will ultimately bring peace and inaugurate his reign of righteousness. The other point worth noting is the contrast between formal religion and a genuine inward faith and devotion. Verse 6 expresses this contrast neatly by its metaphorical use of the word *circumcise*: what was needed was not the purely physical sign of Jewishness—a permanent physical mark—but a permanent change in the lives and attitudes of God's people. A cold and formal religion cannot be the route to God's blessing and favour.

"NOT TOO HARD"

Deuteronomy 30:11–14

[11]"For this commandment which I command you this day is not too hard for you, neither is it far off. [12]It is not in heaven, that you should

say, 'Who will go up for us to heaven, and bring it to us, that we may hear it and do it?' ¹³Neither is it beyond the sea, that you should say, 'Who will go over the sea for us, and bring it to us, that we may hear it and do it?' ¹⁴But the word is very near you; it is in your mouth and in your heart, so that you can do it."

Verses 11–14 are really an answer to an unwritten objection. Among the various reactions to the Exile, some of which we have already noted, was the response that it was all really God's fault: God had bound Israel in a covenant that was simply impossible to keep, so the nation could not justly be blamed for failing to keep it. God had set an impossible target. This must have been the sort of attitude which Deuteronomy is challenging here. In vivid language, the passage insists that God's *commandment* (*ie* the whole of his Law) is well within reach. Verse 14 may be referring to the practice of memorizing and reciting the Law, which devout Jews have so often done throughout their history. If so, then certainly no-one could fairly claim ignorance of the Law, nor claim to have forgotten it.

Perhaps the anonymous objector had a point, all the same. The New Testament puts more emphasis than the Old on man's inborn tendency to sin, and we in the Christian tradition would hesitate to assert that full obedience to God's will was easy. St. Paul, moreover, could describe the Law as burdensome (cf. Gal. 3:10–13). In part, he was no doubt conscious of the enormous edifice of rules and prohibitions which the Pharisees of his era had constructed; but he was also conscious that to adhere to a law code is a constant, unending, and perhaps uninspiring, task. So we may wonder whether it was quite true that God's obligations placed upon Israel were "not too hard".

Yet when we examine the laws of Deuteronomy, we see that many of them were perfectly reasonable and attainable demands; we should not today argue, about our law codes, that to refrain from murder, and to drive our cars on the correct side of the road, were "difficult" laws or impossible targets. It is true that the commands to love God and our neighbour are laws which do set very high standards; but the desire to obey them, and the sincere attempt to do so, would gain God's approval, however far from perfection these first steps might be. So the law of Deuteronomy, at least, was not an impossible ideal.

Verse 14 makes a further point—perhaps responding to a different sort of objection; namely that God's will was mysterious and inaccessible, beyond human knowledge. Any such idea is firmly rejected by verse 14: God's *word* is his self-revelation, which, in every generation, he has made available to men and women. Paul reinforces this assertion in Romans 10:5–13, where he comments on this paragraph of Deuteronomy. To the Christian, God's self-revelation is no longer enshrined primarily in a set of laws, but in the person of Christ himself; and Christ, and all that he offers us, is fully accessible to each one of us.

A STARK CHOICE

Deuteronomy 30:15–20

[15]"See, I have set before you this day life and good, death and evil. [16]If you obey the commandments of the Lord your God which I command you this day, by loving the Lord your God, by walking in his ways, and by keeping his commandments and his statutes and his ordinances, then you shall live and multiply, and the Lord your God will bless you in the land which you are entering to take possession of it. [17]But if your heart turns away, and you will not hear, but are drawn away to worship other gods and serve them, [18]I declare to you this day, that you shall perish; you shall not live long in the land which you are going over the Jordan to enter and possess. [19]I call heaven and earth to witness against you this day, that I have set before you life and death, blessing and curse; therefore choose life, that you and your descendants may live, [20]loving the Lord your God, obeying his voice, and cleaving to him; for that means life to you and length of days, that you may dwell in the land which the Lord swore to your fathers, to Abraham, to Isaac, and to Jacob, to give them."

These verses bring this section of Deuteronomy to a close: chapters 29 and 30 constitute one of the "sermons" of Deuteronomy. It has been said that every good sermon ought to pose a challenge and set a choice before the listeners; and plainly this sermon ends with a very solemn challenge. Chapter 28 set out in great detail the whole range of blessings and catastrophes which could come upon the nation, dependent upon the choice they made. This chapter avoids any hint of overkill and prefers the simple, yet stark, contrast: "life and good" or "death and evil". Material prosperity is thus firmly linked with spiritual well-being. One of the most prized possessions in the ancient world was a long life; but verse 18 applies this idea not to the individual, but to the nation. For a nation to be scattered and uprooted was tantamount to a short lifespan, to premature illness and death. This was the threat that hung over the people of Israel, if they should be "drawn away to worship other gods" (v. 17).

Like many other nations in antiquity, Israel did indeed suffer invasion and depredation, destruction and exile. First the Northern Kingdom endured this fate at the hands of the Assyrians, towards the end of the eighth century B.C., and it was never reconstituted. Then the Kingdom of Judah fell, early in the sixth century B.C., to the Babylonians. As we have seen, the main thrust of chapter 30 was for the exilic generation, who were still offered the chance of restoration. This was a chance they took, and in due course many exiles returned to the Promised Land, where Jerusalem and its temple were eventually rebuilt, and where the Jewish people gradually took steps to eliminate idolatry. So this final appeal of chapter 30 did not fall on totally deaf ears; and history largely vindicated the promise of verse 20. (It can be observed that the promise does not mention the restoration of the monarchy or of political power, which were indeed things of the past.)

The very fact that Deuteronomy was preserved, to be incorporated in both the Jewish and the Christian Bible, proves that its message "got through", and that its contents both demanded and received respect. The threefold obligation of verse 20 was accepted by the Jewish exiles and those who followed them, and has remained the whole basis of the Jewish faith to this day.

It needs little adaptation to serve as the basis of Christian life too. (1) The *first* duty—*loving . . . God*—is a demand that true religion should be internal and genuine, not a mere matter of externals. A genuine faith must exercise the will and stir the emotion. (2) *Second, obeying* God's will is called for. The whole apparatus of the Jewish law is not imposed on the Christian law, but the New Testament is full of guidelines for Christian conduct, from the Sermon on the Mount onwards. A genuine faith, in fact, is not purely a matter of pious thoughts and warm devotion, but of practical action too. (3) *Cleaving to him* means consistency and perseverance. Many a Christian life has started well, with sincerity and the best of intentions; but many people have "fallen by the wayside", as the saying goes. The saying is of course drawn from the Parable of the Sower (Mark 4:3–20), which lists some of the obstacles that obstruct a productive, fruitful and constant Christian life.

PREPARING FOR CHANGE

Deuteronomy 31:1–8

¹So Moses continued to speak these words to all Israel. ²And he said to them, "I am a hundred and twenty years old this day; I am no longer able to go out and come in. The Lord has said to me, 'You shall not go over this Jordan.' ³The Lord your God himself will go over before you; he will destroy these nations before you, so that you shall dispossess them; and Joshua will go over at your head, as the Lord has spoken. ⁴And the Lord will do to them as he did to Sihon and Og, the kings of the Amorites, and to their land, when he destroyed them. ⁵And the Lord will give them over to you, and you shall do to them according to all the commandment which I have commanded you. ⁶Be strong and of good courage, do not fear or be in dread of them: for it is the Lord your God who goes with you; he will not fail you or forsake you."

⁷Then Moses summoned Joshua, and said to him in the sight of all Israel, "Be strong and of good courage; for you shall go with this people into the land which the Lord has sworn to their fathers to give them; and you shall put them in possession of it. ⁸It is the Lord who goes before you; he will be with you, he will not fail you or forsake you; do not fear or be dismayed."

After many chapters of *words*—that is, of speeches incorporating the laws—we return now to the narrative framework of Deuteronomy. Moses and the Israelites reached "the valley opposite Beth-peor" in 3:29, and there the action has remained static ever since. The story now begins to move forward again; this chapter paves the way for the death of *Moses*, and for *Joshua* to succeed him as national leader; a change of leadership which in turn paves the way for the Israelite invasion westwards across the Jordan into Palestine proper. Chapter 34 will record the death of Moses and succession of Joshua, and the book of Joshua will go on to detail the story of the conquest of Canaan.

This section is more than just a necessary part of the narrative, however. It is emphasized, to begin with, that these imminent events were no secret or surprise to Moses himself. He had reached a ripe old age; this much is certainly beyond doubt, even if the age of "a hundred and twenty years" (v. 2) is taken as a symbolic figure, meaning simply, *three generations*. He had in effect completed his work; in the context of Deuteronomy, his major work had been the provision of an appropriate law code which would guide the nation's lifestyle in the land where they were about to settle. The major task of conquering that land was not for Moses to undertake; verse 2 recalls and confirms 1:37–38 in this respect. So the end of Moses' life was not only the natural end of a long and busy career, but also a necessary part in the divine plan, before Israel could move on. Moses is not only resigned to the situation, but is shown to give it his blessing. The chapter gave the Israelite reader the assurance that God had ordered and arranged the nation's leadership in a very critical period of its history. Even today in settled societies, we may from time to time feel a sense of unease or worse, at the death or the resignation of a trusted and capable national leader perhaps, or at a change of government in a democracy. In the ancient world, the death of kings very frequently ushered in periods of political unrest, anarchy, or instability. So this description of God's political arrangements for Israel, with the full co-operation of Moses, must have contrasted with many a later situation.

The *implicit* message, especially for readers of the exilic period, was that God would still overrule in Israel's political future. Even a Moses, unique as he was, had not been irreplaceable; and God could still find a Joshua to lead his people into an unknown and unclear future. The *explicit* message is the call to show faith and *courage* (v. 6), however threatening or depressing the circumstances might be. With this call, comes the promise of verse 8; that of God's unfailing presence. The assertion that "the Lord goes before" his people is a startling one, perhaps. It is a picture drawn from warfare, and it indicates that the real "general" is not Joshua, or any of his successors, but God himself. The New Testament equivalent occurs in Hebrews 12:2, which describes Jesus as the pioneer (and also the perfecter) of our faith.

THE CUSTODY OF THE LAW

Deuteronomy 31:9–13

[9]And Moses wrote this law, and gave it to the priests the sons of Levi, who carried the ark of the covenant of the Lord, and to all the elders of Israel. [10]And Moses commanded them, "At the end of every seven years, at the set time of the year of release, at the feast of booths, [11]when all Israel comes to appear before the Lord your God at the place which he will choose, you shall read this law before all Israel in their hearing. [12]Assemble the people, men, women, and little ones, and the sojourner within your towns, that they may hear and learn to fear the Lord your God, and be careful to do all the words of this law, [13]and that their children, who have not known it, may hear and learn to fear the Lord your God, as long as you live in the land which you are going over the Jordan to possess."

Moses' plan for the future of his people, this chapter asserts, included first and foremost the appointment of a suitable and competent national leader—Joshua, next on the agenda; and scarcely less important, was the preservation and maintenance of the law code enshrined in the book of Deuteronomy. With regard to this new and vital document, three arrangements were to be made: (1) it was to have competent and reliable custodians; (2) it was to be kept in a safe place; (3) it was to be brought to the attention of the whole nation at regular intervals.

(a) The custodians were both *the priests* and *the elders* (v. 9). In other words, this law code was so important that the most senior personnel, both religious and civil, were entrusted with it. This decision was both practical and symbolic. In troubled times, it would be all to the good to have two separate types of custodian; and probably copies began to be made very soon. Also, the joint responsibility of priests and laymen made it clear that Deuteronomy was the supreme guide for both religious practice and also everyday life.

(b) Verse 9 mentions the ark of the covenant, and verse 26 indicates that the book of Deuteronomy was to be kept with or in it, as we know the Ten Commandments had been (10:1–5). This was no doubt the safest possible place in Israel—the most sacred piece of furniture, kept in the Temple.

(c) Verses 10–13 institute a new ceremony: the public reading of Deuteronomy's laws once every seven years, at the autumn feast of booths (or *tabernacles*), which was to become the festival especially associated with the giving of the law at Mount Sinai. A festival was an ideal time for such a public reading, since Israelites were required to make a pilgrimage to the Temple, and so whole families from all over the land would hear the law read. The law-reading would by itself remind the people that they were subject to God's law; in the same way, for many years, the British Army had a ruling that once a year a fixed number of paragraphs (mercifully few in number!) must be read to "other ranks"—a relic of the days of poor literacy. In Israel, by contrast, the *whole* law was to be read; but only once in seven years. The number seems to have been carefully chosen. Not only did it link up conveniently with the regular *year of release* (cf. chapter 15), but it served a good educational purpose (v. 13). Too frequent a reading might become a pure formality, a meaningless ritual, but too rare a reading would result in widespread ignorance of God's will. Of course, no mechanical system will be perfect for everyone, but at least the majority of Israel's citizens—including foreign residents—would be reasonably familiar with the laws which were to govern their lives. Ignorance is no excuse for breaking any law code; but the people of Israel were not intended to be ignorant of their code. As Jeremiah saw clearly, what is needed, where God's wishes are concerned, is that they should be embedded in the hearts and consciences of God's people (Jer. 31:33–34); but the first step towards this desirable goal is a thorough acquaintance with the Scriptures that set out his will. The instinct of our forefathers to train children to memorize key sections of the Bible was not misplaced.

FACING UP TO DISOBEDIENCE

Deuteronomy 31:14–29

14And the Lord said to Moses, "Behold, the days approach when you must die; call Joshua, and present yourselves in the tent of meeting, that I may commission him." And Moses and Joshua went and presented themselves in the tent of meeting. 15And the Lord appeared in the tent in a pillar of cloud; and the pillar of cloud stood by the door of the tent.

16And the Lord said to Moses, "Behold, you are about to sleep with your fathers; then this people will rise and play the harlot after the strange gods of the land, where they go to be among them, and they will forsake me and break my covenant which I have made with them. 17Then my anger will be kindled against them in that day, and I will forsake them and hide my face from them, and they will be devoured; and many evils and troubles will come upon them, so that they will say in that day, 'Have not these evils come upon us because our God is not among us?' 18And I will surely hide my face in that day on account of all the evil which they have done, because they have turned to other gods. 19Now therefore write this song, and teach it to the people of Israel; put it in their mouths, that this song may be a witness for me against the people of Israel. 20For when I have brought them into the land flowing with milk and honey, which I swore to give to their fathers, and they have eaten and are full and grown fat, they will turn to other gods and serve them, and despise me and break my covenant. 21And when many evils and troubles have come upon them, this song shall confront them as a witness (for it will live unforgotten in the mouths of their descendants); for I know the purposes which they are already forming, before I have brought them into the land that I swore to give." 22So Moses wrote this song the same day, and taught it to the people of Israel.

23And the Lord commissioned Joshua the son of Nun and said, "Be strong and of good courage; for you shall bring the children of Israel into the land which I swore to give them: I will be with you."

²⁴When Moses had finished writing the words of this law in a book, to the very end, ²⁵Moses commanded the Levites who carried the ark of the covenant of the Lord, ²⁶"Take this book of the law, and put it by the side of the ark of the covenant of the Lord your God, that it may be there for a witness against you. ²⁷For I know how rebellious and stubborn you are; behold, while I am yet alive with you, today you have been rebellious against the Lord; how much more after my death! ²⁸Assemble to me all the elders of your tribes, and your officers, that I may speak these words in their ears and call heaven and earth to witness against them. ²⁹For I know that after my death you will surely act corruptly, and turn aside from the way which I have commanded you; and in the days to come evil will befall you, because you will do what is evil in the sight of the Lord, provoking him to anger through the work of your hands."

The rest of the chapter is chiefly concerned with elaborating the two themes of verses 1–13; namely the commissioning of Joshua, and the safe custody of the book of Deuteronomy. To us there seems to be considerable repetition; and indeed many scholars think that this chapter was added to in the course of time. With regards to Joshua's appointment, at least, there is a clear sequence in the narrative: in verses 7–8 he is instructed by Moses; in verses 14–15 he is summoned into the presence of God (symbolized by "the tent of meeting" and the miraculous "pillar of cloud", cf. Exod. 13:21; 33:9); and in verse 23, God proceeds to ratify Moses' action, and *commissions* Joshua himself. The leadership of Joshua was not merely Moses' choice, but God's decision for Israel's welfare.

The last paragraph, verses 24–29, repeats the instruction of verse 9 entrusting Deuteronomy to *the Levites* (although without any mention now of the elders, except as listeners, v. 28) for safe-keeping with "the ark of the covenant". The emphasis is very different, however. In this paragraph, as in verses 16–22, Israel's disobedience and disobedient spirit are highlighted. Deuteronomy is now presented not so much as a law book for regular reference, but as a "witness against" those who persistently break its laws.

Why should such emphasis be put on Israel's disobedience? Part of the reason is to convince the Jews of a later period that their nation's history of disobedience (and disaster because of it) had been no surprise to God. Paul was equally convinced that the widespread Jewish rejection of Christianity, in his era, fitted into God's design of history (Rom. 9–11). Another reason was reassurance, based on God's foreknowledge of his people's conduct. If God had known all along how generations of Israelites would despise his laws, then he must have had long-range plans, beyond these rebellious generations. Otherwise his laws, his design for life, could have no real purpose. So the generation reading Deuteronomy could be reassured of God's favour, provided that they changed course as a nation, and sought to embody Deuteronomy's laws in their daily lives.

Perhaps the chief reason of all is expressed in verse 17: it may take God's people a long time and many painful experiences before they come to realize that "our God is not among us". The very phrase, *our God*, asserted a relationship, and was both arrogant and mistaken all the while the Israelites broke their covenant with him. Some of the prophets tell us that all too often there was an odious complacency in both Israel and Judah; a confident assurance that all was well between them and God. There is nobody more beyond the reach of reason than a religious man; but at the last, Israel would wake up to the truth of their experience, their history and their need. Christian Churches may need to learn similar lessons: see, for instance, Revelation 3:14–22, with its warning to a lukewarm and complacent local congregation.

The song mentioned in verses 19–22 follows in chapter 32.

A SERMON IN SONG

Deuteronomy 31:30–32:7

30Then Moses spoke the words of this song until they were finished, in the ears of all the assembly of Israel:

1"Give ear, O heavens, and I will speak;
   and let the earth hear the words of my mouth.
2May my teaching drop as the rain,
      my speech distil as the dew,
   as the gentle rain upon the tender grass,
      and as the showers upon the herb.
3For I will proclaim the name of the Lord.
      Ascribe greatness to our God!

4"The Rock, his work is perfect;
      for all his ways are justice.
   A God of faithfulness and without iniquity,
      just and right is he.
5They have dealt corruptly with him,
      they are no longer his children because of their blemish;
   they are a perverse and crooked generation.
6Do you thus requite the Lord,
      you foolish and senseless people?
   Is not he your father, who created you,
      who made you and established you?
7Remember the days of old,
      consider the years of many generations;
   ask your father, and he will show you;
      your elders, and they will tell you."

Deuteronomy's closing chapters are very concerned with preventing Israel, in later generations, from forgetting or abandon-
ing God's laws. Various provisions have been made to achieve
this aim: proper leadership, the careful preservation of the book
of Deuteronomy itself, and a ceremony for its public reading,
have all been instituted in chapter 31. The *song* has exactly the
same general purpose, set as it is in the context of Deuteronomy.
It is a didactic song, *ie* one designed to instruct those who heard it
and learned its words—we can be sure Deuteronomy meant it to
be a "pop song", its words familiar to everyone. It has also been
classed as a prophetic song; the prophets were the great moral
and religious teachers of Israel, whose words were a constant
reminder of the dangers of ignoring God's will concerning them.
This song (as 31:19 has already indicated) not only gives instruc-

tion about God, but also points out some home truths about Israel's conduct. It is true that Israel showed a rebellious spirit throughout its history, including Moses' own lifetime (according to Stephen in Acts 7); but it is generally held that this song was composed at a much later period, and reflects on all Israel's sins during the period of the monarchy. If so, Moses is the source of its authority, rather than its author (31:30).

The song is rich in metaphor and figurative language; it begins with an appeal to *the heavens* and *the earth* to listen—which is obviously not meant to be taken literally. Verses 1 and 2 together maintain that the song's message deserves the widest possible audience, and will have a very beneficial effect on its audience.

The praise given to God in verses 3 and 4 is typical of many of the hymns found in the book of Psalms; but here the sting is in the tail. The description of God in verse 4 is in no way strange or unusual, but it is used to set up a contrast with Israel, as verse 5 soon shows. God's *faithfulness* is matched by the *perverse* disloyalty of his covenant people. The Old Testament here, as elsewhere, calls God "the Rock", to symbolize his utter reliability and unshakable trustworthiness; but how different is Israel's character! The accusations of verses 5 and 6, stern as they are, are not meant as rebukes, but as the basis of the appeal that follows in verse 7, and indeed the appeal of the whole poem.

There is a double appeal to the reader's emotions in verses 6 and 7, centred in the repeated phrase, *your father*. In verse 6 it refers to God, and draws attention to the close and loving relationship that ought to exist between God and his people; but as verse 5 has already stated, Israel has forfeited the right to be called *his children*. The covenant was not an artificial bond which linked two unrelated parties (as a legal contract usually is); it was the outworking of an existing relationship, elsewhere described in terms of husband and wife.

In verse 7, *your father* refers to earlier generations of Israelites, who could testify to God's goodness, from the time of the Exodus onwards. If the generation who read or heard this song chose to be *perverse and crooked*, they would be turning their backs on both their heavenly Father and their ancestors. In both respects they would be breaching the Commandment to honour their parents (5:16).

EVIDENCE OF GOD'S CARE

Deuteronomy 32:8–14

8"When the Most High gave to the nations their inheritance,
  when he separated the sons of men,
he fixed the bounds of the peoples
  according to the number of the sons of God.
9For the Lord's portion is his people,
  Jacob his allotted heritage.

10"He found him in a desert land,
  and in the howling waste of the wilderness;
he encircled him, he cared for him,
  he kept him as the apple of his eye.
11Like an eagle that stirs up its nest,
  that flutters over its young,
spreading out its wings, catching them,
  bearing them on its pinions,
12the Lord alone did lead him,
  and there was no foreign god with him.
13He made him ride on the high places of the earth,
  and he ate the produce of the field;
and he made him suck honey out of the rock,
  and oil out of the flinty rock.
14Curds from the herd, and milk from the flock,
  with fat of lambs and rams,
  herds of Bashan and goats,
with the finest of the wheat—
  and of the blood of the grape you drank wine."

The song now illustrates God's goodness and care for Israel in highly pictorial and symbolic language, some of which seems very obscure to us. Verse 8 is the most difficult verse, partly because of an uncertainty in the wording. If the traditional Hebrew reading (translated in the RSV footnote) is correct, then the verse indicates that the number of nations in the world corresponded with the number of citizens in Israel; but this seems unlikely. More likely "the sons of God" is correct, in which case the meaning is roughly that the God of Israel "assigned to each nation a god" (GNB). This statement, however surprising it seems at first, takes seriously the fact that the nations of the ancient world had not only their own frontiers (their *bounds*), but also their own gods and systems of worship. The song attacks polytheism at the practical level (v. 12), but in verse 8, all it seeks to affirm is that the God of Israel stands supreme over the whole world—over nations and their gods alike. If so, he is incomparable, and the worship of any other god is folly indeed. The remarkable thing for Israel is that this supreme, majestic Deity, who had created and organized the world, had chosen *them* for his people. (*Jacob* in v. 9 is not the individual of the book of Genesis, but another name for the nation Israel.)

Verses 8–9 then describe God's choice long ago of Israel to be his people, and verses 10–14 spell out the practical results: God's choice had been followed by his unfailing care. Verse 10 pictures God as having *found* Israel, as if they had been lost in the *desert*; the harsh *wilderness* conditions of the Sinai peninsula and the Negev could have seen the embryo nation of Israel perish, but for God's superintending care. The picture of verse 11 speaks for itself, describing God's practical love for Israel, and verses 13–14, in poetic language, say something about the rich fertility of the Promised Land, in contrast to the wilderness: Palestine and its environs are still a land of sharp contrasts, even today.

This past national experience of God's care, verse 12 points out, occurred at a time before Israelites became infected by Canaanite idolatry, at least on a large scale. Quite obviously, when isolated in wilderness regions, the Israelites had not been open to alien cultural influences; after their invasion of Canaan, they were only too readily affected by their new neighbours' customs and practices. So this passage argues forcefully that all the early blessings received by Israel could only have come from Yahweh, not from gods she had not yet started to worship. This sort of argument seems foreign to us, largely because we are so unfamiliar with polytheism; if our contemporaries refuse, or neglect, to be grateful to God for our blessings in life, they are more likely nowadays to give the credit to blind chance or to impersonal fate. The Christian of today can just as easily be affected by our cultural environment as the ancient Israelites were by their Canaanite neighbours.

LIVING DANGEROUSLY

Deuteronomy 32:15–25

15"But Jeshurun waxed fat, and kicked;
    you waxed fat, you grew thick, you became sleek;
  then he forsook God who made him,
    and scoffed at the Rock of his salvation.
16They stirred him to jealousy with strange gods;
    with abominable practices they provoked him to anger.
17They sacrificed to demons which were no gods,
    to gods they had never known,
  to new gods that had come in of late,
    whom your fathers had never dreaded.
18You were unmindful of the Rock that begot you,
    and you forgot the God who gave you birth.

19"The Lord saw it, and spurned them,
    because of the provocation of his sons and his daughters.
20And he said, 'I will hide my face from them,
    I will see what their end will be,
  for they are a perverse generation,
    children in whom is no faithfulness.
21They have stirred me to jealousy with what is no god;
    they have provoked me with their idols.
  So I will stir them to jealousy with those who are no people;
    I will provoke them with a foolish nation.
22For a fire is kindled by my anger,
    and it burns to the depths of Sheol,
  devours the earth and its increase,
    and sets on fire the foundations of the mountains.

23"'And I will heap evils upon them;
    I will spend my arrows upon them;

²⁴they shall be wasted with hunger,
  and devoured with burning heat
  and poisonous pestilence;
and I will send the teeth of beasts against them,
  with venom of crawling things of the dust.
²⁵In the open the sword shall bereave,
  and in the chambers shall be terror,
destroying both young man and virgin,
  the sucking child with the man of grey hairs.'"

Verses 10–14 have described the care God showed to Israel; verses 15–18 now depict Israel's ungrateful response. *Jeshurun* is a rare name for Israel, which is portrayed in verse 15 like an overfed farm animal, which goes its own way without feeling the least gratitude towards the owner that feeds it and looks after it. It was a case of prosperity leading to contempt, and contempt to disloyalty—the disloyalty of false worship. Verse 17 complains that the gods, which the Israelites began to worship in Canaan, were hitherto unknown to them; in other words, they owed no gratitude to such gods whatsoever. Such gods are classed as *demons*—evil and hurtful. We nowadays approach such issues philosophically, and simply deny the existence of a multitude of gods; the Old Testament usually prefers to take a practical approach, very conscious of the harm which false cults could do to their devotees. Verse 18 reminds the reader that Israel's true God was no demon, no unreal fantasy of the imagination, but the God who had brought Israel into being.

Israel's persistent idolatrous conduct over the generations was sheer *provocation* to God (v. 19). Verses 19–22 are just as pictorial as earlier paragraphs, but there is no doubting the reality of God's anger. The Bible—both Testaments, although not in equal measure—has much to say about God's love and mercy on the one hand, and his anger and his punishments on the other. There is no real contradiction in this, only a contrast. The underlying imagery is that of a father who has wilful sons; the dominant theme is his love for them, but discipline will often be necessary. Perhaps the most important lesson for us is that we should be aware of the *personal* qualities of God. In our scientific age, we are easily conditioned into seeing God in impersonal, mechanical terms, as if he had constructed and wound up the machine we call the universe, and left it to its own devices, distancing himself from individuals. That is by no means the God of the Bible.

Verses 23–25 remind us of some of the things that can go wrong in our world: for example, *hunger* on a large scale is still no stranger to human experience, as the Third World knows only too well. The lesson of these verses is not really to threaten Israel with famine and other communal disasters as a punishment direct from God, but rather to remind the people of Israel of the precariousness of their existence, and so to remind them of the need to put their total reliance upon God—the very God who created this dangerous and unpredictable world in which we live. Such is human nature, we are more awake to our dependence upon God in times of adversity than in times when, it seems, "we have never had it so good". It is certainly true that adversity often serves to bring out the best qualities in human nature, such as courage, endurance, and altruism.

FROM POWERLESSNESS TO VINDICATION

Deuteronomy 32:26–52

26"'I would have said, "I will scatter them afar,
    I will make the remembrance of them cease from among men,"
27had I not feared provocation by the enemy,
    lest their adversaries should judge amiss,
  lest they should say, "Our hand is triumphant,
    the Lord has not wrought all this."'

28"For they are a nation void of counsel,
    and there is no understanding in them.
29If they were wise, they would understand this,
    they would discern their latter end!
30How should one chase a thousand,
    and two put ten thousand to flight,
  unless their Rock had sold them,
    and the Lord had given them up?

31For their rock is not as our Rock,
      even our enemies themselves being judges.
32For their vine comes from the vine of Sodom,
      and from the fields of Gomorrah;
   their grapes are grapes of poison,
      their clusters are bitter;
33their wine is the poison of serpents,
      and the cruel venom of asps.

34"Is not this laid up in store with me,
      sealed up in my treasuries?
35Vengeance is mine, and recompense,
      for the time when their foot shall slip;
   for the day of their calamity is at hand,
      and their doom comes swiftly.
36For the Lord will vindicate his people
      and have compassion on his servants,
   when he sees that their power is gone,
      and there is none remaining, bond or free.
37Then he will say, 'Where are their gods,
      the rock in which they took refuge,
38who ate the fat of their sacrifices,
      and drank the wine of their drink offering?
   Let them rise up and help you,
      let them be your protection!

39"'See now that I, even I, am he,
      and there is no god beside me;
   I kill and I make alive;
      I wound and I heal;
      and there is none that can deliver out of my hand.
40For I lift up my hand to heaven,
      and swear, As I live for ever,
41if I whet my glittering sword,
      and my hand takes hold on judgment,
   I will take vengeance on my adversaries
      and will requite those who hate me.
42I will make my arrows drunk with blood,
      and my sword shall devour flesh—
   with the blood of the slain and the captives
      from the long-haired heads of the enemy.'

43"Praise his people, O you nations;
>   for he avenges the blood of his servants,
> and takes vengeance on his adversaries,
>   and makes expiation for the land of his people."

44Moses came and recited all the words of this song in the hearing of the people, he and Joshua the son of Nun. 45And when Moses had finished speaking all these words to all Israel, 46he said to them, "Lay to heart all the words which I enjoin upon you this day, that you may command them to your children, that they may be careful to do all the words of this law. 47For it is no trifle for you, but it is your life, and thereby you shall live long in the land which you are going over the Jordan to possess."

48And the Lord said to Moses that very day, 49"Ascend this mountain of the Abarim, Mount Nebo, which is in the land of Moab, opposite Jericho; and view the land of Canaan, which I give to the people of Israel for a possession; 50and die on the mountain which you ascend, and be gathered to your people, as Aaron your brother died in Mount Hor and was gathered to his people; 51because you broke faith with me in the midst of the people of Israel at the waters of Meribath-kadesh, in the wilderness of Zin; because you did not revere me as holy in the midst of the people of Israel. 52For you shall see the land before you; but you shall not go there, into the land which I give to the people of Israel."

Much of the Song of Moses has God as the speaker. In verses 20–25 we find a declaration by God, expressing his anger with Israel and threatening disaster, as we have seen. In verse 26, again we find words as if spoken by God himself, but with an interesting difference; here we have not what "God said" but what he *would have said*—but did not! God is still the speaker in the verses that follow, up to verse 35. Finally, verses 37–42 tell the reader what God *will say*. There is a clear sequence of ideas in these paragraphs outlining what God has to say to his wayward people. The threats of verses 20–25 were frightening, and are meant to be, but they were in no way *final*; God had no intention of destroying Israel totally, as verses 26–27 make clear. Israel was supremely foolish (vv. 28–29), it is true, but that is not to say that other nations were either wiser or more moral (on the contrary, vv. 32–33 insist). So the day would come when God would reverse the military disasters suffered by Israel, and bring swift *calamity* on her enemies (v. 35). Initially, however, Israel must reach an extremity of powerlessness (v. 36), and at last come to see that idolatry had achieved absolutely nothing (vv. 37–38). The poem ends with a call to acknowledge the power of God, both to bring adversity and prosperity (v. 39), and the promise of full rescue from Israel's powerful enemies, such as the Assyrians and Babylonians (vv. 40–42). A call to *praise* rounds off the song (v. 43).

It is not difficult, if we can get behind the dramatic imagery, to see the mixture of rebuke, warning, appeal and promise, which are here given in the name of God. As the poem was memorized and sung at different times and epochs, it will have often challenged the people's thinking.

Verse 35 begins with familiar words; St. Paul quotes them in Romans 12:19, although to very different effect. Paul was concerned to prevent his readers from exercising private vengeance, since God had said, "Vengeance is mine", and Christian people must leave it to him. In Deuteronomy 32, the lesson is rather that God can be trusted to look after his people. As a humiliated and defeated and exiled nation, Israel's desperate need was for military deliverance, and this is promised in verse 35. The promise came true when the Medes and Persians, under King Cyrus, defeated the Babylonians and took over their empire; the Persian policy towards Israel was altogether different, and could be seen as providential. We can see, however, that the promise was fulfilled in a way Israel neither expected nor hoped; and that is, in a way, Paul's point too: God does ultimately remedy his people's problems, and he does not ignore the injustices they suffer, but his mode of action is entirely in *his* hands.

Verses 44–52 pick up the narrative thread from chapter 31, and again point forward to the death of Moses and to the leadership of Joshua. The function and value of Deuteronomy are underlined in these verses. God's laws, as contained in Deuteronomy, are no trifle (v. 47); rather, they are Israel's very life, in two senses: they provide the whole framework and content of everyday life, and they guarantee long life, not so much to the individual, as to the nation.

THE BLESSING OF MOSES

Deuteronomy 33:1–29

¹This is the blessing with which Moses the man of God blessed the children of Israel before his death.
²He said,
"The Lord came from Sinai,
and dawned from Seir upon us;
he shone forth from Mount Paran,
he came from the ten thousands of holy ones,
with flaming fire at his right hand.
³Yea, he loved his people;
all those consecrated to him were in his hand;
so they followed in thy steps,
receiving direction from thee,
⁴when Moses commanded us a law,
as a possession for the assembly of Jacob.
⁵Thus the Lord became king in Jeshurun,
when the heads of the people were gathered,
all the tribes of Israel together.
⁶"Let Reuben live, and not die,
nor let his men be few."

⁷And this he said of Judah:
"Hear, O Lord, the voice of Judah,
and bring him in to his people.
With thy hands contend for him,
and be a help against his adversaries."

⁸And of Levi he said,
"Give to Levi thy Thummim,
and thy Urim to thy godly one,
whom thou didst test at Massah,
with whom thou didst strive at the waters of Meribah;
⁹who said of his father and mother,
'I regard them not';
he disowned his brothers,
and ignored his children.
For they observed thy word,
and kept thy covenant.

¹⁰They shall teach Jacob thy ordinances,
　　and Israel thy law;
　they shall put incense before thee,
　　and whole burnt offering upon thy altar.
¹¹Bless, O Lord, his substance,
　　and accept the work of his hands;
　crush the loins of his adversaries,
　　of those that hate him, that they rise not again."

¹²Of Benjamin he said,
　"The beloved of the Lord,
　　he dwells in safety by him;
　he encompasses him all the day long,
　　and makes his dwelling between his shoulders."

¹³And of Joseph he said,
　"Blessed by the Lord be his land,
　　with the choicest gifts of heaven above,
　　and of the deep that couches beneath,
¹⁴with the choicest fruits of the sun,
　　and the rich yield of the months,
¹⁵with the finest produce of the ancient mountains,
　　and the abundance of the everlasting hills,
¹⁶with the best gifts of the earth and its fullness,
　　and the favour of him that dwelt in the bush.
　Let these come upon the head of Joseph,
　　and upon the crown of the head of him that is
　　　prince among his brothers.
¹⁷His firstling bull has majesty,
　　and his horns are the horns of a wild ox;
　with them he shall push the peoples,
　　all of them, to the ends of the earth;
　such are the ten thousands of Ephraim,
　　and such are the thousands of Manasseh."

¹⁸And of Zebulun he said,
　"Rejoice, Zebulun, in your going out;
　　and Issachar, in your tents.
¹⁹They shall call peoples to their mountain;
　　there they offer right sacrifices;
　for they suck the affluence of the seas
　　and the hidden treasures of the sand."

²⁰And of Gad he said,
  "Blessed be he who enlarges Gad!
    Gad couches like a lion.
    he tears the arm, and the crown of the head.
²¹He chose the best of the land for himself,
    for there a commander's portion was reserved;
  and he came to the heads of the people,
    with Israel he executed the commands
    and just decrees of the Lord."

²²And of Dan he said,
  "Dan is a lion's whelp,
    that leaps forth from Bashan."

²³And of Naphtali he said,
  "O Naphtali, satisfied with favour,
    and full of the blessing of the Lord,
    possess the lake and the south."

²⁴And of Asher he said,
  "Blessed above sons be Asher;
    let him be the favourite of his brothers,
    and let him dip his foot in oil.
²⁵Your bars shall be iron and bronze;
    and as your days, so shall your strength be.

²⁶"There is none like God, O Jeshurun,
    who rides through the heavens to your help,
    and in his majesty through the skies.
²⁷The eternal God is your dwelling place,
    and underneath are the everlasting arms.
  And he thrust out the enemy before you,
    and said, Destroy.
²⁸So Israel dwelt in safety,
    the fountain of Jacob alone,
  in a land of grain and wine;
    yea, his heavens drop down dew.
²⁹Happy are you, O Israel! Who is like you,
    a people saved by the Lord,
  the shield of your help,
    and the sword of your triumph!
  Your enemies shall come fawning to you;
    and you shall tread upon their high places."

(i)

The Song of Moses in chapter 32 is now followed by the Blessing of Moses; the whole of chapter 33 is another poem attributed to Moses, as his dying *blessing* upon *the children of Israel*. In this context, *blessing* means very much more than mere good wishes on parting; the scene envisaged is like the one in Genesis 27, where Jacob tricked his father into giving him the "blessing" which was intended for his older brother Esau. Esau's bitter reaction (Gen. 27:34–41) adequately shows how seriously death-bed blessings were taken—just as seriously as a matter of property left under somebody's will might be taken nowadays. In fact, the Blessing of Moses is a sort of spiritual testament, made not to Moses' own sons, but to the whole nation, both contemporary and (more particularly) future. A parallel scene and situation are to be found in Genesis 49: the Blessing of Jacob. Jacob, in that chapter, foresaw the fortunes of his sons (or rather, in the solemn act of blessing them, *determined* their future); but the sons were not merely individuals, but the ancestors of Israelite tribes. Those tribes were not constituted as a nation until Moses; so it seems fully appropriate that Moses should reinforce in this way the future which God had determined for the tribes. (The Simeonites are not mentioned, probably because they eventually became absorbed into the tribe of Judah; Ephraim and Manasseh are briefly mentioned by name, in verse 17, but they are understood by the name *Joseph*, in v. 13.)

In one way, Deuteronomy 33 reaffirms Genesis 49. From another point of view, it reaffirms the prophetic poem of chapter 32. The Song of Moses ends with the conviction that ultimately God would bring victory and well-being to Israel by defeating her enemies. Chapter 33 now reinforces that message by applying it to each tribe's individual future.

Although it is impossible to date the various layers and component parts of this chapter, it is easy to see how it took shape. The tribal blessings (vv. 6–25) may well have been pronounced one by one, perhaps at different periods of Israel's history. This is suggested, for instance, by the very different length and style of the individual sayings. However, they were collected and placed together, as we see. Verses 2–5 and 26–29 really form a single poem, which probably had a life of its own; but it provided a perfect literary setting for the tribal blessings. The next stage was to supply verse 1 as an editorial introduction when the enlarged poem was made part of the complete book of Deuteronomy.

In passing, it may be observed that to visualize the structure and growth of Deuteronomy 33 in this way does not, by itself, rule out the authorship of Moses, who could in theory have been responsible for each of the three stages. However, we must take seriously the evidence contained in the chapter: verse 23 already places *Naphtali* by *lake* Galilee, and verse 22 places *Dan* in the north-east (*Bashan*); a territory to which the Danites moved from much further south, during the period of the Judges (cf. Judg. 18). Even then, prophetic insight is not ruled out, of course; but verse 4 seems to be *about* Moses, not *by* him. As has been remarked earlier, the *authority* of Moses is far more important for an understanding of Deuteronomy than his authorship.

Deuteronomy 33:1–29 (*cont'd*)

(ii)

The introductory poem (vv. 2–5) is very ancient and highly figurative, so that parts of it seem strange or obscure to us. Indeed, there *are* some obscurities and uncertainties of meaning (see the RSV footnotes). The general picture is that of a royal procession, with Yahweh himself as *king* (v. 5). The procession begins at *Sinai* and marches north into the land of Israel, called here by its ancient name of *Jeshurun* (as in 32:15). God is accompanied by his courtiers and followed by his subjects. The subjects are of course *his people* Israel, while the courtiers are *the ten thousands* of heavenly beings (almost certainly we must change "from" to "with" the ten thousands, cf. NEB, GNB). The procession already possesses the *law* of *Moses* as they enter the Promised Land, where it provides the constitutional basis of Israel's existence. God is of course king from start to finish, but in a practical sense, he only *became king* in the Promised Land, his proper territory. The passage is by no means denying either the cosmic or the eternal sovereignty of God; it is however setting out Israel's special relationship with God in an extended metaphor, which speaks of Yahweh as if he were an ordinary human king entering his rightful realm and establishing his laws there.

It may be that this picture of God and Israel is metaphorical in every respect, but it is equally possible that it reflects an actual ceremony which was practised from time to time, perhaps annually, in ancient Israel. If so, there could have been a literal procession (although certainly not all the way from Sinai!), watched by *the heads of the people, gathered* in special assembly. It is even possible that, by some ceremonial means, Yahweh was re-enthroned as king; Psalm 47 is often thought to have been linked with some such ritual. One can suppose that Deuteronomy 33:2–5 was part of the liturgy.

But all this is conjectural; our precise knowledge of the customs and rituals of ancient Israel is severely limited. It is clear, at any rate, that in some sense, God *became king* in Israel, even although he was always king of the universe. We may be tempted to dismiss this as a mere paradox, but there are two practical points to be made, The *first* is that by means of this concept the nearness of God to his people, and his love for them (v. 3), could be emphasized. In Christian terms, the Incarnation and the Lord's Supper serve to bring God near, in Christ. The *second* lesson, and one which is never far below the surface in Deuteronomy, is that in some sense, God is only king where his law is enshrined and obeyed. The teachings of Jesus about the Kingdom of God similarly insist that (although God is universal king) many people are located outside his Kingdom, and need to enter into it.

Deuteronomy 33:1–29 (*cont'd*)

(iii)

Reuben (v. 6) was the most senior tribe (cf. Gen. 29:31–35), but it was one of the weakest numerically; the blessing recognizes this historical reality, if we retranslate it as the Good News Bible does—"may Reuben never die out, *although* their people are few". *Judah* (v. 7) was under pressure of a different sort during its early history; it was cut off from the Israelite tribes north of it by a strip of land dominated by Canaanite cities. The blessing, a prayer to God to "unite" Judah (GNB, for RSV "bring him in"), was fulfilled in the reign of David, who conquered Jerusalem. So the first two blessings look to God to protect the tribes concerned.

Levi (vv. 8–11) was a tribe of a different kind; it was the priestly tribe, and had no tribal territory of its own. The tone of this blessing suggests that initially the Levites were somewhat despised or ignored by other Israelites. At any rate, the blessing emphasizes their loyalty to God (v. 9), and also draws attention to their God-given rôles in Israel. *First*, they were the channel for ascertaining the will of God, by use of the *Urim* and *Thummim* (v. 8). This was a piece of priestly apparatus, the exact mechanics of which are unknown; but we can see how it was used from such stories as 1 Samuel 14:37–42. *Second*, they had a teaching rôle, to instruct the Israelite populace, particularly in the laws of the covenant; and *third*, they were in charge of the rituals of worship (v. 10). In seeking to protect and enhance the Levites' rôle, this blessing is also concerned for Israel's spiritual welfare; if the average Israelite ignored the Levites, he would be effectively cutting himself off from the will, the law, and the worship of God. Contempt for the ministers of God, in any era, is but a step from contempt for God himself.

Benjamin (v. 12) was the most junior of all the tribes (cf. Gen. 35:16–26), and was never a big tribe. It was far from weak and insignificant, however; the first king of Israel, Saul, was a Benjaminite. The blessing expresses a note of serene confidence.

The two *Joseph* tribes, Ephraim and Manasseh (vv. 13–17), were centrally located in Palestine, and were prosperous with fertile lands and large numbers. The blessing expresses gratitude to God for all this, and acknowledges the importance of Ephraim, "the prince among his brothers" (v. 16). After Solomon's death, when the kingdom split into two, Ephraim was the dominant tribe in the Northern Kingdom, which was bigger and stronger than the Kingdom of Judah. The Assyrians eventually crushed Ephraim and the whole Northern Kingdom, but for the two centuries until 722 B.C., this blessing fully applied.

Zebulun and *Issachar* are linked together in verses 18–19. The latter evidently prospered from sea-trade, while Zebulun, an inland territory, was best known for a sanctuary which attracted many pilgrims. It is of interest that it is called a place of "right sacrifices", in spite of Deuteronomy's sustained emphasis on one single sanctuary in the whole of Israel. Presumably it was free from any idolatrous practices or associations. It is thought to have been located at Mount Tabor.

Deuteronomy 33:1–29 (*cont'd*)

(iv)

The remaining tribes of *Gad, Dan, Naphtali* and *Asher* are given blessings of a generally similar kind (vv. 20–25). All of them are depicted as sharing the general prosperity of Israel. With verse 26, the poem of verses 2 to 5 is resumed, and it continues the same theme of the well-being of Israel (or *Jeshurun*). The poet was gratefully conscious that Israel was uniquely favoured (v. 29) because she had a unique and incomparable God (v. 26). Such sentiments can readily be shared by Christian people, who have often treasured the image of God's loving care at the start of verse 27. The triumphant, or rather triumphalist, note of the second half of the verse is less to our taste; and so are the closing lines of verse 29.

It is plain that the poem reflects an era in Israel's history marked by economic prosperity and political security; *enemies* were not absent, but they posed no serious threat. Reading the poem against such a background, we can better understand its sentiments. Israel's wars were nearly all of a defensive character; she was not an aggressive nation, but was constantly compelled to repel invaders and encroachment. Victory meant security and peace; the defeat of invading armies gave a chance for prosperity. Those of us who live in secure and prosperous countries should not despise the fact that military matters played a large part in Israelite thinking.

It is important, moreover, to remember the setting of Deuteronomy 33. This poem no doubt originated in a prosperous era, but its incorporation in Deuteronomy gave it a very different setting and therefore a very different function. The main thrust of Deuteronomy was a message for Judah in the exilic period; a time when the fortunes of God's people were at their lowest ebb. It is a measure of the faith of those who published Deuteronomy (if we dare use the term "publish") that they *still* believed that their God was incomparable, and still believed that prosperity and victory could be theirs. The poem, read in the light of Deuteronomy's message, is a document of remarkable faith and trust; and it also reinforces the Deuteronomic call to be loyal to the covenant and obedient to the laws of God, because that was the only possible route to future blessing and well-being.

Finally, it is worthwhile to notice the horizons of the chapter. Even before the Babylonian Exile, some Israelite tribes must have almost or totally disappeared. The Kingdom of Judah consisted only of Benjamin and Judah itself. No edition of Deuteronomy, however, saw fit to omit any of the tribal blessings as obsolete. Judah never forgot that God's people were a much larger entity than themselves, both in past history and (they were sure) in future history once again. Such a perspective is a necessary part of trust in God and perception of his purposes. In Western Europe today, we are often pessimistic over the slow but steady numerical decline of the Church; but in other parts of the world, the story is very different, and we should share the triumphant confidence of "the church militant".

THE END OF AN ERA

Deuteronomy 34:1–12

¹And Moses went up from the plains of Moab to Mount Nebo, to the top of Pisgah, which is opposite Jericho. And the Lord showed him all the land, Gilead as far as Dan, ²all Naphtali, the land of Ephraim and Manasseh, all the land of Judah as far as the Western Sea, ³the Negeb, and the Plain, that is, the valley of Jericho the city of palm trees, as far

as Zoar. ⁴And the Lord said to him, "This is the land of which I swore to Abraham, to Isaac, and to Jacob, 'I will give it to your descendants.' I have let you see it with your eyes, but you shall not go over there." ⁵So Moses the servant of the Lord died there in the land of Moab, according to the word of the Lord, ⁶and he buried him in the valley in the land of Moab opposite Beth-peor; but no man knows the place of his burial to this day. ⁷Moses was a hundred and twenty years old when he died; his eye was not dim, nor his natural force abated. ⁸And the people of Israel wept for Moses in the plains of Moab thirty days; then the days of weeping and mourning for Moses were ended.

⁹And Joshua the son of Nun was full of the spirit of wisdom, for Moses had laid his hands upon him; so the people of Israel obeyed him, and did as the Lord had commanded Moses. ¹⁰And there has not arisen a prophet since in Israel like Moses, whom the Lord knew face to face, ¹¹none like him for all the signs and the wonders which the Lord sent him to do in the land of Egypt, to Pharaoh and to all his servants and to all his land, ¹²and for all the mighty power and all the great and terrible deeds which Moses wrought in the sight of all Israel.

The story and the book come to a natural and appropriate end with the death of Moses. The story of Israel did not end here, of course, and in fact the book of Joshua continues the history without a break; but the death of Moses nevertheless marked the end of an era—an unforgettable and unrepeatable era—in the life of the nation. Before his death, we are told, he was given a panoramic view of "all the land" (v. 1); the passage is symbolic, as if to show Moses laying claim to the whole Promised Land, even although he would never set foot in it. He *died* and was *buried* in *Moab*, not Canaan (vv. 5–6).

A sceptic once said that the only certain historical fact about Moses is that he was buried in an unknown grave in Moab. Whatever historical questions may be raised about the stories in Exodus, there is no good reason to doubt that Moses was a great man, who welded Israel into an embryonic nation and gave it a collection of laws to guide and control it. Certainly the Jewish people have always considered him the incomparable founder of the nation.

This chapter not only records his death but offers us his obituary (vv. 10–12). It may seem surprising that these verses say nothing of his rôle as law-giver, even although the book of Deuteronomy has dedicated many chapters to his laws. However, the emphasis on his rôle as *prophet* is intended to include the law-giving, since prophets were the men who made known God's will to his people. Moses was a prophet without equal; later prophets simply reinforced the laws he had promulgated, reapplying his principles to later situations. The last two verses of the chapter make the further claim that he was incomparable in his achievements for Israel—recalling the miraculous way he had rescued the people from *Egypt*. Miracles always invite scepticism in our modern age; but there is no doubt that Moses' achievements impressed his people as miraculous. This reminder of Moses' achievements was appropriate for Israelite readers of Deuteronomy in troubled times, such as the Exile. Moses may have been incomparable, but it was *the Lord* who had *sent him* to transform Israel's whole situation; and God could always raise another, if lesser, Moses to transform the disastrous circumstances of later epochs (cf. 18:18).

Moses was not immortal, and he died in the natural way of things. Moses' God lived on; the very next verse (Josh. 1:1) portrays him speaking to Moses' successor and giving him the guidance he needed. As a modern hymn expresses it, "The God who lived in Moses' time, is just the same today".

FURTHER READING

Commentaries

P. C. Craigie, *The Book of Deuteronomy* (New International Commentary on the Old Testament) (W. B. Eerdmans, 1976)

A. D. H. Mayes, *Deuteronomy* (New Century Bible Commentary) (Marshall, Morgan & Scott, 1981)

A. Phillips, *Deuteronomy* (Cambridge Bible Commentary) (Cambridge University Press, 1973)

G. von Rad, *Deuteronomy* (Old Testament Library) (SCM Press, 1966)

J. A. Thompson, *Deuteronomy: an introduction and commentary* (Tyndale Old Testament Commentaries) (Inter-Varsity Press, 1974)

Other Studies

S. Blanch, *The Ten Commandments* (Hodder and Stoughton, 1981)

C. M. Carmichael, *The Laws of Deuteronomy* (Cornell University Press, 1974)

R. E. Clements, *God's Chosen People* (SCM Press, 1968)

M. G. Kline, *The Treaty of the Great King* (W. B. Eerdmans, 1963)

E. W. Nicholson, *Deuteronomy and Tradition* (Blackwell, 1967)

J. J. Stamm and M. E. Andrew, *The Ten Commandments in recent research* (SCM Press, 1967)

W. Vischer, *The Witness of the Old Testament to Christ*, Volume I, *The Pentateuch* (Lutterworth Press, 1949)

M. Weinfeld, *Deuteronomy and the Deuteronomic School* (Clarendon Press, 1972)